THE MAKING OF A COACH

GOLDEN PAT RUEL

THE MAKING OF A COACH

FOREWARD BY PETE CARROL

SGM

The Making of a Coach

Some of our authors do participate in speaking arrangements. If interested, please visit the website below.
www.sillygoatmedia.com

ISBN: 978-1-961181-28-1

CONTENTS

Foreword by Coach Pete Carroll 7

Acknowledgements 9

Chapter 1. The Journey Begins 11

Chapter 2. Everything Is New 25

Chapter 3. Leaving Home 37

Chapter 4. Culture Shock 55

Chapter 5. A Coach is Born 65

Chapter 6. Coaching-101 75

Chapter 7. The Crash 87

Chapter 8. Struggling 99

Chapter 9. Goodbye Miami, Hello Arkansas 109

Chapter 10. Going Bowling 123

Chapter 11. Heading to the Evergreen State 133

Chapter 12. Death, Anger, Achievement and then Chapter 155

Chapter 13. Back to a Great Culture 173

Chapter 14. Jayhawk Journey 187

Chapter 15. Success Becomes Us 197

Chapter 16. Reconnecting With My Family 211

Chapter 17. Michigan State 227

Chapter 18. What Is Next? 247

Chapter 19. NFL, Here I Come!.............................. 261

Chapter 20. Money and No Job.............................. 279

Chapter 21. You Can't Capture Me.......................... 295

Chapter 22. Shuffling Out of Buffalo 307

Chapter 23. I Found Gold................................... 323

Chapter 24. Carroll's Magic 341

Chapter 25. The Charge to the Natty 359

Chapter 26. Learning About Greed and Effort............... 371

Chapter 27. NCAA Ambush................................. 379

Chapter 28. The Good, The Bad and The Ugly 389

Chapter 29. Not Invited.................................... 401

Chapter 30. Seattle Seahawks 411

Chapter 31. The Draft 419

Chapter 32. Super Bowl................................... 427

Chapter 33. The Wedding.................................. 437

Epilogue...445

Final Thoughts... 453

FOREWORD BY
COACH PETE CARROLL

In 1977, a couple of aspiring young coaches showed up in Fayetteville, Arkansas with the highest hopes and dreams of someday creating a career in coaching football. We had no idea of the value of being around great coaches and the influence they would have on our futures.

At the time, few people realized that Lou Holtz would become an iconic name in college coaching. Or that Monte Kiffin would be a recognized NFL Hall of Fame coach for his masterful defensive genius. The great staff created by Coach Holtz would play such an integral role in affecting the lives and careers of a couple of young graduate assistant coaches just hoping to get a full-time job.

The 1978 Orange Bowl catapulted the careers of the entire staff, and for the two of us, the rest is history. Golden Pat Ruel and I have shared a life in the game of football and have been connected by a love and passion that was fostered with the Arkansas Razorbacks. We have been committed to a principled style of teaching and enthusiasm. The passion that we were introduced to in our first season together has remained eternally with us. Neither one of us has ever backed off of generating that passion and love for the game.

This book will take you deep into the minds and hearts of all great coaches. We learned how to do things right, and how not to do things. We were so fortunate to have competed with our crisscrossing careers. It is with my ultimate respect that I contribute to this extraordinary inside look at the life of Golden Pat Ruel, a great competitor, friend, and partner. I am forever grateful for having shared the sidelines with a lifelong friend, competitor, and teammate.

Always Compete,
—Coach Pete Carroll

ACKNOWLEDGEMENTS

First and foremost, I would like to express my deepest
appreciation to my family for their love and support.
Dad, Mom, Marti (wife), Sabra (daughter),
and David (son -in-law).

I am extremely grateful to Ingrid Ricks who, as
an author, mentored me and kept this two-
fingered hunt-and-pecker (me) on a schedule.

To my high school coaches Coach Castle and Coach
Injaychock, who molded me with their words and actions.

I would also like to extend my deepest gratitude to all those
coaches who taught me the right way to do things, and to
those who demonstrated by actions or words how NOT to
do things. I was paying attention—thanks for the lessons.

To Pete Carroll, Nick Saban, Jerry Pettibone, and
Hal Allen I am deeply indebted for teaching
me the secrets of great coaching.

I would also like to offer my sincere thanks
to the NFL. For its organization,
the opportunity to represent, and of course my pension.

Special thanks to all the teammates at Coral
Gables HS and University of Miami.

Finally, a Big Thank You to Ditto Nowakoski, Susan
Frederick, Brenda Reiss, and Amy Kriewaldt who,
along with Ingrid Ricks, critiqued my chapters.

Finally, to a young man named Mason Moore
who taught me anything can be achieved with
effort and attitude. Thank you, thank you.

CHAPTER 1

THE JOURNEY BEGINS

The greatest game of all time took place after Hurricane Betsy hit South Florida with force on September 8, 1965. I was fourteen and the oldest of five boys. My yard was the natural hub for all of our neighborhood football games. The field was twenty yards long and ten yards across with the goal lines marked by a driveway on one end and a hibiscus bush on the other. But on this day, we decided to change the venue to the Biltmore Golf Club's 15th fairway, which was located within a two-block radius of all the neighborhood boys. This was ideal, as it was flooded, which changed our game from touch to tackle.

John Allen and I were the oldest, so we chose sides. The game began, and what ensued was pure magic. Twelve neighborhood kids throwing, catching, blocking, and tackling in eight inches of water. The entire fairway was covered, making it impossible to establish goal lines. Instead, when any of us caught or ran the ball, we just continued propelling our bodies forward until we were tackled. We were sliding, slipping, and making diving catches. Doing all of this in a deep cushion of water was unimaginable fun. I was a little bigger and a little faster—the star of the game that day. This game was full of life lessons: camaraderie, brotherhood, failure, success, laughter, love, and of course how to handle a few scrapes and bruises.

The game started at two in the afternoon and ended at dark. When my brothers and I arrived home, we were sopping wet and covered in grass clippings. Our fingers were wrinkled from being in water for four hours straight. On Mom's orders, we stripped off our wet clothes at the back door and proceeded to our bathrooms in nothing but our underwear.

As we headed down the hall, we passed by Dad, who was sitting in the family room reading the newspaper. Dad was a big kid who loved to have fun and usually joined us in our neighborhood football games, but this time we had purposely excluded him because we knew we were trespassing. He was a former FBI agent, and we worried he wouldn't approve. But when his eyes caught mine, his face broke into a huge smile that told me he wished he had been there too.

When school resumed a week later and I found myself standing in the football locker room as an incoming sophomore at Coral Gables High School, all of the self-confidence and glory from that day on the 15th fairway had dissolved.

The locker room had the classic smell of sweaty, dirty clothes and shoes. I was in a foreign land. My dad always stressed the importance of having the courage to participate, and to do so with passion. But my courage felt out of reach; I was legitimately scared. I looked around at the huge seniors putting on their gear—shoulder pads, thigh pads, knee pads, hip pads, and hell, even jock straps. It was all foreign to me. Getting dressed was going to be a challenge. I tried to casually glance around the room and make sure I was doing things right. When I finally put my helmet on, I felt like an astronaut.

I was covered head to toe in big, bulky gear, and nothing seemed to fit correctly. I instinctively knew that I was out of place in some way.

The coaches had coned up a practice field, and we were ordered to get in alphabetical lines for stretching and calisthenics, which was a big word for jumping jacks, sit-ups, push-ups and up-downs. The up-downs had to have been invented by some sadistic person. They were done in one continuous motion but consisted of three phases: First, going from a standing position to your chest lying flat on the ground; second, while flat on your chest, snapping up to a squat position; and third, standing straight up before repeating the process.

We seemed to do a lot of these, as it was a great conditioner for football—getting knocked to the ground and getting back up. After 20 of them, I'd be exhausted. Moments of doubt would creep into my head. Did I really want to do this? But there was no way I was quitting; my dad would have been devastated. Whenever I told him I felt like I couldn't do something, he always said, "Yes you can, and you will." It never sounded like a statement, but more like a command from God, with a deep and unwavering voice.

There was another reason I couldn't quit: The only organized sport I competed in before high school was swimming, and I was good at it. My room was full of ribbons and medals from winning the freestyle and breaststroke events. I told Dad that summer I did not want to swim in high school; instead, I wanted to play football.

He said, "Okay, but I expect you to give great effort like you did with swimming."

Confident, I responded, "I will." The deal was done.

Football is played in a highly social setting; that's what I enjoyed about it. Huddling up to call the play, the eye-to-eye and non-verbal communication, and of course, the shit-talking. It just seemed to fit me better. The physical contact of football that day on the 15th fairway was like mustard on a hot dog—a natural fit.

After surviving the agony of calisthenics, Coaches Injaychock and Castle announced that it was time for one-on-one drills. There was an offensive side and a defensive side. It was about blocking or shedding the block. Panic shot through me. My thoughts raced as I tried to figure out a way to avoid this drill. This was so unfamiliar, being covered with all this heavy equipment and going head-to-head with someone else in uniform. This was far different from the game played on the 15th fairway. Now we were all in combat gear, totally designed to keep us safe; it felt more like being locked in a closet. My body had never felt so restricted.

I was scared standing there watching two bodies dressed in combat gear attacking each other on a coach's command. There was the sound of helmets colliding and legs digging, along with some grunting and groaning.

I loved watching football on TV, but now that it was up close and personal, I was having doubts about my desire to play and my ability to do this one-on-one drill. I really wanted to catch and run the ball, but it seemed that because of my size the coaches thought I would be a good blocker. I was no longer the star of the 15th fairway; I was designated to pave the way for the runners and catchers.

At this point, my courage had left on a flight to the Bahamas. But the one thing I could always count on myself to do was find a logical solution to my problems. That's when it occurred to me that I could just make sure I was always at the end of the line. When each player took his turn and came back, I politely put my hand out to show them they were supposed to be in front of me.

As I waited out the drill, I became more aware that my helmet did not fit—I felt like the original bobblehead. On top of that, my thigh pads that I had placed in my pants kept pinching my crotch. Upon examination of some other players, I realized that my thigh pads were supposed to point outward, not inward. I thought to myself, *Damn, I put them in wrong!* This was not my day. To try to fix it on the field would have brought laughter from the varsity players and snickers from my fellow sophomores. It was too late to change it now. Besides, that would be like admitting that I had no idea what I was doing. I just hoped no one else noticed.

For a few minutes, it appeared my plan was working to perfection. Players would take a spot in front of me, and I would remain at the back of the line.

Then I heard Coach Castle's bellowing voice, "Ruel, get up here and take your turn!"

I was caught. As I walked to the front of the line, I acted like it was some sort of misunderstanding, knowing full well that my courage was now sunning itself on a beach in the Bahamas.

Coach Castle signaled me the cadence with his fingers. It was pretty simple: either on one or two. I was hoping for one because I knew that if I had to wait any longer, I would die of stress. I wasn't listening to Coach as he was instructing me. I was just thinking about how my teammates were about to judge me, evaluate me, or make fun of me. I got down in a three-point stance and looked across at the defensive player. We made eye contact for a brief moment. It was then that I realized he looked as scared as I was. We were just two soph-omores doing battle for all the varsity linemen to watch.

I could hear my dad's voice echoing in my head: "Whatever you do, do it with passion."

Coach Castle started the snap count, and I must admit I jumped the gun by a milli-second. I drove my legs like pis-tons in a racecar. They were churning back and forth with no signs of quitting. I drove my opponent back, straining out of fear of failure. Then the whistle blew to signal us to stop. I could hardly breathe. It only lasted five seconds, but it felt like five minutes.

I was unsure whether I was successful or not, but instinctu-ally, I felt that I was. Before I could even look to Coach Castle for approval, he yelled, "That is the best block I've seen by a sophomore in four years!"

I thought that was weird since I heard he'd only been coaching for two years, but it didn't matter; I ate up those words like buttered popcorn at the movies.

My courage picked itself up off the beach and landed back in my soul. I spent the rest of the practice participating fully and giving every drill my all. I was going to be okay.

That evening, I was bursting with excitement as I arrived home and waited for Mom and Dad to ask me how it went. But when they did, I didn't even tell them what Coach Castle had said.

"I did some good things," I said, "but I need to get better."

I knew that was what my dad wanted to hear. Inside, I was saying to myself, *I executed the best block by a sophomore that he's ever seen!* Yes, with those words, Coach Castle performed CPR on my ego.

* * *

48 years later, I was a coach with the Seattle Seahawks in New York preparing to play the real greatest game of all-time: THE SUPER BOWL! We had the traditional pre-game meal at the hotel five hours before the game. It was time to board the buses and head to Metlife Stadium. The bus was deathly quiet. It was February 2nd, and they had predicted snow for the game day, but the adjusted forecast now called for snow to hit late that night with game time temperatures to be a balmy 50 degrees.

When we arrived, it was four hours before game time. As we entered the stadium parking lot, it was buzzing with people. Fans were tailgating with their team's flag proudly displayed, vendors were organizing and selling game paraphernalia, and security personnel were making sure we were going in the right direction.

I thought back to six weeks before, where on December 15th we had played in the same stadium against the New York Giants and beaten them 23-0.

After the game, one of the employees of Metlife Stadium said, "Thank you for coming," then smiled and added, "I'll see you in February."

I smiled back with an ear-to-ear grin and said, "See you then!" Then I thought, *Will I really see him again?*

As we got off the bus, the cool air was refreshing; "Perfect for playing Seahawk Football," we all said.

TV cameras were already documenting the experience, filming us as we proceeded to the locker room. I was trying to take it all in. I always enjoyed walking through the bowels of the stadiums. Most feel emotionally cold and distant with gray cement, visible pipes of various sizes on the ceiling, and signs designating which group belongs where. It's not fancy or impressive until you add the people that make it all work—the officials, food service workers, janitorial staff, management, and security. Then it becomes alive, like a complete metamorphosis: the egg, larva, and then the beautiful butterfly.

Often these essential workers would line the edges of the hallway to greet us and get a glimpse of Coach Carroll, Russell Wilson, or their favorite player. As we approached the visitors' locker room, I imagined the stadium's underbelly as a larger version of the ant farm I had as a kid. We were all moving with a purpose, and now the cold, lifeless stadium was full of life and personality.

When we entered our locker room, trainers, doctors, and equipment personnel were waiting for us. I was instantly grabbed by the thought, *It's really happening!* The locker room had huge banners that said, "NFC Champions," and "Super Bowl XLVIII," and everybody had a specialized Super Bowl name plate over their locker. I thought to myself, *Now that's cool!* I stared at the name plate on my own locker. It had "Pat Ruel" written on it, sitting on top of a picture of the New York City skyline at night. To the left of my name was the Lombardi Trophy with "XLVIII Super Bowl" written underneath it. So many who dream of this will never get here, and yet here I was. The sense of accomplishment was overwhelming—we did it!

Players sat at their lockers, most of them with headsets on listening to their favorite music. Some were on the phone describing the environment to their kids, wives, or close friends. The air was electric. It was as if every molecule in the room had connected us all in this moment of time. Everyone was excited, but we were all acting as though we had been there before.

Coach Carroll had trained his coaches and players to view every game as a championship game. He was totally convicted to this method of preparation, as it created better focus and communication. It was specifically designed to handle moments like the Conference Championship and the Super Bowl. We had practiced it all year; it was who we were—champions! Many of the players had routines that they used in game day preparation, and Coach had told them earlier in the week not to change them.

Coach was normalizing the game to take away some of the anxieties. We had a saying: "Don't make shit up!" It simply meant to trust your preparation and fundamentals. There is another, older saying: "We don't rise to the occasion, we rise to the level of our training."

During game days in the NFL, I traditionally ran stadium steps to calm down. Coaches will often work out or give extra work to players who are not playing. As I walked the sideline around the field after my workout, I became fully mindful of the atmosphere. It was like finding my happy place to the tenth power. The air was crisp and clean, the fans were filing in, and I had this feeling that we were in a moment of destiny. As I walked around the field, there were celebrities everywhere:

broadcasters, former players, and even Bruno Mars for the half-time show.

I looked up into the stands where the Seahawk fans were gathering. They called themselves the 12s because there are 11 players on the field, and so they became the 12th. Proudly dressed in team colors, they were already chanting, "Seahawks!" We loved our fans because of their enthusiasm and passion for the team. Coach Carroll had always said we had the best fans in the world, but he would remind us that there were a few 13s, and to be careful, as they could take things too far. It always made the players and coaches laugh.

As I continued my stroll around the field, the stadium was growing with fans by the minute. I thought about Russell Wilson, our quarterback who would sometimes ask, "Why not us?" It was a reminder that we were there for a purpose: to finish what we started.

It was time for the pregame, where we would all leave the field and then come back out by position. While in the locker room, Cam Chancellor (our All-Pro safety) and I had a tradition. He would look at the clock, and in his anxiety to warm up and get this game started, he would yell at me, "Pat, is that clock broke?"

"I don't think so!" I would yell back.

Cam's voice would get louder; "I think it is."

"Are you sure?"

"You would think that the NFL would get a clock that works!"

"Damn NFL," I would say in agreement. It was then that we would exchange smiles, as we knew it was just a game of nervous energy we were playing.

The pregame was an organized warm-up. It lasted about 15 minutes. As we re-entered the locker room, the game was about 20 minutes from starting. Coach Carroll always loved good team energy before a game, and if he sensed it was low, the assistant coaches would start buzzing around the locker room like bees in a garden. We would create an atmosphere of chaotic excitement in the locker room with music playing and coaches motivating. It was not needed on this day, though; the locker room was filled with energy and a certain craziness that you can only experience in team sports.

It was game time.

As both teams entered the field, it was a little before 5 p.m., and it was already dark. The stadium lights were on, and it felt as if everything was slowing down. Seconds felt like minutes. I was about to participate in the greatest game of all time, not as player but as a coach. That day was all Seahawks. Everything we did was successful. Even 48 years later, it reminded me of Biltmore's 15th fairway in eight inches of water.

Our defense scored first, sacking Denver's quarterback Peyton Manning, for a safety. Then it became the Russell Wilson/Percy Harvin show. The fun was unimaginable.

We defeated the Broncos 43-8. I was standing on the field with my family as the confetti fell. The tears of happiness flowed, and we began to sing a song that Frank Sinatra made great, "New York, New York." As I looked around in a moment of reflection, I wished my father could have been there. Players and coaches hugged each other and their families as we watched the presentation of the Lombardi Trophy to Paul Allen and Coach Pete Carroll.

I asked myself, *How did I get here?* Coach Carroll was an obvious reason, but my thoughts went to Coach Lew Castle, who was a tipping point in my life and, like my father, played a significant part in igniting my passion to be something special.

I decided I should call Coach Castle. For whatever reason, I waited until after the parade, the ring celebration, and our visit to the White House before I looked him up on Facebook. Then I tracked down his phone number through a former teammate. It had been 48 years since I had spoken to Coach, and it was the 48th Super Bowl. Some things just seem to synchronize.

As I dialed his phone number, my anxiety rose; the phone rang a couple of times. Would he remember me? He had to be in his mid-eighties by now. Was he even still alive?

My thought was interrupted when he finally answered in a quiet voice and said, "Hello?"

Excited, I quickly said, "Coach, it's Golden Pat Ruel."

There was a pause, and I briefly closed my eyes, thinking, *Please remember me.*

Then he said, as if we were long-lost friends. "Pat, it's so great to hear from you! I've been following your career."

My nervousness became a rush of love—he remembered me! I jumped the conversation past the usual "How are you?" and with the excitement that only a young child on Christmas day would understand, I said, "Coach, I want you to know that those words that you said to me on the practice field my sophomore year, 'That was the best block by a sophomore in four years,' started my life's journey."

There was a brief moment of silence as I pictured my young athletic-looking Coach now as a gray-haired man.

Coach Castle said, "You made my day!" I was beaming as he continued, "I didn't realize the impact that had on you. I am very proud of you."

All the things he taught me exploded to the surface: Do the little things; don't be afraid to try; teach the younger players; be a great teammate. My journey had come full circle, from my first day of organized football to coaching the Super Bowl.

It was then that I finally said, "How are you?"

"Just getting your call made this a great day."

He is such a caring person, I thought. "Coach, I don't know why I waited so long to tell you."

Coach Castle, like my father, was a diamond. He was hard and unyielding in principal but could shine and sparkle when it came to expressions of love.

CHAPTER 2

EVERYTHING IS NEW

High school was a list of firsts. First time playing organized football, first time I drove a car, first time I went on a date, first time I kissed a girl, and the first time I fell in love. Another first was the integration of Coral Gables High School.

It was the summer of 1965 when my father and mother had the discussion of private school versus public school. My father refused my mom's wishes to send us to a private Catholic high school. He told Mom, "They need the world view, not the closet view." I had no idea what that meant at the time, but my dad won out.

Prior to 1965, there were no black students at Coral Gables High School. They went to the all-black George Washington Carver High School on the other side of the U.S. Route 1 (the main highway). This all changed with court-ordered desegregation. The new black students' choice to be part of our previously all-white school was a testament to their courage and will to grow in a new environment. Culturally, we all benefitted from the exposure as we grew in our understanding that all of us were different in some minute way, and it was our differences that made us all unique. Included in those incoming students was a young man named Craig Curry. His leadership skills and athletic talent were evidence that he was special, and he became our star quarterback.

By the time I was a senior, our football team was recognized as one of the best in the state. It stemmed from our coaches who were disciplined, tough, and most of all, caring! It seemed that they were as much interested in us as people as they were interested in us as football players.

Our Head Coach, Nick Kotys, was a masterful coach! He taught us toughness and had a knack for devious motivation. Nick was a gray-haired man, about 5'10", with bowed legs and a portly body. His face was round like the Cheshire Cat's. He was from Pennsylvania, and he loved coaching. He coached his assistants as well as players. Coach Kotys was a stickler for the little things. He often said, "Don't worry about the big things, boys. Take care of the little things, and the big things will take care of themselves!"

I loved his intensity. What made him special was his philosophy and a smile that could stretch across an eight-lane freeway! He was tough, but he was able to connect us in a way that made hard work seem fun.

The days before the games, we had review practices. After those practices were over, Coach Kotys would call the team up and we would all take a knee, forming a crescent moon shape as Coach stood before us like a general addressing his troops. He would remind us that the preparation was not over, then he would say, "Take your shoes and helmets home and polish them, make the shoes look brand new, and make those silver helmets shine so that your opponent can see the fear of God in your helmet's reflection."

We would then quickly go to the locker room to shower and put our shoes and helmets in our mesh laundry bags. Then we would go to our designated pick-up area for the bus home. Often, we would board the bus and compare helmet scars, then show the girls the marks on the helmets with the sole purpose of proving our masculinity. Playing offensive tackle, I was 6'4" and 215 pounds, and we had a lot of helmet-to-helmet contact.

We would say, "Look at this ding," and some of the girls would look at us like dogs do when they're unsure what you're talking about, heads tilted to one side.

A girl named Becky seemed to be unimpressed as she uttered, "You can make those dings at home with a butter knife." It made me mad, but she was right, and maybe some guys did. Regardless, to us they were the marks of a warrior.

When I got home, I went to my room. I would do my homework then polish my shoes, which were black with black laces. First, I would wipe them clean. Then, I would carefully grab a shoe, put it on my left hand, and apply the polish, making sure I completely covered it. Finally, I would put a shoe on my foot and then my foot on the frame of the bed and buff it until it shined.

Then it was the helmet's turn. Our helmets were already a shiny silver color. I would place it on my lap, clean it with soap and water, and apply a clear wax polish. Then I would take a clean cloth and buff it until it reflected the light. The whole process took about 30 minutes. I knew that my opponents wouldn't see the "fear of God," but, just in case, I made it shine! I guess you could say I bought in fully to Coach Kotys' tactics. When getting dressed for games, I would look around to see if anyone did it as good as I did. When they didn't—and they never did—I felt as if I'd won.

There was something special about each game because Coach seemed to have a unique motivational plan for each of us. We couldn't wait to hear his speeches! We didn't know when they were coming, but we knew he had a plan.

Once, about three days before we played Columbus High School, an all-boys Catholic school, he ordered us to go to the locker room and sit down in front of our lockers. As we filed in, there were not enough benches to sit on, so some players sat on the floor. The room was quiet, and as Coach Kotys entered, all eyes focused on him. We noticed he had a bunch of papers in his hand which he immediately thrust above his head.

"This is Columbus High School's scouting report on us."

We were impressed; most of us wondered how he got that. As we sat silently on the wood benches and on the floor in front of our lockers, he began to read the scathing scouting report aloud in front of the whole team. It was critical about our style, our fundamentals, and our effort. We were in shock! Then Coach read some critiques of individual players, and we hung on every word, hoping our names wouldn't be mentioned. But then it happened.

"Number seventy-two struggles at pass protection."

Are you fucking kidding me? I thought. I was number 72! Well, you can imagine the focus at practice was razor sharp. We were going to show them and Coach that this scouting report was wrong.

And with that, Coach achieved his first victory of the week: a focused team!

Our game against Pompano Beach was a demonstration that Coach would not only use a psychological ploy on us, but sometimes on the other team. That week, Coach told us that Pompano had new jerseys for our game, and that they looked just like Miami High School's jerseys—our biggest rival! Coach seemed upset as he expressed that they were trying to intimidate us. Later that week on Friday, we bussed to Pompano's stadium.

On arrival, we unloaded the bus, and the team went to an open grass area. Coach told us to sit down; it was like being at an outdoor concert, and we were about to hear the main act.

"Listen carefully." His voice commanded our attention. "We will enter the field one at a time, single file, three feet apart around the goalpost and to our bench area. Seniors will lead the way."

We lined up into what must have looked like a humongous centipede and began to slowly walk to the entrance of the stadium. We were all thinking that this was weird, as we usually ran out as a group. We had 100 players on the team because we were a successful football program, and Coach always said, "If you come out for the team, you dress for games." I believe he thought that the more he had to work with, the more gems he would find.

The other team was already on the field with their 40+ players. Then it happened: we ran out single file and they watched and watched and watched as what seemed like a never-ending line of Coral Gables Cavaliers grew toward them, all with shining helmets and polished shoes.

We looked at each other, then across the field, and realized that they must have been thinking, *Oh my god, how many of them are there?*

One of my teammates, Walter Lightburn, knew. He smiled at me and said, "Well, that's a new one," and laughed. We also noticed that, although Pompano's jerseys were new, it was a real stretch to say that they looked like Miami High's jerseys.

We won 41-0.

A couple weeks later, we played our rival, the Miami High Stingarees, in front of 40,000 people. We were both undefeated. The city was growing with excitement. Most high schools had never witnessed that kind of fan support. The Orange Bowl was delirious with frenzied fans.

Earlier in the week at practice, Coach Kotys had called up the team with 15 minutes remaining in practice to announce, "You think you're going to win by throwing your jocks on the field." That was Coach's way of saying that we lacked the effort and concentration to win. He then turned to the rest of his coaching staff and said, "Let them figure this out on their own."

At that moment, Coach Kotys and his staff threw their practice scripts on the ground and walked off the field.

"What the hell is going on?" players were asking. The seniors knew that it was another motivational ploy. We picked up the practice scripts that the coaches had purposefully thrown on the ground and began to run plays. For the next 45 minutes, the seniors were coaching the little things and running plays till we got them right. The coaches achieved their goal. We were now taking ownership of the preparation.

We won against the Stingarees 16-0.

Coach had his devious ways at half-time too. Our final regular season game was Southwest High School. We were 0-0 at halftime. The offense had fumbled three times. Coach came walking down the aisle of the locker room with newspaper sections and started singling out players.

"Bo Dunn," he said, "I guess you've been reading about yourself in the newspaper and have forgotten how to play."

Then he tossed the paper at him angrily, and Bo dropped his head in shame before Coach turned to me.

"Ruel—here, you want to read about yourself?"

I dropped my head for a moment as he tossed the paper at me, but as he cleared the area, I quickly opened up the paper to see my name. It wasn't there; it wasn't even in the sports section. I was bewildered, then Bo shook his head and said that we better pick it up.

We beat Southwest 40-0.

We bussed to all of our games from the high school parking lot. Coach wanted a totally silent bus on the way to the game, as he felt it would keep us focused and show our seriousness about winning. We complied religiously, but with one exception: the last railroad tracks before the stadium. The bus driver always stopped to make sure the tracks were cleared to cross. It was a tradition that a senior in the back of the bus would make a train sound, "*Whooooooo a hooooooooo,*" and Coach would snap his head around with a look that could scare a lion. He would say nothing, just stare as we all tried to become invisible. As a junior, I couldn't understand why anyone would defy Coach's command, then I realized it seemed to be a tradition. Now, as a senior, I couldn't wait to make that train sound. Coach created the atmosphere he wanted but didn't seem to mind us crossing his line for fun; it was like he knew that it was a sign that we loved and respected him and his discipline.

My senior year in high school was truly magical. I was 1st team, all-city! It was December 15, 1967. Our team was 12-0, and we were headed to Jacksonville for the State Championship game against Jacksonville Wolfson. During our six-hour bus ride, we talked quietly about everything, including girls, college, and mostly about going undefeated. As seniors, we tried to talk younger players into making the train sound, but they were both afraid and knew it was a right reserved only for seniors.

It was an unparalleled time for me—undefeated, in love with football, and feeling truly special. There's a unique bond that's developed on championship teams. It was like we were one, connected together like a chain, and our purpose was to demonstrate that it was unbreakable. As we neared the stadium, the day turned to dusk, and I had only one thought: *Can this dream come true?*

As we pulled into the lot, I thought, *Wolfson, we have arrived.* Coach had no devious plan for this one; it was the State Championship Game. We all knew what was on the line. Last-minute preparations for the game were being made and there was an air of excitement and a bit of arrogance.

It was Friday night at the Gator Bowl and time to finish the season. There had been rain earlier in the day. It was a damp 50 degrees. Fans, in their respective school colors, were streaming in. Our fans wore their scarlet and gray proudly. As we started the pregame warm-up, it was common for players to search the crowd for their family or girlfriends. My girlfriend was a cheerleader, and she was always particularly hard to find, as she had an identical twin sister, so I never knew who I was waving at.

On this day, that habit was missing. There was no scanning the 25,000 fans who packed the stadium. Instead, we were focused perhaps too much on each other, making direct eye contact, as if we were checking each other's readiness. At this moment, my family and my girlfriend didn't exist. I was thinking about two things: to make sure that I did "the little things," like Coach always said, and wondering what it was going to be like to go the whole way undefeated.

The first half was filled with mistakes as we fumbled a punt, roughed the kicker, and missed an interception that turned into a touchdown for Wolfson. For the first time all season, we did not have the lead at the end of the third quarter. Instead, we were tied 7-7. It didn't matter, though; we knew who we were.

Championship teams have a high pain tolerance; no matter how bad the situation is, they believe that they will eventually emerge victorious. We finished by dominating the fourth quarter with two touchdowns and held Wolfson to one first down. We won 21-7!

There was no music in the locker room after the game, but we didn't need any. We were dancing and hugging each other in an energetic display of camaraderie that only sports seem to bring.

Out on the field, a reporter was asking the Wolfson Head Coach what it was like to lose to a Negro quarterback. But inside our locker room, we were connected. There was no color barrier, no religious barrier, and no wealth barrier. It was just a group of boys who had caring coaches achieving the ultimate goal. Maybe that day we defeated more than Jacksonville Wolfson.

Coach required all of us to learn the alma mater, and so after games, as our buses got close to the high school, we would all sing:

"On Miami's southern border reared against the sky,
Proudly stands our alma mater Coral Gables High,
Onward, upward be our watchword, conquer and prevail,
Hail to thee our alma mater Coral Gables, hail."

There is something very unifying about singing as a group in celebration of an accomplishment. But this day, we didn't wait to get back to the high school. It seemed as though going undefeated required more, so once the buses were loaded and pulling away from the stadium as our parents, peers, and fans were cheering, we started to sing the alma mater and continued to sing it at least five or six times. It got louder each time. It was a euphoric moment. Coach let us act the fool on the bus home as we sang "Wooly Bully" by Sam the Sham and the Pharaohs.

With each repeat of the song, the whole bus including the coaches would sing "Wooly Bully" until we all laughed.

The celebration quieted for a brief second and then Walter Lightburn, our offensive guard, started to sing "My Girl" by the Temptations. We all knew the words, and his voice was awesome, so again we all joined in for the chorus.

By the time we were 100 miles outside of Jacksonville, the bus went totally quiet. We were spent; our energy was gone.

The seniors were taking the college entrance exams at 9 a.m. We slept the rest of the way.

The next six weeks were a whirlwind of excitement. There was a constant flow of college recruiters coming by the high school, making home visits, each trying to convince us that they were our best choice. It was fun to get called out of class because there was a recruiter in the office waiting for you. Classmates always wanted the scuttlebutt on who everyone was talking to.

During that time, we were declared National Champions! We were the best high school football team in the nation. Seven senior players from our team would go on to play NCAA Division I football.

40 years later, the Florida High School Athletic Association declared the 1967 Coral Gables football team the "Team of the Century."

CHAPTER 3

LEAVING HOME

College football, here I come! I was recruited by the Air Force, North Carolina State, and Memphis State. I signed with Memphis State, and I thought my dad was going to kill me. He asked why I chose Memphis.

I said, "Dad, they hung my name on a banner in the airport. It said 'Memphis State Tigers welcome Golden Pat Ruel.'" Again, I was surprised at his response.

He smiled and said, "Pat, it's your decision, and you must make it work."

I was soaring on top of the world, but a few months before entering college, the world seem to turn upside down. First Martin Luther King was assassinated on April 4th in Memphis, and then Robert F. Kennedy was assassinated on June 5th in Los Angeles, and the Vietnam War was raging.

Even closer to home, during my first days at Memphis State, I learned that it was nothing like the culture I just came from. The coaches were less caring, and the team was a blend of rednecks with their confederate flags, some outlaws who tried to rob a bank, and the normal craziness of teenagers away from home. I quickly joined the latter group. I was about to be involved in some new firsts; first time I was away from home; first time I drank beer; first time I joined a protest; first time I had knee surgery; first time being kicked out of the Air Force ROTC program; and first time arrested! Seems like a lot for a year and a half.

I joined Air Force ROTC training the first week of college because it promised me a deferment from the draft. Lucky me, I got the one "Napoleon" asshole squad leader. He was 5'6" and 150 pounds with a military-style haircut, who never smiled and absolutely loved his power way too much. And here I thought Napoleon was dead.

He asked, "What is your name, cadet?"

I responded, "Cadet Ruel, sir."

"Give me twenty-five push-ups."

I had accomplished this routine several times. One day, I had decided that the no-reason push-up routine was over.

He said, "Ruel."

I said, "Yes, sir."

"You don't like me," he said disdainfully.

"No sir, I do not." It was the truth.

He then pointed to the ground and said, "Give me twenty-five."

I said, "Sergeant, you get down and give me twenty-five."

He sent me to the commander's office, where I was told I would be going to Vietnam if I continued my insubordination. I did continue my insubordination, mostly because I sincerely disliked the Sergeant's infatuation with the abuse of power. Therefore, within two weeks I was kicked out, making me eligible to be drafted. I think this was the beginning of me standing up to the world of toxic authority.

Later that year, I joined the protests against the Vietnam War. The Administration Building's steps were full of students.

Naturally, I was looking for a cute girl to sit next to. I spotted her—she had long black hair and a beautiful smile.

I asked her, "You mind if I sit here?"

She said, "No, not at all."

I nervously said, "Why are you here?"

Her face had that "you're an idiot" look.

I quickly said, "Just kidding."

She smiled, her blue eyes sparkling. I was hooked. She said, "Our boys are dying eight thousand miles away, for what?"

I said, "What about communism?"

The guy on the other side of her exclaimed, "Ideologies will fail on their own, JFK!"

She looked at me and I said, "Great point," hoping to see that beautiful smile again; she obliged. I was now involved in deep conversations for the first time in my life, talking about things that were much bigger and more complicated than our own existence. It gave me a sense of importance. We were not only questioning war, death, and foreign policy. We were discussing the meaning of one's existence. I thought, *If I'm going to be sent to war, I might as well try and stop it before I have to go.* I knew some of this would land me in hot water with Dad, but I was away from home and out of the corral like a wild horse roaming the plains.

A few days later, this wild horse was riding on a bus to Hattiesburg, Mississippi. The freshmen team was going to play the Southern Miss Golden Eagles. It was 300 miles from Memphis, a five-hour bus ride. Varsity took airplanes to anything over 250 miles. This was just like high school; get off the bus and go play. I played some defensive line, offensive line, and was on the kickoff return team and the punt team.

It was a night game in early October, cold with a light fog. As we entered the field, I told Bill Reddish, one of my team-mates, "Spookie should be here." Our head coach at Memphis State was Bill 'Spook' Murphy.

We laughed and he said, "Why do they call him Spook?"

"I have no idea," I said.

It was an eerie, chilly night, the temperature in the 40s. The fog hung over the stadium, amplified in the lights. Fresh-men games were not usually big venues for fan attendance, but this one was strictly for those who loved you a lot.

The second quarter of the game had started. Our offense had stalled. Fourth down, we had to punt. I was on the punt team and stayed on the field. My job was to block my area, then release to tackle the punt returner. I was the first down the field, which was an awesome feeling—running full-speed and feeling the strength of my legs and rhythm of my arms churning away to tackle the punt returner.

I was like a pilot diving in at high speed to fire on a lone ship in the water. The pleasure of high-speed contact was totally exhilarating. It felt intrinsic to proving your manhood to the rest of the tribe.

Bearing down ten yards away, the punt returner was look-ing up with his hands extended, the ball near.

I am going to crush this guy, I thought. The ball and I would arrive at the same time. I was less than two yards when the ball went through his hands—he had fumbled. I made an effort to leap over him, but my legs hit his helmet and shoulder pads. Suddenly, I was doing a great impression of Simone Biles, the world's greatest gymnast, as I was flying through the air, arms flailing and legs searching. I landed perfectly on my face and chest. The ball was between my legs. Before I could reach it, several players came crashing in on my legs.

That's when I heard what sounded like someone ripping paper. We un-piled. We had recovered the ball. I was jogging toward Coach at the sideline. I thought I was ok. Coach signaled me to stay in. I pivoted, my right knee buckled, and I fell to the ground.

Oh no, please don't let this be bad, I thought. The trainer had run onto the field and was now examining me. He moved my knee. It was loose.

He said apologetically, "Pat, you're done."

"And that means?" I asked.

He said, "We'll get the doctors to look at it."

The game was over. We loaded the bus for home. I was given no aspirin or pain killers. I didn't care; I thought it would demonstrate my toughness.

That toughness went on vacation about one hour into our five-hour trip back to Memphis. The pain was excruciating. Most everyone had fallen asleep. It was like having one of those brain freezes you get from drinking something really cold on hot day, only it was in my knee, and it wouldn't stop. Seconds became minutes, minutes became hours, and hours became days.

A couple of times I moaned out load, one of the players said, "You'll be ok."

I said, "It really fucking hurts."

Another teammate said, "You guys shut up, I'm trying to sleep."

It was 2:30 a.m. We made it back. My leg had locked in a 90% angle. I needed help getting off the bus. The trainer handed me crutches and said, "Be at the training room at 7:30 a.m. The doc will be there."

What the fuck? I have to crutch a quarter of a mile and climb three flights of stairs? I looked at him with disgust and said angrily, "Great." A few of my teammates offered to help me, but there was nothing they could do except keep me company on my trek to my room.

I didn't stay in my room long. I had taken aspirin, which was not working. I was grunting and moaning while lying on my bed.

My roommate Bill said, "You want to go to the hospital?"

I said, "No, I'm going to the training room and waiting for the trainers." I knew he was being caring, and I felt I should show him the same respect for his sleep. My second trek across campus, it was almost 4 a.m. The pain seemed to be declining, or maybe I was getting used to it. I waited patiently, but I was filled with anxiety about my future. Sitting on the cold cement steps, I was actively reprimanding all those who seemed not to care.

Finally, the trainer and the doctor arrived. It was 7:15 a.m. They walked me into the training room, and I immediately hoisted myself onto an examining table. The doc grabbed my lower leg and moved it back and forth. It ached, but there was no throbbing pain like I'd had for the previous ten hours.

He looked at me, shook his head sadly, and said, "I think you tore your posterior cruciate completely."

I immediately realized that was the sound of paper tearing.

He then turned to the trainer who was nearby and said, "Get him to the hospital immediately."

"What does this mean?" I asked him.

He replied, "You need surgery to repair the ligament."

The trainer helped me get in his car. As we drove to hospital, I was thinking, *I need to have a good attitude.* I remembered Coach Injaychock saying, "Attitude is everything."

We drove up to the entrance of the emergency room. It was like they knew I was coming. A nurse was pushing a wheelchair toward the car.

I opened the door, and she said, "Hi, let us take care of you."

Working on my attitude, I said, "Hiiii," in a happy voice. The nurse rolled the wheelchair through the front door, and I was shoved off to the side as she left to attend to somebody else.

The trainer said, "You're all set, paperwork is done. I'll come back later."

In the following 45 minutes, I watched the emergency room become like a football game. Everyone was communicating in a professional manner, like they were running medical plays on patients. It felt a bit like organized chaos—nurses and doctors moving in every direction. The smell of antiseptic alcohol was pungent. Then they rolled a man on a gurney past who was sitting up and bleeding profusely from his head. The blood was dripping down his face.

I asked the nurse with concern, "What happened to him?"

"I think the wife hit him in the head with a porcelain plate," she answered dolefully.

A few moments later, they rolled another gurney by. This patient was sitting up as well, and he had two bloody spots on his abdomen. They rolled him in the room right across from me. I watched as doctors and nurses were trying to get him to lay down.

The same nurse walked by, and I asked, "What happened to him?"

This time she answered in disbelief, "I think he was shot."

Early Sunday morning at the ER was a whole new world that I knew nothing about. I was beginning to feel abandoned when they finally gave me a room.

A doctor entered and said, "We will prep you for your surgery in about an hour, then we'll repair your ligament."

Being away from home was like being forgotten. *Did anyone call my family?* I wondered. As if on cue, my room phone rang, and I picked it up. It was my mom.

"Are you ok, sweetheart?"

I said, "Yes, they're taking me in for surgery in an hour. Does Dad know?"

Mom said, "Of course, he's on his way up." There was a brief silence, then I said, "Mom, I'll be fine."

Conversations with Mom and Dad on the phone were always brief. I could sense something was not right with Mom. She was slurring her words, which seemed odd to me. We exchanged goodbyes, and as I hung up the phone, I was both worried about Mom and relieved that Dad was coming.

When I woke up from surgery, there was a huge gift basket from the Memphis State Tigers booster club. I had a cast all the way to the top of my leg. When my teammates started coming by, I was disoriented, the drugs in control, but still glad they came.

Then Dad entered the room. *He's here...* I tried to talk, but my words were garbled. I had no control over my tongue. I heard some laughing, then Dad leaned over and said, "I talked to the doctors. Everything went fine." He put his hand on my shoulder, and I fell asleep.

The next couple of months was all physical therapy. The trainers did a good job; my right thigh was a one quarter inch bigger than my left thigh—now that's some good rehab.

During my recovery, Jay McCoy, a running back from Southwest High School in Miami, took me under his wing, with us being Florida boys. I liked having a wingman like Jay. He was a year older and tried to educate me on college life.

I was almost done with rehab when Jay and a few of the older guys decided I was going on a trip to Hernando, Mississippi. The drinking age was 18 in Mississippi at the time. My birthday was December 5th.

"I'm seventeen, and I can't drink until my eighteenth birthday, which is four days away," I told them.

"Just get in the car, we got you," Jay said.

We loaded up in a blue Ford Fairlane and picked up three six-packs of Schiltz beer at a convenience store as soon as we entered Mississippi. Then we headed to Hernando. It was less than 30 minutes from campus. They handed me a beer in the back seat. I had never drank any kind of alcohol in my life. I sipped it, didn't like the taste, then surreptitiously poured half of it out the back window. I was determined to stay in control as I handed them my empty can, and they gave me another. I had the equivalent of three cans of beer, and I knew something was wrong when the taste was all of sudden a moot point, and I was laughing at everything.

We pulled into a country western bar. No one asked for ID, and soon I'd had three more beers.

There was a group of Marines being loud and boisterous. My Florida wingman Jay McCoy said laughingly, "Shut those Marines up, Ruel."

I was too drunk to realize they were taking advantage of me. I got up, climbed up on top of the table, and hopped over to their table, knocking customers' beers over along the way. When I reached my destination, they quickly tilted it, and I fell to the ground, causing a bar room brawl.

We were thrown out, and while in the parking lot, I exchanged words with the Marines who were now in a car pulling out. I chased their car on foot. They literally left me in the dust. Acting like I was some kind of tough guy, I walked back into the parking lot with red and blue lights flashing behind me. Jay and some others were cheering my idiocy. The police grabbed me and told me to put my hands on the hood of their car.

I was suddenly scared. *What was happening?* Police told me to spread my legs. I thought I did, but he hit me on the inside of my left leg with his baton. It hurt a lot, and I pushed my legs farther apart.

"Don't do that again!" I said.

The cop quickly hit my right knee, the one they operated on. Without thinking, I spun around, snatched the baton out of his hands, and threw it deep into the bushes. Within seconds, my face was on the hood of the car, and I was handcuffed. It was then I thought, *What am I doing? I just ruined my life.* I was being arrested for public drunkenness, disorderly conduct, and resisting arrest. The cops put me in the back seat of a police car.

I was frightened but was in solution mode. I was often complimented by my dad for never getting into trouble. It wasn't that I didn't participate in some shenanigans here and there—I just always knew when to skedaddle. Not this time; the alcohol destroyed my instincts. As we proceeded to the jail, I vacillated from terror to humor.

I pleaded with the cops. "I've never drank beer before. I'm away from home and I'm going to lose my scholarship," I said, digging hard for some compassion. They were ignoring me, so I continued, "Well, how come I don't get the siren?"

One of them turned on the siren, laughed, and said, "Now shut up."

Arriving at the Hernando jail, they took me out of the car, and I made my final plea. "Watch me walk a straight line." I held my head high in concentration and put one foot in front of the other. After about five steps, I was flat on my face in the grass as I heard them laughing. The sidewalk had taken a right angle which I didn't see.

They picked me up, and one of them said, "Good try," as they both laughed.

Once inside the police station, they uncuffed me and told me to put my hands on the counter as they patted me down and emptied my pockets. One of them was calling out the items as the other was writing them down. "Eight dollars and twenty-five cents, wallet, and Thomas Jefferson." He was referring to a plastic presidential coin I acquired from a purchase at a drug store.

I laughed nervously and said, "How did Thomas Jefferson get in my pocket?"

They laughed, and one of them said, "Maybe he'll read you your Bill of Rights." We all laughed.

They escorted me to my jail cell. When they slammed the door shut, I felt like my soul was being evicted from its home. I laid on the bed and closed my eyes, hoping this was all a bad dream. The room was spinning. I tried to put my legs on the floor to make it stop.

It did not stop.

When I woke up in the morning, I was lying on the cold cement floor in my own vomit. There was a gross sour smell that almost made throw up again.

My life is over, I thought. *I let everybody down. My family, my team, and myself.* I wanted to cry, but there was a piece of me that was tough, unrelenting, and extraordinarily positive. As I lied there, I was telling myself, *Be a man, be accountable, and get back on the right track.* In actuality, it was my dad who was in control of my inner voice.

They pushed a breakfast of powdered eggs and grits through the jail door slot on the floor. Just looking at it almost made me puke again. *How could this be happening? Why did I drink the beer? Will the coaches take away my scholarship? Will Dad find out?* My thoughts were racing around in my mind like a frustrated dog chasing his tail. I was in a state of confusion.

A cop finally came to my cell and said, "We're supposed to hold you for twelve hours, but one of the guys on your team paid the hundred and twenty-five dollar fine, and because you're seventeen, it won't go on your record. You can leave an hour early."

Finally, things were beginning to look up. I was escorted to the lobby. The police gave me back my money, wallet, and

Thomas Jefferson plastic coin. My teammate, Jay, was waiting for me with a huge grin. As we walked to his car, there was silence, but the fresh air felt good.

Then Jay said, "What a crazy night, huh?"

"Yes, it was, Jay. You got me drunk, and you got me into a fight."

"Sorry." Jay smirked as he thrust a piece of paper into my hand. "We paid your fine. Here's who you owe one hundred and twenty-five dollars."

It was lined school paper with a list of 30 players who contributed. It was a crazy list, mostly freshmen like me, contributions of one to twelve dollars.

"Thanks," I said sarcastically. As far as I was concerned, he was the culprit.

Jay waited until we were in his car, then dropped the atom bomb. "You made the papers."

"The coaches know?" I said as my heart fell on the floor.

"I think you know the answer to that." He smiled, then quickly added, "You're going to be okay."

My head hurt from the alcohol, my body was sore from fighting Marines, and my knees ached from being whacked with a baton. I just wanted to take a shower and escape—get into deep sleep hoping it all would go away.

But I can't. I have a debt to pay. Where do I get a hundred and twenty-five dollars? I had an idea.

No way I could ever tell my dad what happened, and lying to him was very tricky, as he always seemed to know. I thought acting excited about something would be a great cover.

I called Dad, and the second he answered, I nearly shouted, "Guess what? I have a date to a formal!"

Dad said, "That's great."

Without hesitation, I continued, "I need some money for a tux, corsage, and dinner."

He curiously said, "How much?"

"Ummmm, about a hundred and twenty-five dollars."

"I'll wire you the money. Have a good time."

That was too easy. "Thanks, Dad!" I said. I pulled it off.

The next day, I went to Western Union and picked up the money from Dad. I paid everybody off and successfully hid it from him.

Dealing with the coaches was different; they had read the paper. Coach Murray Armstrong was in charge of the freshmen and was a dorm supervisor. He informed me that my punishment was running. I was to meet him at the track at 5:30 a.m., where I would run laps until he was satisfied. I ran laps around the track for two weeks.

Coach Armstrong always gave everybody nicknames. As I ran the laps for about 30 minutes, he would yell, "Hernando Hurricane, you need to pick it up." I was in the best shape of my life, but my world was upside down.

I felt I was heading in the wrong direction for the first time in my life. I was so far away from home; the atmosphere there was nothing like I experienced in high school; the life I knew had disappeared. I wanted that feeling of my senior year in high school back. I felt empty.

I called Bo Dunn, my good friend and high school teammate. He had received a scholarship from the University of Miami. I asked, "How do you like Miami?"

He said, "It's great. I like the coaches too."

It was time to tell Dad. I wanted out of my bad choices. I wanted a do-over. I called Dad.

He said, "How are you doing?"

"Dad, I want to come home."

"Why?"

"I don't think this is a good place for me."

Again, Dad uttered, "Why?"

It was then I finally said, "Dad, I got kicked out of ROTC, and there are a lot of bad people here. They go to Mississippi to drink and get into fights."

He responded, "Ok, come home, and we'll talk about your future."

"Thanks, Dad. I want to transfer over to University of Miami to play for the Miami Hurricanes. I talked with Bo Dunn. He said he liked Charlie Tate, the Head Coach," I said enthusiastically.

As I said goodbye, it occurred to me that I was the problem; I was the one making the bad choices. My first action of accepting responsibility was the elimination of beer. That time in Hernando, Mississippi was the last time I drank a beer, ever!

Arriving back in Coral Gables, I received a gut punch. I was informed first by my brothers and then by my dad that my mom had a problem with alcohol. She refused rehab. Dad had felt it was too toxic for the kids.

My mom and dad had separated; Mom was filing for divorce. I had friends in high school that had suffered through a divorce, but I never thought it could happen to our family. I was old enough to accept it but trying to understand it was like a problem without a solution.

Dad assured me that everything would be ok. "Take care of you, and let me handle this," he said.

Later that week, I met with Coach Tate, and he told me to go get an AA degree. I could transfer into Miami on a full scholarship. My dad seemed to be pleased with me pursuing a course of action. He was happy with my decision but quickly pointed out my reason for signing with Memphis was a lousy one and explained why more thought should go into future decisions.

I asked, "Why didn't you stop me?"

"You will learn more from your decisions than if I make them for you."

After being home for a week, my dad strategically waited for a dinner with my brothers to pop me a few questions.

He said, "How was your formal date?"

Puzzled, I said, "What formal date?"

"The one you needed a hundred and twenty-five dollars for," he said.

"Oh! Yes, that was a great time."

Dad laughed and said, "Where did you go for dinner?"

I said, "Some steak place."

He said, "What was the name of it?"

My eyes started to water up. I knew that he knew everything and was seeing how far I would take this lie. I said, "Dad, I'm sorry I let you and the family down." I started to explain why it happened, telling him, "Jay McCoy gave me too much beer."

He then said a couple of things that impacted me for the rest of my life. He said, "Pat, ninety-nine point nine percent of all the problems you have in your life are either directly or indirectly related to decisions you made." Then after taking a bite of his spaghetti, he looked me directly in the eyes and said, "Don't ever lie to me and don't ever try to explain your lousy behavior by using somebody else's lousy behavior."

It was in that moment I learned three things: Lying is unacceptable; be accountable for your behavior; and don't mess with a former FBI agent. Dad knew the minute I asked him for money something was up. He called the coaches, and they told him. He then waited three months until I arrived home and was sitting at the dinner table—where he could look me in the eye and make an example of me in front of my brothers—to tell me, man to boy, to "grow up."

CHAPTER 4

CULTURE SHOCK

I arrived at the University of Miami all fired up. With an AA degree in hand, I was ready for spring training with the Miami Hurricanes. I showed up for the team meeting full of excitement, but it quickly turned to concern. Just a few weeks earlier, Miami fired Charlie Tate. It was immediately clear that the new coach, Fran Curci, didn't have the same genuine attitude or warmth. When he spoke, he sounded disingenuous. It had a feeling of US versus THEM from the very start.

"Let me introduce you to two of my henchmen," he said, motioning to his assistant coaches. "This is Coach Mirilovich and Coach Baily, and we're going to find out who's serious about playing football."

It was the era of four-year scholarships; you could only lose them by quitting, flunking out of school, or committing a criminal act. It was clear in the days to come that they were going to make players quit to make way for new ones that they had picked.

I thought the up-downs were tough in high school, but things just got way tougher. Most of the drills in the off-season program were weed-out drills, taking us to the point of exhaustion. The coaches were militaristic in their style. Tuesdays and Thursdays were particularly rough. Knowing what we were about to go through, nobody could even eat lunch. We would sit at the dining table staring off into the distance with nausea and anxiety. We knew in three hours we were going to be in hand-to-hand combat.

As we walked over to the athletic facility, guys would bitch about what we were about to do. Steve Robey, an offensive guard who was always philosophical, said: "How important is this bullshit going to be five years from now?"

I laughed. Steve could make me laugh in the most stressful moments.

Entering the locker room on those afternoons was like going on a trip to hell. As we dressed in tennis shoes, shorts, and T-shirts, my only thought was, *Who am I going to fight today?* Then I would say to myself, *Does it matter? Just get in and get it over with.*

We would stand outside the "Insanity Room," as I called it, waiting our turn. It was an artificially turfed room, 30' by 30', with no windows. The walls were cement block painted yellow. The room was originally used for stretching and pre-practice walk-throughs, but now it was a war room where we were expected to use any method necessary. We would elbow, kick, punch, headbutt, and sometimes bite. We all knew the coaches were trying to make us tough and run off the weak ones. We knew it was wrong that we were disrespecting each other, and it was the opposite of what we knew team sports to be.

As we congregated around the door of the Insanity Room, waiting for our turn to enter, the air was always stifling with tension and nervousness as we wondered whether we were going to win, or at least survive. There would be a lot of yelling and screaming going on inside, then suddenly the door would open. When it did, the heat would pour out. The players were covered in sweat, some were bleeding, and they all looked exhausted. As they passed into the locker room, they spoke with their eyes: "This is such bullshit."

It was our turn to go. We ran into the room and aligned ourselves in pods around the perimeter, then ran in place until we heard our names called out. The air in the room was thick and smelled musty, like an old, deserted house, and the heat was at least 95 degrees. We were in full sweat after two minutes. In the middle of the room, my opponent and I would kneel down facing each other and grab a towel with an inside grip and an outside grip. The point of this was to either pin the opponent or get him to let go of the towel.

We were in the third week of the Insanity Room, a Thursday. I was 6'4" and weighed 245 pounds. I was quicker than most of the bigger linemen, and I knew I could handle myself, but I was sick of this shit. My roommate, Bill Murphy, had quit the week before, transferring to Maryland. I made no effort to talk him out of leaving. I knew his reasons were justified. It was then that I realized that the ones that left the program were not weak; they were smart. They did not want to subject themselves to the abuse.

While I was running in place, drenched in my own sweat, I heard it: "Ritchie and Ruel, you're up."

Fucking great, I said to myself. Ritchie was one of the most naturally strong players on the team.

My position coach, Jon Mirilovich, was 6'2" with broad shoulders. He looked like a Marine, acted like one, and had a mean streak a mile wide. This day was no different.

Ritchie and I knelt down, grabbing the towel, and as the battle began, my coach yelled, "Ruel, you're pathetic. You can't get that towel." As I continued to fight, he yelled, "You're a pussy, Ruel."

I'd had enough of the degradation. Dropping down to their level, I quickly headbutted my opponent, opening up a three-inch gash in his forehead. He let go of the towel as blood dripped down his face. I was not a human in that moment; I was an animal without cerebral thought or compassion. I won and immediately thought about punching Mirilovich—he was turning me into something I did not like.

The Insanity Room was disgraceful, a showcase of how fragile we are when pushed to the brink with no morality, just the will to survive and come out on top. It was football at its worst. Morale was low, as 25% of the team quit in the off-season program. The henchmen were winning.

I thought back to when I was seven years old. We'd lived in an apartment building in Chicago, Illinois. The apartment was called the Paddington, and it was on Irving Park road in downtown near Lake Michigan. One Saturday, Mom asked me if I wanted to go to the playground.

"YES!" I exclaimed. It had swings, a seesaw, and a sandbox. My mom walked me down and sent me out to play as she stood outside the fence and watched. I would occasionally glance over to Mom to make sure she was watching.

On this day, a nine-year-old boy, who was 2-3 inches taller, confronted me as I walked into the playground.

He said, "You have to leave."

When I ignored his command, he shoved me to the ground. I had already started to cry, and as I got up, he knocked me down again. I was in full crying mode by this time. I ran to Mom, who tried to console me.

"We'll come back when he's not there." She grabbed my hand and walked me back to our apartment. "Honey, it will be okay, he's just a mean boy."

As we neared the door to our apartment, I wondered, as tears rolled down my face, if Dad was going to be mad. When Mom opened the door to our apartment, we walked toward the kitchen. Dad said curiously, "Why are you crying?"

I guess I was too busy crying to answer, so Mom answered for me: "He was shoved on the ground by another boy who was just being mean."

For a second, Dad did not speak, then he assumed his usual calm manner and said, "Quit crying."

My crying turned to sniffles.

"I'll take you back to the playground," he said simply.

Mom shot Dad a warning look. "Honey, that's not a good idea."

Even at seven years old, I knew the look on his face; he was no longer entertaining opposite points of view. "He needs to learn from this."

He grabbed my hand and started to walk me out of the apartment and to the playground. I felt a source of strength that he was by my side, but as we got closer to the playground, he announced, "I want you to punch him in the nose."

I started to plead with Dad, telling him, "No, I can't."

He said, "You have to."

As we got close to the scene of the crime, he instructed me to enter the playground. He was not coming. I was terrified. My dad stood back and away from the fence. I glanced at him several times as he gave me the go-ahead nod. It didn't take long for my nemesis to spot me. As he walked toward me, I stopped; I was confused and scared. As he got closer, I glanced in my dad's direction, and again, he gave me the nod.

We were now face-to-face.

"I told you to leave," he barked.

Still sniffling with semi-dried tears on my face, I landed a punch right on his nose! He fell to the ground, his nose bleeding, and I ran back to my dad, seeking safety.

Dad looked down at me and smiled. "He won't bother you again." I smiled half-heartedly, then Dad said, "Pat, you have to stand up for yourself."

I wasn't sure as a seven-year-old what it all meant, but at that moment, it felt good. I punched a bully, and my dad had his supportive hand on my shoulder. He was proud of me, and I was pretty happy with myself as well. I don't think I could have ever punched that bully in the nose without his affirmation.

A week after my headbutting incident, the Florida State football program was criticized in the newspaper for running an identical off-season program. The story went national, and the Insanity Room died. But the abuse continued.

We started spring practice, and some coaches would grab players by their face masks and jerk them around as if we were deaf and couldn't hear them. Steve Gaunt and I discussed how it wasn't right and decided it was time for us to say something to our position coach. We gave each other the go-ahead nod. Arriving at the coaches' offices, I had the same anxiety I had as that seven-year-old on the playground. I readied myself to confront one of the most abusive coaches on the staff.

"What do you fucking want?" he barked as we entered his office.

Oh, my god, I wanted to punch him. We sat down, looking at each other, then our eyes locked on the coach, and I blurted out, "If you grab us again, we'll punch you."

He laughed evilly and said, "Get the fuck out of my office." As we left the facility, we looked at each other.

"That did not go well," Steve said.

We weren't the only ones who had reached their limit. My offensive line teammate, Wiley Matthews, who was 6'5"and 290 pounds, usually had a wonderful disposition. But now he was rumbling like a volcano, and two days after our useless meeting with the coach, he erupted.

We were doing a three-on-three drill, and every time Wiley got into a three-point stance, Coach would put his foot on Wiley's butt and shove him into the block. After the third time, he snapped. He got up and threw his helmet about 20 yards from where we were standing.

"Go get your fucking helmet," Coach yelled.

But Wiley wasn't listening—he'd had enough. He took off his jersey, then his shoulder pads, before slamming them to the ground.

Coach yelled at him again, "You fuckin' baby!"

Wiley walked toward him and then in a sudden move grabbed Coach by sliding his hand inside his collared shirt. In a twisting motion, he lifted Coach up onto his toes and walked him backward, threatening to kick his ass.

"I am sick and tired of you!" he screamed.

Coach looked stunned. His eyes were big, and everyone could see he was scared. I was cheering inside, *Please deck this asshole!*

"Don't ever fucking touch me again," he bellowed. Wiley shoved him, then turned and left the field.

We were worried about his mental state. I yelled, "It's okay, Wiley!" Others offered him words of encouragement as well, and no one even bothered to ask Coach if he was okay—we didn't care.

The next day, we had a team meeting because the Head Coach had kicked Wiley Matthews off the team for assaulting Coach Mirilovich.

This time, it was Steve who stood up and said, "You can't treat us this way!" His words fell on deaf ears. Nothing resulted from the meeting.

Ironically, a mile and a half away from our practice fields at the University of Miami was Coral Gables High School's practice fields, where Coach Kotys, Injaychock, Castle, Coughlin, and Scarnecchia were treating a new group of players with dignity and respect.

Outside of practice, we very rarely talked about anything other than survivability, classes, and girls. Football was an afterthought. We had a saying among the players: "Win, lose, or tie, there's always Big Daddy's after the game." Big Daddy's was a local bar not far from campus. It was where we found a bit of joy. Football was no longer primary. We loved the competition of games, but we lacked the cohesiveness and camaraderie that makes team sports so special.

Being close to my dad, I told him what was going on, looking for advice.

His answer was, "Pat, there are always hurdles in one's life—you must become a good hurdler."

How he simplified everything always amazed me. I fully understood this piece of advice. When obstacles are thrown in your path, jump over them and keep going. Dad's advice fueled me. I had decided that my abusive coach couldn't beat me.

At the end of my senior season, we turned in our equipment, grabbed our jocks, and headed out to the field for the "burning of the jocks." It was a senior tradition. It was symbolic of what was past and what was to come. I was glad it was over. Coach Curci and his staff were burning their jocks as well. They knew it was over for them, and Curci managed to secure himself a new head coaching job at the University of Kentucky. Though we did not have a winning season, we had talent, and some went on to play in the NFL.

NFL scouts came by and asked if I was interested in an opportunity to play. I said to myself and to them, "I'm done."

CHAPTER 5

A COACH IS BORN

I was walking across campus after a clinical psychology class, when I ran into Bo Dunn, my high school teammate who had encouraged me to transfer to Miami.

"Hey," he said, "the new coaches are at the football office."

It was the spring semester of my senior year. I was done with the football shit.

Looking at Bo with my "who gives a rat's ass" face, I said, "And?"

Bo glared at me with contempt. "I thought you'd like know."

I could feel Bo's anger, so I quickly changed my attitude. "You know what, I'll go over and say hi."

Bo smiled. "I knew you would," he said, as if he knew me better than I knew myself.

When I had burned my jock two weeks earlier, I thought I was done with the football facility. Two years of its toxicity was enough. But now, as I walked the quarter mile, I was relieved that Curci and his henchman were gone. Now I was curious about the new staff.

Entering the football offices parking lot, I ran into Coach Whitey Campbell who was the freshmen coach under Curci. He was one of the few likable coaches on Curci's staff.

"Golden Pat Ruel, just who I was looking for." He said that to everybody, but it always made me feel good.

Coach started to give me the low-down on the new coaches and told me that he and coach Harold Allen, our defensive line coach, were retained. Just then, the new head coach, Pete Elliott, walked out of the football facility and headed toward me. I guessed he was about 6'1". He had a slender build, blond hair, a square jaw and a warm smile. I could tell he was an athlete.

I extended my hand, and he grabbed it with both of his, as if we were friends in a previous life. He pulled me close, his face less than eight inches from mine. That only happened when I was about to be kissed by my mom or my girlfriend. It made me a little uncomfortable.

"It's great to meet you. I've heard some good things." Before I could utter a word, he added, "How would you like to be a graduate assistant coach?"

I was shocked, as I had just come to grips with being divorced from football. Again, before I could respond, he continued with his pitch. "You will have room and board, and we'll take care of any graduate classes you need." He talked with such joy and passion. I was fascinated by his enthusiasm. It was if I was the only thing that mattered.

I really hadn't given much thought to my direction after graduation, but I knew I liked psychology and needed a master's degree, and now someone wanted to pay for it.

I finally responded, "I would love to."

He was still holding my hand between both of his, and I could feel him squeezing my hand like the deal was done. "Great, Patrick! You'll love this opportunity—you'll work with Coach Selmer, our offensive line coach and offensive coordinator."

I was so caught up in Coach Elliott's emotional warmth. In less than two minutes, I cancelled the divorce and was on a honeymoon with football again. This time as a coach.

As I walked back to my apartment on campus, my thoughts were already bursting with ideas about coaching. I wasn't a great player, but I was going to be a great coach. I was already developing my mindset. Plus, I had a special secret. It was given to me by Curci and Mirilovich. The secret: What not to do! I was already 50% better.

It was a euphoric moment. Like Coach Castle, Coach Elliott had just given me a path for my future and I couldn't wait to tell Dad. Arriving at my apartment, I didn't even go in. I jumped in my car and made the mile drive to Dad's house.

I was like a rocket ready to launch. My inner excitement was now rushing out of my soul like a dam that had just broken, but I forced myself to act like I had done this before.

I could hear my dad talking to my twelve-year-old brother Jeff as I entered the house. He was obviously giving him a lecture on something. I stood in the foyer impatiently waiting for the discussion to end. When it did, I stepped into the family room to make my presence known.

"Oh, hi Pat, you need laundry done?" Dad said with a chuckle.

"No Dad," I snapped like a bolt of lightning. "I came to tell you that University of Miami's new head coach offered me a job coaching."

"And...?"

"I'll bring the laundry over tomorrow."

His eyes lit up, and he smiled like he had won the Super Lotto. "That's great, Pat. I'm very proud you! When do you start?"

I beamed. "Monday."

He opened his arms and gave me the famous go-ahead nod. I stepped in, and we embraced in an emotional hug. I could feel the rush of love and happiness that I had just given him. As we broke the embrace, he laughingly said, "You do know how to use the washer and dryer?"

During those twenty-two years of my life, my father had been my disciplinarian, my guidance counselor, and my mentor. Now he was becoming my best friend.

When I reported to work, I could already tell that the players' attitudes were more upbeat. There was a halo of positivity hanging over their heads. Could the genuine enthusiasm of one man have that effect? I loved his energy and was soaking it in; so were the players. I was still puzzled from my initial meeting with the head coach in the parking lot. *Why did he get so close to my face? Why was he holding my hand with two hands?* I wondered if I should even ask that question. I didn't want to offend him, I but needed to know. My father always said I ask too many questions.

I was trying to find the right time, and this was it—it was the end of the day, and I spotted him in the hallway heading to the parking lot.

I gathered up my courage and approached him.

"Coach, why do you get so close to my face when talking to me?"

He smiled, moved closer, and said, "Dale Carnegie wrote a book called *How to Win Friends and Influence People.* This book describes how important it is to make a connection to whoever you talk with, make eye contact, be sincere, listen, and have a genuine appreciation for them. You should read it. You're half there already."

I smiled, then said, "I will."

He winked at me, turned, and headed to the parking lot.

Later that week, I went to the college library and checked it out. I read a chapter a day. It was all about treating people with respect. Making them feel good. I felt like sending a copy of the book to Curci and Mirilovich, as they were the antithesis of this book. Curci was a manipulator, and Mirilovich was an abuser.

This book sparked my interest in another coach on Curci's staff who was retained by Coach Elliott. His name was Hal Allen. He survived seven head coaches and spent two decades at the University of Miami. He coached Ted Hendricks, Ruben Carter, Eddie Edwards, Tony Christiani, Don Latimer, Gary Dunn, Don Smith, Jim Burt, Lester Williams, and Jerome Brown. All of them were All-Americans or NFL first-round picks. He hardly raised his voice at practice. He was the opposite of my position coach. All the players admired him. What was his secret? I wanted to know.

I was walking toward his office after two weeks on the staff, determined to pick his brain.

"Can I ask you a couple of questions?" I said, as soon as I stepped inside.

"Of course," he responded. It was like he already knew he was about to teach me something. There was something infectious about Coach Allen. Though he was in his early 50s, he had a boyish grin that made him seem a lot younger. He was built like a defensive lineman. He had square shoulders and athletic legs. His hair was always combed with a frontal wave. It reminded me of pictures we would take as a family on Easter after church; my brothers and I had the same wave.

Now my hair was long like the Beatles', and I wore a necklace made of Hawaiian puka shells. I was a true sign of the times.

I pulled up a chair next to his desk and settled in. "You know all the players wanted to play for you," I said. "We hated Mirilovich."

He quickly came to Mirilovich's defense. "Pat, there are a lot of coaching styles. John was a hard-ass, and he didn't connect with the players like he should, but he was an excellent technician."

His response really surprised me because Mirilovich was universally despised by the offensive linemen. But I was not there to talk about Mirilovich; I wanted coach Allen's secret.

"How come you don't yell and scream at players like some of the other coaches?"

He laughed and said, "Pat, that's not my style."

"You were always telling players secrets," I continued. "You would put your hand on their shoulder, lean in close, and whisper through the earhole of their helmet. What was that about?"

He flashed his boyish grin at me. "Go home tonight, and sometime after dinner, put down the newspaper, look at your girlfriend, and say, 'I love you.'"

I smiled and said, "That's it?"

"Yes, just do it—it's your homework assignment."

My girlfriend Marti was a senior cheerleader for the University of Miami. We had been dating for two years.

On the way to her apartment, I reviewed my homework assignment and laughed to myself. Easiest homework ever. But I was wondering, *What is the purpose of this?*

Later that evening in Marti's apartment, I was sitting on the couch reading the sports section of the newspaper. Just like he told me, after five minutes, I quickly pulled the newspaper down toward my lap, making that ruffling sound.

"Hey," I said, grabbing her attention. "I love you." I never told her she was part of a homework assignment.

She smiled and said, "I love you too."

There, I was done. *I should get a good grade for that,* I thought.

The following morning, I was anxious to tell coach I had completed my assignment. I walked down the hall to his office. When I entered, before I could say anything, he smiled and asked, "Did you do your homework?"

"Yes. It was easy," I replied.

"Tonight's homework will be tougher," he said, chuckling.

"Really?" I gave him a doubtful look.

"You're going to do the exact same thing as last night, except when you put the paper down, you're going to get up and go to her. You're going to hold her in your arms. Gently push her hair away from her ear, then put your lips close and whisper, "I love you."

I laughed. "Seriously, Coach, are you pulling my leg?"

"You want to learn or not?" he retorted.

I was beginning to wonder if I was the recipient of a staff joke. It was a thought that continued to play through my mind as I drove to Marti's apartment that evening. I decided to go along with it.

Like the night before, I settled on the couch, hiding behind the sports section of the Miami Herald. Marti was sitting at the kitchen table studying. A few minutes had passed; it was time. I folded the newspaper and laid it down on the table.

I walked toward her and said, "Can you stand up?"

"Why?" she asked.

I said, "Because it's part of a homework assignment."

She laughed. "Well, ok."

I immediately grabbed her around the waist. She turned as if to get away. I was now behind her and thinking my homework was not as easy as I thought. I tightened my grip around her waist with my left arm, and she started to giggle. Then I raised up my right hand to her hair and pushed it aside. I moved my lips close to her ear and whispered, "I love you."

My homework was done, but it became the catalyst for a two-hour physical education period. Wish all homework was like this.

That next morning, I went to the football office earlier than usual. I couldn't wait to get my next homework assignment!

Coach Allen was already in his office when I entered. "Homework part two is done," I announced.

He looked up from his desk. "What did you learn?"

I sat in silence for about a minute as he stared at me.

I finally said, "Whispering is much better than talking."

He shook his head, making it clear I had missed the point. "Well, not exactly, Pat. It's about strengthening your message. When you want to connect deeply with someone, it helps to be more intimate. To share something between one another that only you and that person know is powerful. That's why I often whisper to my players—it creates a connection. If I whisper,

'Great job putting your hands inside and maintaining leverage,' the other players want to know what I said. That player now becomes the teacher as they ask, 'What did Coach say?' They usually can't wait if it was complimentary, but if I whisper, 'That's not a championship effort,' then it's between him and me. The player never has to wonder what the other players are thinking because it was never shared."

Everything he was saying made complete sense. It seemed so elementary. How come I never read about this or even thought about it? I was shocked that in all my psychology classes the power of intimacy was never addressed. Dale Carnegie, Pete Elliot, and Hal Allen knew.

"Who taught you this?" I asked.

"My father." He continued, "When my mom was upset, Dad would often put his arms around her waist and whisper in her ear. She immediately calmed down, as if she had been shot with a tranquilizer."

"So, it's more powerful to whisper in a player's ear that what he did was unacceptable when I'm upset?"

Coach smiled and said, "It's disrespectful to yell negative things at anybody. Let me tell you a story. It was Christmas time, and a mother had taken her five-year-old son with her to Macy's to pick up some last-minute gifts. Walking by the toy section, the young boy spotted a truck. He told his mom he wanted the truck.

"The mom said, 'No. Christmas is almost here.' The boy immediately fell to the ground, throwing a temper tantrum. Kicking his legs and flailing his arms while crying, he yelled, 'I want a truck now!' A sales lady in the toy department said, 'Miss, we can't sell toys with that going on.'

"The mom responded, 'I'm trying.' A manager stepped in and offered a sucker to the boy lying on the floor. The boy said, 'I don't want a sucker. I want the truck.'

"'Get the company psychologist,' the manager said to the sales lady. Within minutes, the company psychologist arrived, the boy still crying and pleading for the truck. The psychologist said, 'Listen to me. You're being a bad boy, and if you continue, not only will you not get a truck, you might not get anything for Christmas.' The young boy continued his tantrum, and the psychologist said in frustration, 'Get Santa. Maybe he can help.'"

Coach Allen paused for a second, and I sensed he was getting to the climax.

"Santa arrived on the scene. The young boy, unrelenting, kept demanding the truck. Santa bent over and whispered in the young boy's ear. The boy got up, sniffling and trying to wipe his tears, no longer pleading for the truck. As the young boy and his mom departed, the others asked, 'What did you say?'

"Santa said, 'I told him if he didn't stop crying, I was going to break his fucking arm.'"

Coach Allen and I laughed, and I got the message of the whisper. It was about making a connection, an intimate one.

"Thanks, Coach," I said as I got up to leave.

He flashed his boyish grin. "Pat, just be you, and you'll do great."

CHAPTER 6

COACHING-101

Wow, what a change in culture. Coach Elliott and Coach Allen gave me the main ingredients to creating better relationships and better communication. I was so excited; I could feel myself growing like a sapling, being watered every day and soaking up the sunlight. My attitude was full throttle. The Curci years were filled with storm clouds, and now, under Pete Elliott, the sun was shining.

After a week on the job as a graduate assistant, I was learning what it was to be a coach. We usually started with a staff meeting in which Coach Elliott would address the staff, going over things he wanted to get done. He always spoke in terms of the team: we must, we can, and we will. Then he would add, "This is so exciting, what an opportunity we have."

I was blown away at the amount of organizational planning for practice, the detail in the teaching. I never really thought much as a player about what a coach's daily life was about. I was in uncharted waters.

There were four areas that Coach Elliott emphasized. The first was evaluation of the players we had on campus. We wanted to put the best players on the field, playing their best position. We would talk about players who were flexible enough to play other positions as well. Speed, strength, and ultimately the athletic skills for every position were discussed about each player. We often tried to put size dimensions on each position. Certain players did not fit the profile, but they were remarkably good because they had natural instincts for the game.

The second area was recruiting. It was an evaluation of possible prospects. We each had an area to recruit. It was the first time I heard, "Recruiting is like shaving—if you don't do it every day, you'll start to look like a bum." Recruiting is the lifeblood to any athletic program. We needed to evaluate and target the players we wanted. This included letter writing, phone calls, and building relationships with the athlete, the mom, the dad, the brothers and sisters, and even the dog, if need be.

The third area was the design of the offense and defense. This was primarily done to take advantage of our personnel and to create difficulty for opposing teams. This included situational drills that would help develop our execution. The drills used were first- and second-down play calls, third-down play calls, blitz pick-up, and goal-line and short yardage.

The fourth area was Coach Elliott's real talent: creating a positive atmosphere and developing bonds between the players and the coaches. Dale Carnegie had nothing on Coach; he was a natural. Having done my undergrad studying in psychology, I was eating up his approach like a starving man at a buffet.

Going into the office each day was a joy. My first stop was always Coach Campbell's office because he started my day with an emotional boost.

"Here's one of the all-time greats," he would say, or another, "Just who I was looking for."

He said these phrases all the time, but they never got old. He had a way of making both players and coaches feel special. His desk was covered with papers three to four inches high. You would ask him for a schedule, or a ticket request, and he knew which pile to look in and how deep to go, handing it to you in less than ten seconds. I was mesmerized by his chaotic efficiency.

After leaving his office, I would head down the hallway to Coach Selmer's office and immediately put on my serious face. There was nothing playful about Coach Selmer. He was mathematical and methodical. His balding head and constant scowl reminded me of an aging accountant. The truth was that he was one of the top offensive line coaches in the country. Just the year earlier, he had helped lead the University of Nebraska to back-to-back National Championships. Despite our personality differences, I was very eager to learn from him.

Coach Selmer was all about detail; he planned drills, practice, and office time down to the minute. Every drill was designed to teach specific fundamentals. When Coach Kotys said, "Do the little things and the big things will take care of themselves," it was if they were raised by the same parents. When I was around Coach Selmer, I was intimidated by how much he knew and scared that I would not meet his expectations.

Each day was the same. It was like I had been there a thousand times already. We would review practice drills and watch film from Nebraska. He was teaching me the drills we were going to use.

I usually pulled up a chair next to his desk and listened as he pointed out proper fundamentals and techniques. Toward the end of the week, he switched it up.

"Take a seat at my desk and look over the practice drills for the first week," he said, "I'll be back in a few."

As I settled into his black leather chair, I reached into my back pocket to pull out my pen. "Oh no." I felt something wet; my fingers were covered in black ink. The cap had come off and was leaking in my pocket.

Quickly, I ran down the stairs to the locker room to change and clean up. When I returned five minutes later, Coach was sitting in his chair. My eyes darted from his face to his tan slacks. He started to review drills, and I kept looking to see if his pants had black ink on them—they did! I suddenly felt queasy. He spotted me looking and put his hand down where I was staring. He pulled up black fingertips. The oxygen had left the room.

Oh shit, he's going to kill me.

He gritted his teeth and his lips pulled back; it was a classic pit bull expression.

"Coach, my pen broke in my back pocket," I said, then quickly added, "I ran downstairs to clean up and thought I would be back before you."

"Look what you did to my chair and my tan slacks!" he growled.

I was sure that he was going to fire me. "I am so sorry," I managed. "Let me clean the chair."

"What about my pants?" he snapped.

"I'll pay for new ones," I replied remorsefully.

For a few seconds that felt like hours, he didn't speak. Finally, he sighed, "I have to coach you and the offensive line; they're not paying me enough."

"Sorry, Coach," I said again. There was another long pause.

Then he looked at me and smiled. "Are we going to let a little ink get in our way?"

I was thankful to be re-invited into his world of offensive line fundamentals. He was different from Mirilovich in that he never cussed, never allowed his anger to consume him, and after criticisms, he would occasionally smile and let you know everything was good.

There was an enthusiasm that suddenly had overtaken the football program. Coach was connecting with the team, university, and community. I was very happy to be back in a good culture. I was back in love with football.

We were scheduled to open the 1973 season with the Texas Longhorns, which Sports Illustrated had just named preseason number one.

We were sitting in the offensive staff room talking personnel when Coach Campbell stepped in and held up a copy of the magazine. There on the cover was the University of Texas pennant with a "#1" next to it and a hand symbolizing their motto: "Hook 'em, Horns."

"Here you go. Something to make you start drinking and smoking," he said as he tossed the magazine on the conference table.

There was an immediate bit of anxiety in the room. But that dissipated moments later when Coach Elliott walked in. He grabbed the magazine, held it up, and said, "Miami beats Texas in opening season upset."

His optimistic, playful tone immediately shifted the mood in the room. Coach tossed the magazine back on the table, but it was immediately snagged by Coach Selmer, who conveyed in a serious tone, "We are going to play the number one team in the nation right out of the box, and we have secret weapons."

"And those are?" Coach Elliott said inquiringly.

"Ruel and Endicott." Selmer started laughing. It was so unlike Coach Selmer to be funny that everyone joined in. Endicott was the other graduate assistant coach. He and I smiled graciously. We were the worker bees and usually the targets of their ribbing.

Coach Elliot flashed his wide Dale Carnegie grin. "Of course, we can't lose with those two."

I loved the fellowship of being part of this coaching staff. We had a large task in front us: turning around a floundering football program.

Our schedule was a bit scary. We were independent and had no conference affiliation. We were scheduled to play Texas, Alabama, Notre Dame, Oklahoma, Florida, and Houston, all of whom were ranked in the top 20 in preseason polls. Those teams scheduled us because we were an easy mark, a sure win. Did we schedule them because we wanted to make our mark in the college football community? Or was the athletic director on drugs? I never did get the answer to that question. *But Miami* is *the cocaine capital*, I thought jokingly. It's prudent in any college athletic program not to schedule yourself out of a job.

Texas, here we come.

I was on an emotional high, my kilowatt meter off the charts, and yet I was filled with concern. I knew we had the right attitude, but how good were we? Could we beat the number one ranked team in the nation? My thoughts jumped to a phone conversation I had with my dad earlier in the week.

"Are you ready for Texas?" he asked.

"Not yet. We have to do the goal line and short yardage game plan. Then we have to cover all substitutions for all the game situations—" Before I could add more and impress him with all that I had been learning, he cut in.

"Don't tell me how stormy the sea is, just bring in the ship," he chuckled.

My dad had trained as a Navy pilot, and he had a few sayings from his Navy days that seemed to always arise at the appropriate moment.

Game day finally arrived. How could I be totally excited and filled with concern at the same time? It was like I was two people going back and forth, like a walking metronome. The team boarded the bus. It was eerily quiet. It stayed that way until we pulled into the stadium parking lot, then the chatter started.

"Let's do this!" someone barked.

Then another yelled, "Fuck the Longhorns."

As we unloaded, another chimed in, "I'll be selling Longhorn hamburgers after the game."

For a moment, I felt like a player and wanted to yell something, but I caught myself. I could feel the confidence as we entered the locker room at the Orange Bowl.

For the first time, I understood what it was like to be a coach.

Did we work enough blitz pick up? Did we cover the substitutions? We just need to be close in the fourth quarter—that will give us a chance to win.

Our preparation and the attitude and desire to compete showed up. Watching our players play and execute fundamentals that we taught them was exhilarating. During the game, I was constantly telling offensive players, "We can do this!" I even cheered the defensive team as they stuffed the Texas Wishbone attack. I wasn't really coaching, I was transformed into a cheerleader, like my girlfriend Marti, who was now a senior cheerleader.

I was not involved too much in the strategy of the game. Instead, I helped with charting our plays and the results. Texas scored first, and it was 6-0. We were playing them tough. We scored twice in the second quarter and went into the locker room at halftime with a 13-6 lead. The enthusiasm was in abundance. We all were acting as if we had already won. It was an affirmation that the positive attitude that Coach had created was working.

Coach Elliott called up the team. It was suddenly as quiet as a vacant church.

"Winning the first half was great, but we must win the second half," he stressed. "We are right where we need to be. Now let's finish it."

I ran out on the field for the start of the third quarter as if I had just won a championship and now was going for another.

The third quarter ended with us leading 20-12. Then the momentum shifted. Early in the fourth quarter, Texas managed a field goal for three points. Then, with less than three minutes left on the clock, their quarterback pitched the ball to his halfback, who was running down our sideline. He had a clear path to the end zone. As he passed me, my heart sank. I threw out a prayer to the universe: *Please, God, no.* Then there was a divine intervention; he was slinging the ball next to his side, and his own hip pad knocked it loose.

"Get the ball, get the ball!" I yelled to anyone on my team who would listen. The first two of our players ran right by it, but the third player recovered it. Destiny had moved into our hearts. We won the game 20-15.

I was jumping up and down hugging players when I spotted my girlfriend. We ran toward each other, and then she jumped on me, wrapping her legs around my waist and her arms around my neck.

"Oh, my god, we did it, we did it!" she screamed. I was holding her up in my arms, basking in the glory like a conquering hero.

In this moment, I felt separated from the life of the ordinary, and catapulted into the life of the extraordinary. I was hooked. If ever there was a doubt of who I wanted to be, it was gone. I was given the most powerful drug. The drug of belonging to something special. I had this drug in high school, and it was awesome to taste it again. I was addicted to coaching.

By beating Texas, the number one team, we became part of history. We perpetuated the mythical Sports Illustrated Jinx. Whoever they put on the cover had a bad performance immediately following their cover story.

As I walked out of the tunnel of the stadium, I couldn't wait to see my dad. He was standing where he always stood after my games as a player.

We made eye contact as I hurried toward him. Our smiles lit up the night as we hugged. Dad whispered in my ear, "I am very proud of you."

"Thanks, Dad," I said. As I pulled back, both of us had glossy eyes.

"Go celebrate. Your ship has docked."

The following day, I couldn't wait to read the sports page. I picked up the Miami Herald on my way to work. I immediately turned to the sports section.

Oh my god, what the hell is this?

I froze. There, underneath the headline, was a large picture featuring my embrace with Marti after the game. Her legs and arms were wrapped around me, with my hands holding a clipboard which pinned her raised skirt against her back. Her orange cheerleading panties were in full view. The caption read, "Coach and Cheerleader celebrate upset win over Texas."

There was something about it that made me think I was in deep shit.

I arrived at the football facility, thinking that surely everybody would understand that we had been dating for three years. But I was still bracing myself for the backlash.

The first person I encountered was Coach Campbell.

"Just who I was looking for," he boomed before breaking out into laughter. "You have some explaining to do."

My defensive mechanism kicked in. "You're jealous," I shot back.

He continued to laugh. "I am; I was hugging Ruben Carter." Ruben was our 270-pound, all-American defensive lineman.

I continued down the hall to Coach Selmer's office, where we were going to grade the offensive line's performance together. Selmer never said a word about the picture. We were halfway into the film together, when his phone rang.

He picked it up and said, "He's here. I'll send him down."

Then he looked at me and said, "Coach Elliott would like to see you in his office."

I got up and sighed. "I hope I'm back in a few."

Coach had a puzzled look as I left his office.

I was nervously trying to organize my explanation. As I headed to Coach Elliott's office, I was greeted by his secretary. "Go in. He's expecting you."

Taking a deep breath, I stepped into his office.

"Hi, Coach," I said enthusiastically, trying to hide my concern.

Coach, who was seated behind his oversized desk, flashed his trademark smile. "Great win last night. How are you doing?"

I breathed a sigh of relief. "Great, Coach. Thanks for asking."

"Did you hug any coaches?"

Oh, here it is, I thought as my stomach churned. "No, Coach, I didn't," I said in a subdued tone.

He bent to the side and picked up the sports page, then pointed to the picture and said with a smile, "This is more than a hug. It's like you're dating her."

"We *are* dating," I said.

"Well, I know that Pat, I just want your date to start after we depart the stadium." He winked at me.

"Yes, sir," I barked. "That won't be a problem."

I turned to leave his office, relief engulfing my body. I was walking down the hall back to Coach Selmer's office when I spotted Coach Walden, our running back coach.

"Where is my hug?" he asked.

I said teasingly, "Next week."

Coach Allen's door was closed, but he had pinned the now infamous picture on his door. It was clear that the staff had already bantered about the coach-cheerleader picture.

As I returned to Coach Selmer's office, he said, "I'm not going to comment on your post-game activities—let's get back to grading the players."

My serious look was plastered back on my face and we proceeded to grade players' performances. I was right where I was meant to be.

CHAPTER 7

THE CRASH

It was mid-March, and Coach Elliott called a 1 p.m. staff meeting, which was highly unusual, as we always met in the morning. All the coaches were in a good mood. Recruiting was more enjoyable after a winning season.

All the coaches were in the staff room sitting in their usual seats. Coach Elliott and Coach Selmer were not there yet. It was kind of odd, since Selmer was so disciplined with time and Coach Elliott was rarely late. The coaches were talking quietly, giving me a feeling that something new was happening.

Coach Selmer and Coach Elliott finally walked into the staff room five minutes late. Elliott put his hand on Selmer's shoulder and announced, "Carl is taking over as head coach. I will maintain my job as the athletic director."

The announcement stunned me. I respected Coach Selmer, but he was more reserved and calculated; he didn't fit the head coaching type.

We all clapped and started to congratulate Coach Selmer. He suddenly looked much younger, as his smile was stretching into unknown territory. I was happy for him, but then the full weight of the words started to sink in. My mind went immediately to, *Who is going to take over the offensive line?*

My thoughts vacillated between, *I can do this!* and, *Do they think I'm too young?* I knew I was prepared. I spent the last two years absorbing everything I could from one of the best line coaches in the country. I was participating in staff meetings and coaches responded well to my ideas. I was energetic and did everything to prove my worth.

After the congratulatory session for Selmer died down, Elliott flashed one of his Dale Carnegie smiles and said, "Coach Ruel will take over the offensive line duties."

I nearly jumped out of my skin. I was so excited that I wanted to hop on the table and shout my thanks to everyone there like an awards show acceptance speech. I knew I owed my success to them; they had all generously shared their gifts with me. I did my best to stay calm and composed, but I was like a teenager with his first car.

Coach Selmer said, "You had a good teacher."

"I did. Thanks, Coach," I said humbly. The other coaches began shaking my hand. I could feel the wave of exhilaration rushing over my body. After congratulations, I went to my desk and immediately called Marti. She had graduated and was working as a corrective therapist.

The call was brief because she was working, but she was so happy for me. Before we hung up, she asked, "Have you called your dad yet?"

"No, but I will," I replied.

"Do it now. He'll be so excited!"

I was thinking about playing a prank on Dad. I was going to tell him that I quit. Then when he asked why, I would shout, "Because I just got hired as a full-time coach with a real salary!"

I was dialing Dad's office. Soon, I had his secretary, Betty, on the line. "Golden Ruel Insurance." My dad started his own insurance agency after leaving the FBI.

"Hi, this is Pat, is my dad there?"

She happily responded, "Why yes, he is."

After a slight pause, Dad answered the phone. "Hi, Pat."

Any thought of playing the prank went out the window. "Dad, Pete Elliott gave Carl Selmer the head coach job, and he's going to stay on as athletic director." I purposefully paused to wait for his response.

"What does that mean for you?" he asked. It sounded like he already knew.

"I think this is when you should use your FBI skills," I chuckled.

"Well, according to the radio report someone heard here at the office, you're the new offensive line coach," he said with joy.

"You weren't going to call me?" I said in amazement.

"I told my secretary, 'Let's see how long it takes him to deliver the news.' When she smiled at me and nodded confirming it was you, I looked at my watch. It took you three minutes," he said smugly.

"Well, I called Marti first," I snapped pompously.

He laughed and said, "Of course you did. I think we should all go to dinner at the Yorkshire restaurant and celebrate on Saturday."

"That would be great, Dad."

"Invite a few of your friends if you'd like."

When I hung up the phone, I thought how lucky I was to have a dad who had become my best friend.

I was excited about showing my coaching skills and looking forward to exhibiting my talents. I started by developing relationships with my players because I knew that was a primary secret to their success. Every day, I brought my enthusiasm. But there were signs of a looming storm as well.

The first sign was the press guide. During Coach Elliot's tenure, it was first class. But now the press guide looked like it was put together by third graders. On top of that, there was no money for recruiting. It was clear Miami was no longer investing in the football program.

We had worked hard in the off-season to prepare our team, but the Elliott magic was gone. We lost our first four games of the season. Coach Selmer's serious and often defensive tone was picked up by the press. He lacked the charisma and communication skills. I thought he should read *How to Win Friends and Influence People*. The press would ask him tough questions, and he would get angry. I knew he was under a lot of scrutiny, but I also realized being a head coach required a multitude of skills. It's not good enough to be an excellent coach. One must be a lightning bolt for the program, flashing, shining, and gleaming. It was about creating confidence for the players, coaches, and community.

Selmer's one-on-one communication was fine. In front of the team, he was an accountant. He lacked energy. It was like we were at a lecture about spread sheets and ledgers. We played teams tough, losing close ones, finishing 2-8. Some of that amazing drug had worn off. Losing was taking its toll.

When you lose, you start to question everything: coaching, schemes, effort, and commitment.

Coach Elliott, as the athletic director, addressed us at the end of the season. "The University might be thinking about dropping football as a sport. They're not providing us with necessary funds to operate a Division One program." It was evident that Coach Elliott's enthusiastic nature was being crushed, and he was evaluating our losses as well. We had no conference affiliation, and our attendance was dropping.

My dad always said, "Before you evaluate others, evaluate yourself." I was looking at things internally, wondering what more I could have done. Eventually, I came to the conclusion that the problem was much bigger than me.

This was reflected by the 1976 football press guide issued two weeks before our football season was to start. It looked like it had been reduced to kindergartner level. I was so disgusted I stopped by Dad's house and left the press guide on the kitchen counter while he was at work. It was driving me crazy that we were all working so hard, and they weren't investing in us.

On Sunday night, September 12, I was in the football office studying for our season opener versus Florida State. I suddenly thought I should call Dad to ask him what he thought about the crappy press guide.

The phone rang.

Dad answered. "Hi Pat, are you getting ready for Florida State?" he asked as soon as he heard my voice.

"Yes, I'm at the office now."

"We're ready too. We got our season tickets in the mail last week."

"That's great, Dad. Did you see the press guide I left at the house?"

"Yes, I did. And I noticed that you and that other young coach who coaches the special team are the only ones wearing puka shell necklaces. When are you two getting earrings to match?" he said jabbingly.

"Funny, Dad. I'm talking about the actual press guide. What do you think?"

"Well, it definitely looks cheap, and it's missing staples," he said with laugh.

"That's what I think too. It seems to be a harbinger for the future of our football program."

Dad's voice took on the teaching tone; I recognized it immediately, as I had heard it so many times before. "Pat, don't worry about that stuff. Just go be a great coach."

It was just what I needed to hear. I was worried about things I couldn't control. Dad put me back in a good mood and helped me focus on beating Florida State.

The next day was Monday September 13th, my grandmother's birthday and the start of the preparation for game week.

I arrived at the football office early as usual. I immediately dove into studying film and taking notes. After a couple hours of work, I decided to take a break to call Nana (my grandmother) and wish her a happy birthday.

The phone rang several times, but there was no answer. Just then, Coach Allen popped his head in my office. "Why are you here?" he asked.

I glanced at the clock; it was 10 a.m. I knew there wasn't a meeting I was supposed to be attending. I shot him a puzzled look. "What do you mean? I work here."

I noticed his trademark boyish grin was gone. "Have you talked to Coach Selmer?" he asked. I looked into his eyes and they were penetrating, as if he wanted to speak but was afraid to. I became overwhelmed with a fear that something terrible had happened.

"No," I said, concerned.

"Go see him now," he said.

My mind began to spin. Why hadn't Nana answered my call? My enthusiasm for the day was being squandered. I had a slight feeling of nausea. I reluctantly picked up the phone receiver and dialed home. After one ring, Nana answered.

"Nana?"

"Pat, please come home now." I could hear her voice break.

"Why?" I asked. I could feel the waves of panic crashing inside me.

She didn't answer for a moment, but I could hear her crying. "Just please come home," she said finally.

I was consumed with animosity as I hung up the phone. *What the fuck? No one is telling me anything!* I grabbed my car keys as I stepped into the hallway, nearly bumping into Coach Selmer, who had positioned himself just outside my door.

"We got this. Go home."

My stomach was in knots as I drove out of the parking lot. Everything seemed to slow down. Every tree, bush, person walking, and car driving by was caught in a hyper-focus. My mind felt like a camera taking snapshots so I would remember this day.

It was a beautiful day; the sun was shining, the sky was cloudless. But I was feeling the army of anxiety marching through my body telling me something was wrong—really wrong.

As I drove the mile to my dad's house, my thoughts jumped to my grandfather who I called Bampa; he had been struggling with heart issues for the past three years. Maybe he had a heart attack, or maybe one of my brothers had a car accident?

Turning down Santa Maria Street where my dad's house was, I could see 20-30 cars parked on the street and on the grass. I pulled into the driveway, got out of my car, and took a deep breath. The garage door was open, so I took the back way into the house. I opened the door and saw all these people looking sad—many were crying. Then everybody's eyes shifted to me. I could feel the emotional sledgehammer was about to smash me. Suddenly, Bampa was in front of me. His eyes were red and filled with tears.

He reached his arms out to hug me and said in a broken voice, "Your dad was killed in a plane crash."

I stepped back and away from him, looking at him in disbelief. My voice cracked as I said, "No... It's not Dad, it's somebody else..." I was met with silence. "It's not my dad!" I yelled. "It's a mistake!"

I could feel the anguish in the room. It was stealing my breath away. My legs suddenly felt weak. My eyes darted around the room, looking for someone to agree that it was not true. All I could see were sad and crying eyes.

I fell to my knees, tears pouring off my face as I cried uncontrollably. *How could this happen?* "It's not true! It's not true," I said repeatedly. It was like I was trying to end a bad dream. My heartache was like an earthquake sending painful vibrations through the core of my body.

I could hear garbled conversation; "It was a mid-air crash with an Air Force jet"; "He flew his private plane so they could get back in time for one of the passengers' daughter's birthday"; "The weather is perfect. I don't understand how this happened."

Then a hand went under each arm and lifted me up. Two of dad's good friends helped me to my feet and walked me to the guest room. I laid on the bed all alone, going from denial one minute to sobbing the next.

I asked God several times, "Why did you take him? You should have taken me."

After a while, I could hear Dad's voice from the night before replaying in my mind, "Don't worry about that stuff. Just go be a great coach." Dad had found his way into my soul. He was reminding me to let go of what I couldn't control and stay focused on what I was meant to do. Get up, be strong, go thank his friends and employees for coming. I walked out of the room and back into the sea of mourners.

The hard-core pain was dying. I was now an empty vessel adrift in the ocean of sorrow. I walked around thanking them for coming.

Many of them said, "I know how you feel."

No, you don't, I thought angrily to myself.

Nothing made sense until Cleve Allen said, "No one can possibly imagine the pain you're going through. Only time can heal this, Pat."

My anger subsided for a brief moment.

Cleve's son, John, was a great friend and a participant in the greatest game on Biltmore's 15th fairway. Cleve had lost one of his twin sons in a bad car accident. The other son survived with severe injuries. He knew of the pain I was experiencing; I could see it in his eyes. His words hit home. Time was the answer.

I wanted to escape this scene. I looked at Nana; she was completely heartbroken. An extraordinarily strong woman, she had lost one son already to cancer at the age of 27, and now she had lost her last son at the age of 49 on her birthday. She looked at me with the saddest blue eyes, swollen from crying. "Be strong—the family needs you," she said. I was intending to do that, but uncertain that I could accomplish it. I was completely numb but feeling like I was gaining control. I shifted into coach mode.

"Hey everyone," I announced, "I'm going back to the office because I have players there who need me to coach them." My grandfather gave the go-ahead nod.

Others protested, "Stay here, please."

I turned and walked out of the house. Where was the rain, the lightning, the wind? Shouldn't mother nature be just as angry and sad as we were? I got into my car, put my hands and head on the steering wheel, and started crying again. Nana's words kept attacking me. "Be strong—the family needs you." I wiped the tears away and drove back to the office in a fog.

"Why are you here?" Coach Campbell asked when he saw me.

I snapped at him angrily, "Because my dad wants me here."

Finally, stepping into my office, I sat down, just wanting to think about football and my obligation to the team. But I was continually interrupted by a stream of coaches and players that wanted to express condolences. On the outside, I tried to show them I had the heart of a lion, but on the inside, it was the dying heart of a lamb.

Our team secretary stepped into my office with a glass of cold water. "I'm so sorry," she said. Her voice was caring and soft. "I thought you could use this."

I forced a smile. "You're right. My tear ducts are empty."

Despite my attempt at humor, I was still in an angry stage. Everything went on as normal. It was not supposed to be fucking normal; everything should be in chaos. But no, the sun was shining, people attended to their daily routines, and practice was happening in 30 minutes.

My attitude needed to change as I walked out to the field. The staff and players were great, giving me space to breathe and talking about beating Florida State.

As practice progressed, Larry Brown, who was one of my tackles, executed a block perfectly and I said, "Larry, that block is the best thing that has happened to me today." Again, an attempt at humor.

"I wish I could give you a hundred of those, Coach."

I smiled and thanked him.

* * *

Later that week, Coach Selmer told the players they were dedicating the game to Coach Ruel and his father.

I was holding up pretty good, but between meetings, I would stop in the office kitchen and release a few tears.

We beat Florida State 47-0, and they presented me the game ball. I tucked the ball under my arm and walked through the tunnel and out of the stadium. I quickly looked at the spot where my dad had stood so many times. He wasn't there. Tears rolled down my face as I stood on our spot.

I lost two people. The first was my dad, who disciplined me, taught me life lessons, supported me, and loved me. The other person was my best friend, who I shared everything with and loved so much.

"I'm going to miss you," I whispered.

CHAPTER 8

STRUGGLING

Game-winning balls don't fix reality. I was out of sync. It seemed that the natural rhythm that I had been living in was now a road under repair with no end date.

Every day was a challenge. I was exhibiting strength for everybody, but inside I was crippled with grief. I would occasionally take a break from meetings or my daily routine and go to the coffee room and close the door. I had never had a cup of coffee in my life. I was there to cry. Standing over the sink, tears would fall off my face. I was not sobbing. I was draining the pail of pain that resided inside me. Whenever anyone opened the door, I would turn on the faucet and throw water on my face as if I was freshening up.

Nana's words would come marching forward again and again. "Be strong—the family needs you." I hated the weakness inside me, but I knew it was part of what would make me strong again.

After the opening win over Florida State, we lost four games in a row. Then we beat TCU and Boston College, but our attendance was at an all-time low, less than 19,000 a game. Those storm clouds were rolling in.

Coach Selmer was a carpenter without a saw. The football program was under fire, and he was failing at managing the press. We struggled through the season. The atmosphere was beginning to become toxic. The University was openly weighing the future of the program. Players were talking about transferring. Coaches were whispering in their offices about who was to blame.

Some of the players came to my office and asked, "Are they really thinking of dropping football?"

I told them, "No, it's just a ploy to get money from the alums."

I was trying to calm them down, but I didn't know for sure. This had become a very difficult culture to coach in.

We were an 18-wheeler on a steep grade with no brakes. Coach Selmer was battling the press, the team was battling injuries, and I was still battling heartache. We were all battling rumors about the future of the program.

Our last game was to be played in Houston on the first Saturday of December. We were 3-7 playing the number six ranked Houston Cougars. On Friday night before a game, college football teams would traditionally go to a movie together. Instead, Coach Selmer had lined up an exhibition hockey game. I was in no mood to watch a bunch of guys with sticks slap a puck around the ice. I only went because it was the right thing to do.

Halfway into the hockey game, there was a public announcement: "Will Coach Selmer please report to the lobby office—you have an emergency phone call."

A siren went off inside me as Coach got up and proceeded to the lobby. I hoped that everybody in his family was ok. When he came back to his seat, he looked as though someone had punched him in the gut. The team was watching the game, and the coaches were watching Coach Selmer. He sat down, leaned over to his son, Brian, who was our team's kicker, and whispered something. Brian's head immediately dropped down and his eyes closed. *Oh, my god, what's happening?*

Coach Herndon, our offensive coordinator who was sitting behind Selmer, leaned forward. "Coach, is everything okay?"

"They are announcing my firing tomorrow," he said in a defeated tone.

Suddenly their conversation became magnified, and the sounds of the game seemed far away.

"Why are they telling you at a hockey game?" Herndon asked angrily.

That was my question exactly. I could feel my anger consuming me.

Coach Selmer sighed. "Someone leaked it to the press, I guess."

I sat in my hotel room later that night and reviewed our game plan material. Houston had won a share of the Southwest Conference title in its first year in the league. We had a daunting task in front of us that was now complicated by Selmer's firing. I tried to focus, but I could feel the rage bubbling inside me. They didn't even have the decency to fire him in a first-class manner. What a bunch of assholes. I felt bad for Coach Selmer; he was genuine and caring. He worked extremely hard and he gave me the opportunity to prove myself. At the same time, I knew in my gut something had to change.

Miami had all the ingredients for success. A fertile recruiting area in its own backyard. A strong academic institution. Warm weather and beaches. What athlete wouldn't like that?

As I continued to grapple with the situation, I could hear my dad's words: "Don't worry about that stuff. Just go be a great coach." Still, I had a hard time sleeping.

When I woke the next morning, it was game day. My thoughts went to the team. *Do they know? How will this affect them?*

By the time I boarded the bus to the stadium, I had my answer: The news of his firing was spreading like a wildfire in high winds. What was usually a very quiet ride was now a whispering convention. I felt sorry for our team and Coach. Their minds were not on the game. Neither was mine.

The game was played in the Houston Astrodome, which in 1966 had been outfitted with the first artificial grass surface at a major venue. Now, ten years later, that artificial surface has been nicknamed Astroturf.

During pre-game, I walked around the field. It was no longer a soft surface. It was like playing on the freeway. It was compacted, compressed, and hard. I thought to myself, *I'm glad I'm not playing on this crappy turf.*

I caught myself bitching to some of the other coaches. It was then that I realized that my attitude was going in the wrong direction; I needed to right myself and help others as well. I began pep talking the players and considered telling Coach Selmer, "Forget about being fired, let's win this game," but I was afraid to.

Ten minutes before the game was to start, Coach Selmer asked us to gather the team up in the locker room. That is when he amazed me. He was no longer the accountant.

He said in an alpha voice, "Men, I know some of you are worried about me, but don't be. We have an opportunity to beat the number six rated team in the country—now let's show them who we are."

Coach was no longer worried about the press, alumni, or coach critics. He was free and fierce. The team ran out on the field with an air of confidence. I, like the rest of the team, was no longer worried about what we couldn't control. Coach had displayed his grit.

We ditched our conservative style. We were moving the ball and playing good defense. We had a 10-7 lead at half-time. In the second half, Houston took the lead, and by the fourth quarter, they were ahead 21-16. With time running out, we had the ball on offense and proceeded to pound the ball down the field with OJ Anderson, our running back. OJ would go on to play 15 years in the NFL and be named MVP of the 1991 Super Bowl.

The ball was now on their two-yard line. It was first down. We threw the ball. It was incomplete. Now it was second down. Coach Westbrook noticed that the quarterback could have run the ball for the touchdown. He told our quarterback, Frank Glover, to run the same play and run it in, if it was there. The ball was snapped, so Glover rolled to his right. He couldn't run it in because he had a defender in his face, so instead he threw it—and Houston intercepted. Game over.

Coach Harold Sawyer, the team scout, threw his headset out of the press box window. "What the hell are we doing?" he bellowed.

I understood, and we marched down the field to give the ball to our best player, OJ Anderson. Now, in the most critical part of the game, we decided to throw it. OJ Anderson was now watching. Coaches are always open to criticism, but there is an old coach's saying that was once used by Ronald Reagan: "Dance with the one that brought you." We didn't.

I looked out the window and saw the headset dangling on 15 feet of cord from our coaches' press box. It made me snicker for a moment. It was the perfect picture of frustration, anger, and disappointment.

In the locker room, Coach Selmer had tears in eyes. He was proud of his team for their outstanding effort.

When we got on the plane, the players presented me with a small chocolate birthday cake. I was turning 26 the following day, and it was a nice gesture. But I was in no mood to celebrate.

I took a seat next to Coach Jim Walden, our defensive coordinator.

I asked Jim, who was with Selmer at Nebraska, "What is Coach Selmer going to do?"

"I don't know," he said dejectedly.

"I feel bad for him. He's a great coach and a great person," I said.

"I agree. I think he'll be fine," he said, nodding.

"Well, I hope he finds something that suits him. It's been a rough year."

Jim stared at me with a puzzled look. "You know that means you're fired, too."

I wasn't in the mood for a joke. "You're kidding me, right?" It was like a parent telling his child that there was no Santa.

"No, I'm not kidding—that's how it works in coaching. When they fire the Head Coach, all the assistants are fired too."

I felt like I had been slugged. "That's totally unfair. I didn't do anything to deserve this."

"Well, welcome to the real world, Pat."

My heart was crushed, and reality was taking control of my soul. Wanting not to get captured, I said, "Well, tomorrow is my birthday—you want some cake?"

"No, thank you. But you will get a chance to interview with the new head coach," Jim replied.

"That's great," I said.

"Since you have no idea who it is, I suggest you start looking for another job."

I wanted Jim to stop talking; his comments were loaded with reality. I wanted to say goodbye to uncertainty, at least for the airplane ride home. I needed my dad. He would have told me something that would make me feel better.

I suddenly thought I should go see Coach Allen; he always had a good perspective, so maybe he could whisper something to me. I gave myself the go-ahead nod.

I scanned the plane and spotted Coach Allen sitting on an aisle seat. I proceeded up the aisle and stopped in front of him. Leaning over, I whispered, "What do you think about all this?"

He was amazing; he knew why I was there. He reached up and put his hand on my neck, pulling me down so he could whisper in my ear. "You are a really good coach. You will be fine." He was like a doctor shocking my heart back to life.

How quickly my attitude changed. I was suddenly in better spirits.

The next day, they officially fired Coach Selmer. Reporters were calling coaches for comments. I knew that I did not want to say anything controversial or negative.

A Miami Herald sports reporter called me and asked, "What do you think about the job Coach Selmer has done, and do you think he should have been fired?"

I responded defiantly, "Miami never really made a commitment to him, and you don't fire someone over the phone, on the road, before a game."

My Irish temper had found my mouth, and though I caught myself now, I had just given the reporter an opening.

He jumped on it and said, "Explain the lack of commitment."

I knew I had screwed up. I had watched Coach Selmer get angry and defensive and knew that didn't work, so I opted for humor and deflection.

"Look," I replied, "I lost my dad, voted for Gerald Ford, and might be getting fired on my birthday."

"Tough couple of months, Coach Ruel. I'll let you go," he said.

My strategy worked. The interview was over as quickly as it began.

Marti had planned a birthday party that night. Most of the football staff came over and drank beer—a lot of beer. After my arrest, I vowed never to drink beer. Instead, I was drinking Jameson Whiskey on the rocks. Very slowly. I didn't want to complicate an already bad year.

The party started off as a bitch session but quickly went to laughing and joking around. It was what we all needed.

I spent the rest of December recruiting for Miami, selling high school athletes on a university without a head coach. I knew that this action, although extremely difficult, might get me retained.

Miami had its new head coach in place right after Christmas. Lou Saban, the former Buffalo Bills head coach, had accepted the job. He had OJ Simpson at Buffalo, and now he had OJ Anderson.

The first week in January, Pete Elliott called to tell me that Coach Saban would like to interview me. It was just what I wanted hear.

"When?" I responded.

"Tomorrow at nine a.m.," Pete said with his usual enthusiasm.

I hung up and immediately started to prepare and organize my thoughts. *What am I going to wear? Should I wear a tie? Take that puka shell necklace off? I don't need him asking if I have earrings to match.* I wanted to be ready, so I headed to the library to do a little research on his background.

I got magazines and newspaper articles and began to read. He left most of his previous jobs after a one- or two-year stint. He always seemed to cross ways with administration or management. *Why are they hiring this guy?*

It didn't matter; I wanted a job.

I arrived early at the facility and waited in the lobby, wearing my coat, tie, nice pair of slacks, and polished shoes. My first real job interview. I kept staring at the clock, waiting for 9 a.m. Then it passed. It was now 9:15. Did he forget? I told the secretary I was there.

Finally, she said, "He's ready."

Stepping into his office seemed strange, as he was sitting where Coach Elliott and Selmer once sat. He did not get up. He pointed to a chair in front of his desk and said, "Sit down."

This was not a good start.

He asked a couple of questions, then looked at me pointedly and said, "How old are you?"

"Twenty-six," I said.

"You're too young to be my offensive line coach."

My heart was racing. He never asked me a football question. I had this uneasy feeling that this was a complimentary interview for Coach Elliott, who was fighting for me to be retained.

Instinctively, I jumped up, extended my hand, and said, "Coach, as a University of Miami alum, I am with you win or tie." I'd had enough of the bullshit.

He looked puzzled. His forehead wrinkled as he extended his hand, and we shook. Forcing a smile, he said, "Good luck."

Walking out of the building, I was sad, but there was a part of me that was excited about the next adventure. I just didn't know when or where.

I was back in my apartment later that day when Coach Elliott called. "Don't worry, I'm going to get you some interviews." I think he knew that the interview with Lou Saban was a waste of time.

Pete understood that I was new to coaching and didn't have the network. He was my network. True to his word, he secured two interviews: one with Pepper Rodgers at Georgia Tech, and the other at Arkansas with Lou Holtz.

Coach Rodgers offered me a full-time position as the tight end coach and recruiting coordinator. Not my areas of expertise, but I would be making more money than I made at Miami. Coach Holtz offered me a part-time position as an assistant offensive line coach. Arkansas was going to give me a dorm room, meals, and pocket change. I knew on the surface it looked like a step backward, but my instincts told me it was the right move. It was my area of expertise, and Coach Holtz was becoming nationally recognized, so I wanted to learn why he was so good.

Arkansas Razorbacks, here I come.

CHAPTER 9

GOODBYE MIAMI, HELLO ARKANSAS

The Miami coaching staff gathered for one last hoorah at a party hosted by Jerry Wamsley, our defensive backs coach, and his wife, Nita. Everybody had secured new jobs and was excited about future adventures. I was excited to leave my roots in South Florida and head off to the unknown in Arkansas. Still, there was a piece of me that was grappling with the idea that I could be discarded again like a candy wrapper.

We spent the evening laughing and telling stories about things that, three months earlier, were devastating. I glanced around the party, feeling an appreciation of the friendships I had acquired. I would especially miss those who impacted my life in such a unique way.

It was nearly midnight when Nita pointed to the trees in the backyard. They were lit up with some kind of spotlight. "Where is the light coming from? There are no houses behind us, just a canal," she said. I could hear the curiosity in her voice, and it made me curious, too.

"Let's go look," I said.

A few coaches, Nita, and I walked out to see what the source of the light was.

Nita yelled, "Oh, my god, it's a car!"

It was then that we realized that a car had slid into the canal and was almost completely submerged. The headlights were the only part of the car sticking out of the water.

Without much thought, I kicked off my shoes, removed my shirt, and dove into the dark, murky water. I had been in these canals a lot while growing up, but never at night.

On my way to the car, I bumped into something big. My heart was pounding out Morse code. I was hoping it wasn't an alligator or a manatee. I grabbed it. It was a man, face-down in the water.

I had worked as a lifeguard during my college summers, so I had training. I pulled his head up and positioned myself behind him. With my right arm across his chest and my left hand holding his chin up, I scissor kicked to the edge of the canal where his car entered. I was on the opposite side from Jerry's house. I couldn't stand; it was too deep. I kicked while holding him with one hand and hitting his back. I could hear the sirens. Nita had called 911. Then, as if on cue, he started coughing up water. What a relief—I was no longer holding a lifeless body. He was sputtering and mumbling words I couldn't understand.

I grabbed a root sticking out of the canal's edge and held on, exhausted from holding us both up. He never fought me, thank God.

Finally, the flashing lights of the ambulance and police cars were coming down the dirt road. The paramedics rushed out, leaned over, and pulled him out. Now that I was able to look at him, I saw that he was short, heavy-set, and balding, dressed in a tux.

He'd probably had too much to drink. I was about swim back to the other side when the paramedic screamed, "Is there anyone else in the car?"

"I don't know," I said.

"Check the car!" he yelled. By this time, they had put their spotlight on the water.

It was that moment I felt a surge of anxiety. I didn't want to climb into a car that was submerged underwater. But I knew it had to be done. I dove down into dark water that was only slightly illuminated by the spotlight. I was completely blind, unable to see anything. I felt the driver's side door was open. I entered the car. My hands were searching feverishly, feeling around for a body. I found something and quickly got out of the car and back to the surface. I held it up. It was a women's purse.

"Was there anyone in the car?" the paramedic yelled.

"No, just this," I said, holding up a purse.

I could hear the paramedics questioning him, "Was there anyone in that car with you?" they asked multiple times. Finally, a paramedic yelled back, "We're okay, he was the only one in the car." That was good news.

I threw the purse up to the police. I was going to swim back to where I originally dove in, but the police said, "We need your information—let us help you out."

The police and paramedics grabbed my hands and pulled me out. I gave them my information. They congratulated me and said that I saved that man's life. It was gratifying to be a momentary hero. I was filled with a sense of achievement. The police gave me a ride back to the house.

The man I saved had apparently gotten lost. He turned down a dirt road running alongside the canal looking for a place to turn around, and the rear of his car slid off the road and plunged into the canal.

I was soaking wet as I walked back into the house. Everyone congratulated me. But then, moments later, wives were criticizing their husbands for not helping me. Their husbands were all in agreement; they were not going into a canal full of alligators and snakes.

I immediately took charge of the conversation. "I'm the only one who spent my junior high and high school years playing in those Florida canals," I said.

"It was pitch-black, Pat. I admire your courage, but at midnight, I'm not diving into a backyard pool unless the lights are on," Coach Walden shot back.

"You had every right to be concerned. There are snakes, alligators, and an occasional manatee. Growing up with them may have given me a false confidence. Although, I honestly was more scared of getting trapped in that car."

"If Pat had gotten attacked by an alligator, we would be getting praised for being smart," Jim laughed.

The next day was Sunday, and a reporter called to ask me about saving Sampson Horn, age 79. I didn't even know his name until the reporter called. He asked me several questions.

He said, "Most people would never dive into the canal, much less at night."

"I was just reacting to the situation," I said.

On Monday, the story of me saving a man's life was on the front page of the local section. After all that had happened in the last six months, I felt that in some way I had saved my own life that day. My self-worth and identity had gotten a booster shot.

* * *

I headed to Fayetteville, Arkansas, leaving my family and girlfriend in South Florida. Arkansas's campus sat on a hilltop overlooking the Ozark Mountains. It was an absolutely beautiful campus. The athletic facility was completed the year before, and it was state-of-the-art. It featured a weight room three times the size of Miami's, a training room with all the latest equipment, and a huge indoor artificial turf area that opened up to the stadium with five huge retractable doors. On top of that, the coaches' offices overlooked the stadium and felt like executive suites. We didn't even have an on-campus stadium at Miami. It was clear that the Arkansas football program was competing on a national level.

After getting situated, my eyes and ears were set on Head Coach Lou Holtz. I wanted to learn what made him so successful.

He was a frail-looking man, about 5'10" and 150 pounds. He had narrow shoulders and talked with a slight lisp. There was no way he played football; he was a bag of bones covered in skin. Seriously—I thought he would have major problems opening a jar of peanut butter.

About a week into my new stint, Coach Holtz stopped me in the hallway. "You're going to drive me to Little Rock for an Arkansas Alumni event tomorrow."

Wow, I was feeling honored that I was picked for the job. "Great, Coach, what time do we need to leave?"

"We should leave around four, and it's a three-hour drive."

Being unfamiliar with Arkansas, I went to his secretary, Cathy, to see if she had directions to the event. She did, which was a relief.

That night, I thought about what questions I could ask him. I wanted to find out as much as I could.

The next day, about an hour before our departure, he informed me that I was to introduce him.

In a panic, I again went to see Cathy. "Any chance you have his resume?"

"Sure," she said, reaching into a file cabinet. "Let me make a copy."

I now had directions, his resume, and my questions. I was excited about this opportunity to visit with him. I jotted down a few notes from his resume, and I was ready to go. When I got into his car and started to drive, I didn't say anything at first. He was working on his speech. But about an hour into the drive, he appeared to be done working.

I broke the ice by saying, "Coach, I'm really excited that I'm here at Arkansas."

"What is wrong with you?" he asked with contempt. "Why are you going so slow?"

"Coach, I'm going the speed limit."

"The red and blue signs that say Interstate Forty on them are the highway numbers. Now pull over, I'm driving."

I got out of the car and mumbled to myself, "You're lucky I wasn't on Interstate Four Hundred Forty."

He drove 80 mph the rest of the way. It was 120 miles of him talking about himself or bitching about my driving.

We arrived to a packed house, and everybody was excited to hear him speak. He had a reputation for being a good motivational speaker. It was time for me introduce him. I got up and covered his history as a Head Coach of William and Mary, then North Carolina State, where he took them to four straight bowl games. I was doing great until I decided to make a little joke about his time with the New York Jets. I never mentioned that he was 3-10 and quit with one game left.

I merely said, "His last stop was in New York, where he got Jet lag."

The room erupted into laughter.

"Here is Head Coach Lou Holtz," I said.

The audience broke out into thunderous clapping as he stepped to the podium. Coach did a great job entertaining them with a magic trick and stories.

Later, we got in the car to drive back to Fayetteville. I was designated driver again. Then he started...

"Don't you ever bring up the New York Jets again," he barked.

"Sorry, Coach, I apologize. I didn't know you were sensitive about it."

"Because you're ignorant."

I set my jaw and gritted my teeth. "Sorry," I said. I was getting a clear vision that his public persona was nothing like his working life.

Later that spring, Coach Holtz sent me and Coach Pete Cordelli, one of the other part-time coaches, to Wendy's to get burgers for a working lunch. I took the orders down on paper.

Coach Holtz said, "I want a single with cheese, lettuce, pickles, and mustard. No tomato, onions, or ketchup."

"Got it, Coach."

Everybody's order was in, and Coach Cordelli and I were off to Wendy's. Once we arrived back at the facility, we handed out the burgers to the staff. I gave Coach Holtz his, and he unwrapped it and lifted the bun up for inspection.

"What is this?" he fumed, pointing to a single ring of onion that was left on his burger.

Offering a unique solution, I said, "Take it off, Coach."

The hamburger was now coming at me at high speed. With no time to dodge the airborne burger, it collided with my shirt. *He didn't just throw a Wendy's single with cheese at me—what the fuck is wrong with this guy?*

"You can't even get a hamburger order right, and you want to be a coach?" he yelled.

I knew full well that I was dealing with a narcissistic asshole. If my dad was there and gave me the go-ahead nod, I would have given him a fist sandwich. Instead, I looked at him in disbelief. *Who acts like this?*

I knew who. That asshole sergeant I had in the Air Force ROTC. He was enthralled with his authority. Nothing was ever his fault, and he was quick to place blame.

Holtz had this reputation of perception. He entertained people with his motivational talks and demeaned people in the office and on the field. Treating people with respect was not his specialty. He was a coral snake: small with beautiful colors and a venomous bite.

Despite Holtz being a dysfunctional adult, our staff was amiable and well versed in football. It was obvious that Coach Holtz knew how to hire excellent coaches; he found those with good characteristics for recruiting and a passion to coach.

I had a fortunate assignment. I was working with Larry Beightol, the offensive line coach and offensive coordinator. Coach Beightol was an intense teacher. Footwork was a huge part of his principled approach. I was impressed with his ability to break down the minute details of blocking into footwork, leverage position, and hand placement. Beck, as he was called, was a good, hard-working coach. He had a big heart, and he cared about his players. He was also fierce, blunt, and crude. At times, this was accompanied by a hair-trigger temper.

During a spring practice, Steve Little, who was our All-American kicker, kicked the ball, and it hit Beck in the back of the head. Beck chased him around the field and up into the stands. He was overweight for his 5'9" frame and bow-legged.

The team watched and laughed, as Beck had no chance of catching him. Watching him run was almost cartoonish, as he had a unique waddle. Halfway up the stands, Beck stopped and sat down. We all laughed, as what we thought might be an assault turned out to be a Road Runner versus Wile E. Coyote cartoon.

* * *

Spring practice was described by Coach Holtz as "Not any tougher than your average death march."

The death march wasn't always on the field. Beck and Coach Holtz would often get into arguments, mainly because Holtz would purposefully antagonize him. We were in an offensive staff meeting when Holtz told Beck he didn't have a clue what he was doing. His intent was clearly to aggravate him. Beck got charged up, and they threw verbal grenades at each other. This became a weekly occurrence, and it was uncomfortable to be in the same room with the disrespect.

On one occasion, Coach Holtz was sitting at a table in front of the room. He started launching insults at Beck again. Beck, who was sitting in the middle of the room by the projector, fired back. Holtz then started picking up cannisters of 16mm film and throwing them at Beck. Beck picked up the projector and threw it toward Holtz. Neither one of them hit the other.

I was beginning to think I was working in a school for kids with behavioral problems.

Beck headed to his office; he'd had enough. I waited a couple of minutes, then went to check on him. He was packing his stuff. I wanted to protect him like he protected me after the hamburger incident.

"Pat, the asshole threw cannisters of film at me," Beck said angrily.

"Well, throwing the projector back at him was impressive." I was trying to make him laugh. He didn't; he was mad. Taking one more shot at calming him down, I said, "He threw a Wendy's single with cheese at me." That one did the trick, and we both laughed.

The coaches were like a team that protected each other from snake bites. We supported each other and kept the atmosphere from becoming toxic. No one was immune to Holtz's outbursts. Players, coaches, trainers, and even the athletic director were all targets.

During one staff meeting, Holtz said, "Pat, get Dean Weber on the phone and tell him to get up here." Dean was the head athletic trainer.

I called Dean to relay Coach Holtz's order.

"When?" Dean asked nervously.

"Right now." For a few seconds, there was silence.

"What is it about?"

"Don't know, just hurry up." I had a feeling he was about to get bit by the coral snake.

Within a few minutes, Dean popped in and said, "Hi, Coach." He was acting happy, but we all knew he was about to be verbally assaulted.

Holtz glared at him. "Why are we having ankle sprains?" he hissed.

"Don't know the reason, Coach. Sometimes they just happen."

Holtz glared at him. "Are you taping the ankles correctly?"

The staff watched, feeling bad for Dean. We had all been there before. It was bad enough when it was in his office one-on-one, but horrible when it was in front of the staff.

"Yes, Coach, we are doing it correctly," he said.

That afternoon, another player sprained his ankle. That was a total of four players. Fall camp was about to be a miserable experience for our trainer.

The next morning, we repeated the same scenario.

"Pat, tell Dean Weber I want him up here now."

I called the training room. It rang twice, and I hung up. "Coach, I'll go to the training room and get him," I said as I left the staff room. I didn't want Dean to go in the snake pit without some idea of Coach's anger, so I ran down to the training room and grabbed Dean.

"Coach Holtz has reached a full boil. So, I would wear some protective gear, like a helmet and shoulder pads," I said, laughing.

It wasn't funny to Dean. We walked back to the staff room together. When we entered, I sat down in the back. I did not want to get hit by verbal shrapnel.

Holtz was in striking pose. "Dean, we had another ankle sprain. You're doing something wrong. I want a list of the top fifty trainers in America."

The air in the room suddenly got heavy, like we were all breathing the fumes of misery. The following morning, I stopped by the training room in an effort to deliver the cure before our staff meeting.

"You have that list ready?" I was trying to make fun of Coach Holtz's demand. Dean was not laughing. "It'll be alright, Dean. You're an excellent trainer." I was trying to keep him from being captured by the Holtz rage.

He had his list. It was written on a sheet of school notebook paper. He was ready. I told him I would call him when Coach wanted him at the staff meeting. His look was that of a man who was about to attend his own funeral.

The staff meeting started. Holtz immediately asked me to get Dean. This time, he answered the phone after one ring. He was waiting for my call.

"It's time," I said.

When Dean stepped into the room, it went totally quiet. He headed straight to Holtz and handed him the sheet of paper. Coach examined the list that had two columns of 25 names each. Coach dramatically put his finger on the top of the first column and slowly dragged it down the page. As he reached the bottom, his finger went to the top of the second column. He repeated the process.

He lifted his head and said with disdain, "Just what I thought, Dean. Your name is not even on the list." Then he added, "You better get this solved."

Dean said nothing. *Smart move,* I thought, *no point in furthering a discussion with a coral snake.*

After the staff meeting, I headed to the training room to ask what we were all thinking: "Why didn't you put your name first on the list?"

Dean shrugged. "He would have said, 'Why the hell is your name on the list?'"

"Dean, you're exactly right. It was a lose-lose situation." I instinctively put my arm on his shoulder, and like a good friend, I said, "Welcome to the club."

Holtz wanted his staff walking on hot coals. It was his method to combat his Napoleon complex. He was always looking for ways to inflate himself. He was a manipulator.

He later supported Jesse Helms from North Carolina, a known racist, by doing campaign ads from his office in Arkansas. By 1983, Arkansas had had enough and fired him.

CHAPTER 10

GOING BOWLING

Despite all of Holtz's chaotic and manipulative antics, we had an excellent team. It was a blast. I was working 15 to 18 hours, enjoying every minute of my destiny, and when I did have moments of down time, I would occasionally hang out with Pete Carroll.

He was full of energy and was a graduate coach like me. Pete worked with the defensive backs. He had a very natural way about himself. I gravitated toward him because of how he lived in the moment. He was extremely positive, and he had a passion for coaching. We just seemed to naturally hit it off. A couple of times I wanted to ask Pete what he thought of Holtz's managing methods, but Pete was always focused on the positive. The negative stuff didn't interest him. To Pete, life was meant to be fun and enjoyable.

There's a Christmas story about two kids. They were about the same age. Their father had put horse manure in two boxes, wrapped them up like gifts, and placed them under the tree. On Christmas morning, excited to open the gifts, they tore the paper away.

The first one opened his box and screamed, "I got poop! Why did I get poop?"

The second son opened his box and shouted, "Where is my horse?" That was Pete. I loved his attitude.

After beating Southern Methodist 47-7 in Dallas, we boarded the plane to head back to Fayetteville. We were 9-1 and several post-season bowls were courting us. One in particular was the Orange Bowl in Miami. That's where I wanted to go. It was surreal to think that I could be back home with my family and Marti to celebrate a great season. When we arrived back in Fayetteville that night, we were buzzing with energy and ready for a little post-game celebration. Pete had the idea to go entertain the other coaches.

We decided to start with Beck. By the time we pulled into his driveway, the house was already dark. Pete, his wife Glena, and I stood on the front lawn where we began belting out the Arkansas fight song.

Not just once, or twice, but three times. It was going to be our first bowl game. We were ecstatic.

The next week, it became official after beating Texas Tech; the Orange Bowl gave Arkansas an official invitation. I was more excited than a young boy getting his first bike.

We were ranked number six and were going to play number two, Oklahoma. After a couple weeks of bowl practice in Fayetteville, three of our student athletes, Ben Cowens, Donny Bobo, and Michael Forrest, were involved in an assault on a woman in the dorm. The woman had not yet pressed charges, but the police had investigated—it was a serious matter.

Although these players were responsible for 70% of our offensive scoring, Coach Holtz suspended them from the Orange Bowl game. The choice shocked me because I knew he wouldn't sacrifice winning over a moral issue. He had stated that the process should be decided by the law. The rumor was that the attorney general for the state of Arkansas flew in and told Holtz he had to suspend them. The mood was somber. Whenever a player or players committed acts of evil, the whole team felt as if they had been betrayed.

I was furious. How could they commit this vile act against a defenseless woman? It was like rebranding all the good that we had accomplished.

In the midst of this crisis, Holtz summoned me to his office. I was scared. *What did I do?* Cathy, his secretary, gave me the "I don't know" look. I braced myself as I stepped into his office. His face was missing the usual scowl.

"Pat, why don't you go down to Miami early and check things out?"

I immediately became suspicious. "Check out what, Coach?"

"The facilities. And, you know, see your family."

Did the narcissistic asshole just say that? I quickly studied his face for clues. It was a puzzling gesture, but I wasn't about to give him the opportunity to change his mind. I thanked him and hurried out the door.

The day I was set to leave, I received a big surprise. Jim Walden, who had become the Head Coach at Washington State University, called me and offered me the offensive line job. He wanted me to bring the split-back veer offense to Washington State.

I accepted so fast that I never even asked about my salary. I'd gambled on my future by taking a part-time assistant position at Arkansas, and it paid off. Now I had a full-time position with full-time pay coaching the offensive line.

Exactly what I wanted.

I arrived in Miami three days before Christmas. I had already been given my Christmas gift. I couldn't wait to share my excitement with my family and Marti.

It was an awesome feeling to go back to where I was fired with a successful future on the horizon. It was a "look who's back" moment. Being on a 10-1 team playing in the Orange Bowl was a huge honor. It was then that I was grateful for the leadership that Coach Holtz provided to get us there, though it didn't change how I felt about him personally.

I stayed at my father's house, but it was tough being there. I sat at the dining room table, looking at the chair where he used to sit as he schooled me with life lessons. I was no longer blaming God or the Air Force pilot. I was grateful that I had his presence for as long as I did. He would have been so thrilled about this Orange Bowl game.

The morning after I arrived home, a call came in from Arkansas telling me that Lou Saban, Miami's coach, wanted me to come by. I was surprised, but I couldn't wait to make the call. The request intrigued me.

I had a full-time job offer, was on a 10-1 team, and was playing in the Orange Bowl. I felt like a shooting star that he failed to see the first time.

I could feel the energy shift as soon as I walked into the secretary's office. She greeted me warmly, "Go in. He's expecting you."

This time, he got up out of his chair, walked around his desk, and shook my hand. "Pat, what a fantastic year you guys had!"

I was soaking up the moment. The guy that was too young to be his coach had made his comeback. "Thanks, Coach. It was a blast, but we're not done yet."

He motioned for me to take a seat, then settled into the chair next to me. "Would you have time this afternoon to teach our staff about the Arkansas offense?"

His request stunned me. Eleven months earlier, I was a discarded candy wrapper. Now, I felt like *Time Magazine*'s Man of the Hour.

I smiled. "Absolutely. I would love too."

I spent the next three hours preparing a general outline of what I wanted to cover, including run-game and play-action passes, and the philosophy behind them. I wanted to show them my organizational skills and teaching methods.

That afternoon, I walked into the Miami staff room. I was greeted by eight coaches who were excited to hear my presentation. All of them were older than me. It was my first time presenting to coaches, and I started off a little nervous, but as we interacted, they started nodding, and I knew I was having an impact. My confidence was growing. I was feeling a little full of myself, like I was on top of the world.

When I left the building, I took the same route home that I did the day I lost my father. It was déjà vu. I started tearing up. *What's wrong with me?* I thought. I didn't want to feel weak, but I did want to at the same time. It was if I was trying to tell him with my tears how much I missed him, yet I was trying to be strong. I wanted my dad to see his son was doing it with a passion.

The city was buzzing about the match-up between Oklahoma and Arkansas, and they rolled out the red carpet. They hosted us at the Four Ambassadors, a swanky hotel right on Biscayne Bay. It was a beautiful setting with spectacular views.

As part of the pre-game events, the Orange Bowl hosted a barbecue behind the hotel on a small bridge that went to an island called Brickell Key. The island had not yet been developed, so they had tables set up on the bridge. I was waiting for Marti, who was running late because of work. By the time she arrived, there were no vacancies at any of the tables. We got our food, and I suggested we go sit on the curb away from the main party.

"This is what happens when you're late—you get the curb," I said jokingly.

Just then, a man approached and asked if he could sit with us. He was wearing dress slacks and a long-sleeve shirt. He was dressed a lot better than the players and coaches; we were in our casual clothes.

"Sure, have a curb." I chuckled.

He smiled and settled down next to us. "Hi, I'm Bill Clinton."

I swallowed a bite of baked beans. "Hi, I'm Pat Ruel, and this is my girlfriend, Marti." I explained that I was one of the coaches, and Marti was a corrective therapist.

"That's great. Maybe I can get a few inside tips on the game from you, Pat. Or maybe, Marti, you can teach me what a corrective therapist does."

I was taken back by his smooth and natural communication.

"What do you do?" I asked.

"I'm the attorney general for the state of Arkansas."

Three things hit me at once: First, this was the guy who forced Holtz to suspend those players; second, he looked way too young to hold that position; and third, he obviously had no problem sitting on the curb.

I decided to avoid the suspension topic. Suspending those players was a blessing. I wanted to have a positive conversation. We ate our barbecue and talked about higher education and Arkansas football for about 20 minutes. He used our first names continuously. He was very engaging. I wondered if he'd read Dale Carnegie's book too. When we got up to leave, he thanked us in a way that made us feel special. Again, using our names.

I noticed Marti had really enjoyed the conversation.

"Thank God you were late, or we would have never met the curb or the lawyer," I joked.

"I liked him. He has a lot of charisma," she replied, totally ignoring what I just said.

"Oh, really? I think you like him because he said your name a lot."

"No, I just think he was charming. Maybe he will be the governor someday."

I shot her a sarcastic look. "Why don't you make him president?"

"He's not ready yet," she shot back. We both laughed.

The game was two days away, and the mounting stress was affecting the whole team. Practice was not going particularly well—we were not executing.

During a team drill, Coach Breaux, our running back coach, was frustrated and lost it. "You guys are choking! Get your asses out of your heads!" We all looked puzzled for a moment, then the team started laughing.

Coach Breaux laughed too. "You know what I mean."

I could feel the team pulling together. Practice improved immediately. At the end of practice, Roland Sales, who was battling a bad cold and was now the starter due to the suspensions, asked to speak to the team. We all kneeled and formed a half circle around him. You could tell he was uncomfortable and searching for the right words. We waited anxiously for him to collect his thoughts. His long pause made us realize how difficult this was for him.

"I have a cold, and I'm not feeling that well, but I want you to know that you can count on me. I'll run hard, and I'll block hard, and I'll be there for you."

That was all he said, but it was powerful. For me, it was the emotional string that tied the team together to achieve its goal. Those few moments brought our team back to our purpose.

Game day was magical. Our team, which was a 24-point underdog with the loss of those players, was now on a mission. Oklahoma was on a mission as well. Texas was beaten earlier that day by Notre Dame in the Cotton Bowl, and Oklahoma was now playing for the National Championship. We dominated the game from start to finish.

We made the great Oklahoma team look normal, beating them 31-6. Roland Sales rushed for an Orange Bowl record of 205 yards on 22 carries. He was named MVP. Arkansas finished third in the final poll.

My father once asked me, "What are the three most powerful words in the English language?"

I said, "I love you."

Dad said, "No, Pat. It's 'I'll be there.'"

"Why, Dad?" I asked.

"Because it represents caring, dependability, and accountability."

That was a lesson my dad gave me. Roland Sales gave that same lesson to the team on January 2, 1978.

* * *

I had a three-day break before I had to report for my new job. I called Marti's Dad, Virgil, a couple of days before the game. I asked him if he would give me permission to marry his daughter.

He said, "Yes, Pat. Jane and I would be honored to have you as part of the family." I didn't invite Marti to Arkansas because I knew it was a short stop. I enjoyed my single life, but I was more afraid of losing her than I was of getting married.

The question was: When and how would I do it? I needed to devise a plan. If I did it before the game, it would be a distraction, and immediately after the game, there would be too much going on. We had planned to spend some time with her parents in Juno Beach after the game. *Perfect*, I thought, *I'll do it in front of them.*

After dinner with her parents, we would always play Yahtzee. You rolled five dice, and if all five dice had the same number, it was a Yahtzee. I decided that as soon as I rolled one, I would say, "That's a sign—good luck and good times," then get out of my chair, take a knee, grab her hand, and pop the question. My plan was set.

The day after the game, Marti and I headed to her parents' house, which was about 90 miles from Miami. We were listening to music. The Marshall Tucker Band was playing a song called "Heard It in a Love Song." It was about a wrangler and a rambler who was leaving behind the hardest thing to get off his mind: his girl.

I loved the song, but I turned it off. I could feel there was tension in the air. We made small talk for a couple of minutes. Then silence. I could see Marti's thoughts flying around the car. Marti could no longer contain herself. I didn't ask her before the game, and I didn't ask her after the game. We had dated for seven years. She wanted answers.

"I have a question for you," Marti started. I braced myself for what I knew was coming.

"Go ahead."

"I want to know what your plans are, because this boat is leaving the port." Marti was giving me the "start rowing or get out of the boat" speech.

"Well, I do have something planned."

"And that is?" she asked.

"I'm going to Washington State to be their offensive line coach."

She looked stunned. I was being playfully stubborn, thinking I could hold her off until after dinner. I glanced into her eyes and could tell she was hurting. My heart was not prepared for that.

"I can't do that without you," I said, pausing for a moment to let my words sink in. "Will you marry me?"

I could see tears of joy pooling in her eyes. "Yes," she said, scooting over beside me. I grabbed her hand. I could feel the oneness of our love. It didn't go the way it was planned, but we were excited to be together in life's journey.

CHAPTER 11

HEADING TO
THE EVERGREEN STATE

I seemed to be marching my way across the USA. Miami Hurricanes, Arkansas Razorbacks, and now Washington State Cougars. As the plane neared Spokane, Washington, I looked out my window, and there was a beautiful blanket of snow on the ground. Something about snow and the contrast to its surroundings has always enchanted me. Maybe it was being a kid on my grandfather's farm in Rockford, Illinois. We would often visit around Christmas time. Bampa would hook up the sled to the back of his old black Cadillac and pull my brothers and me around the circular driveway. At seven years old, those moments become unforgettable.

As I got off the plane, Steve Morton, the tight end coach, was there to greet me. He looked me over and shook his head. "Did you think you were landing in California?"

I was wearing a T-shirt with an unzipped wind breaker. "I'll be fine," I said as we headed out to his car.

Leaving the airport, huge evergreen trees decorated with fresh snow dotted the landscape. *That's next year's Christmas card*, I thought. I was a bit apprehensive, as I didn't ask about my salary or take a visit to the WSU campus. I'd made a blind decision, but I trusted Coach Walden.

As we drove south to Pullman on a single-lane road, Steve, who played at and graduated from WSU, filled me in on the history of Cougar football. Within an instant, the beautiful evergreens and snow were gone. I was looking at rolling hills of the blackest dirt I had ever seen in my life.

"What's with all these dirt hills?" I asked.

"We're driving through Whitman County, which is the largest wheat growing county in the world," Steve said, like he was proud of it.

"How far?" I asked.

"It's seventy-five miles, and we've only gone fifteen."

The single-lane road, the rolling hills of black dirt, and my impatience made it feel more like 150 miles. We made small talk, then, all of a sudden, a town materialized.

"Is this it?" I said in disbelief.

Steve laughed. "No, this is Colfax. It's the county seat for the largest wheat growing county in the world."

I shook my head and said, "Well, it has one stop light and looks like it never left the eighteen hundreds."

"Yep, that's Colfax," he replied, smiling at me.

"How much further?" I pushed back, acting like an impatient child.

"About fourteen miles."

Doubt about my decision was creeping in. I'd just left behind the Florida weather and the beautiful beaches. I wondered what Marti would think of this. She had stayed behind to prepare for our June wedding. This was going to be a big cultural shock for her.

We drove for what seemed like another hour. Then, there it was: an oasis with buildings, a stadium, and some large evergreens. I had arrived. The second we got out of the car, I was hit by 25-degree air and a 20-mph wind.

"I need a bigger coat," I said as my teeth vibrated and I zipped up my windbreaker.

Steve just looked at me and laughed. He gave me the grand tour of the stadium and practice fields while I tried to keep from freezing my ass off. He finally took me into the football office, and I was grateful to be in a warm building. I began introducing myself to the staff. They were very amiable and energetic. I was excited, and my doubts were quickly erased— this was my new team. I quickly settled into my new office, which had a big window overlooking the parking lot and a student dorm across the street.

Jim called his first complete staff meeting. He kicked off the meeting talking about the selling points of WSU and the recruiting areas for the coaches. Then Steve stepped in and educated us on the history of WSU. He explained that it was the only school in the new Pac-10 conference that had a true family atmosphere.

Then he dropped the bomb: "WSU has not been to a bowl game in forty-seven years." That was a frightening statistic. It quickly put a red flag on our task at hand. Post-season bowls were a sign of success.

My recruiting area was the San Francisco Bay area. I was so enthused that I bought maps of San Fran and San Jose and started highlighting my schools. I was a rookie to the west coast; it would be my first time in California. The Beach Boys and The Eagles wrote songs about California. I couldn't wait to see what all the music was about.

It was awesome—the weather, the mountains, the farm-land, and of course the spectacular coastline. I was good at charming the recruits and getting them to commit to a visit. But after six weeks of making the hour-and-a-half drive from the airport and repeatedly listening to the same questions from prospective students that I asked Steve on my first trip, I knew something had to change. If I was a farmer, I would have been totally impressed with the richness of those black mounds of dirt. The coach in me was not.

As I headed to Coach Walden's office, my mind was churning with ideas on how to fix the problem. By the time I arrived, a solution had hit me.

"Is there any way we could use an RV to pick up recruits from the Spokane airport?" I asked. "We need to do something to distract them during that ninety-minute drive."

Coach Walden's face lit up in agreement. "That's a good idea. We can put student hostesses in the RV to educate them about WSU."

I could feel his enthusiasm, and it ignited my creative juices. "Yes—snacks, card games, backgammon, and a hostess will make the trip go fast," I agreed.

I left his office fired up; our recruiting problem was solved.

That spring, we all worked day and night to develop our own blueprint for success. My contribution was giving the staff the ingredients of the Arkansas offense. Our staff was creative and very collaborative. We were on our way to building a successful football program.

* * *

It was late April, and I was in my office drawing plays for the playbook. I glanced out the window at the dorm across the street. There was a huge banner that hung across the dorm's third-floor windows. It said, "May 8th Outdoor Intercourse Day." I was puzzled by this banner. So, I summoned our team historian for clarification. When Steve walked in, I motioned to my window.

"What is this?" I asked, pointing at the banner.

Steve looked at me with devilish grin. "What do you think it is?"

"Well, since we're an institution of higher learning, I'm going to say it's outdoor debates on current affairs."

Steve started laughing. "No, Pat. The wheat that grows on those black hills is knee-high in May, so you go out in the field with a blanket and lay down with your girl and..."

"Stop—you're kidding me." It was a true what-the-fuck moment. "No wonder you picked this school."

We both laughed.

Time seemed to be flying by, and before I knew it, my wedding was a week away. Before I got on the flight to Palm Beach, Marti informed me that her mom had signed us up for pre-marriage counseling with the minister. I considered myself spiritually based, but to me, religion was about exclusivity. I agreed to it anyway because I didn't want anything to interfere with our big day.

The minister's office was located in the church where our wedding was to take place. As soon as we arrived, he greeted us and motioned for us to sit down at his mahogany table. Then he positioned himself across from us.

He spent the first five minutes detailing the purpose of pre-marriage counseling. He said it was about religion, past history, sex, money, and children.

Then, without missing a beat, the minister said, "Have you been reborn?"

"No, I'm Catholic. We get baptized," I retorted.

"So, you haven't accepted Christ yet?"

Marti started to say something, but I interrupted. "I don't want this to be a conversion session. Next question." I was getting the idea that this was a total manipulation.

"Have you and Marti had, ummmm, well, ahhhhhh..."

"Sex?" I blurted out, finishing his question.

"Yes, sex," he said.

"Well, of course, we've dated seven years." I was feeling a bit shocked at his timidity.

The minister then asked, "Do you and Marti use, ummmm, well, ahhhhh..."

"Protection?" I said, taking a good guess. Marti kicked me under the table because I was having fun playing the finish-my-sentence game.

"Yes, protection," he said.

"Not always. We used a timing method."

Marti kicked me again.

The minister had a wide-eyed look, but it was the truth. Then he lectured us about becoming reborn. I just wanted some real substance about marriage. I ended the session. I was not interested in being born again three days before our wedding.

* * *

The day of our wedding was beautiful. There was hardly a cloud in the sky. When Marti walked up the aisle, she was stunning. She had the most captivating smile. Her light brown hair graced the top of her shoulders, and her blue eyes sparkled. She was slender, and her gorgeous dress was fitted at the waist to accentuate her beautiful figure. Smooth lines of silk fabric flowed as she walked, and the lace across her neckline was like baby's breath in a vase of roses.

I saw my mom sitting in the front row. I smiled at her, grateful she was there. She had survived alcoholism and a divorce. She looked so happy. I finally grasped alcoholism. I thought it was a weakness, a character flaw. But actually, it was a disease accelerated by addictive behavior. For ten years, I thought my mom was weak and was critical of her. She went to AA and beat her addiction, but there was a cost. She lost her family and her husband. She was starting over, but I was proud of her.

The minister started with a welcome, offering thoughts on marriage. Then he said, "Pat and Marti have not yet accepted Christ into their life."

My eyes went from tears of happiness to penetrating daggers. Marti shot me an "It's okay" look. I was not happy and had to control my Irish temper. If Marti had given me the go-ahead nod, then that minister would have been punched in the nose.

I glanced down at Nana and Bampa, who were devout Catholics; they both looked horrified. I looked at the minister and delivered a look that said, "Don't fuck with me."

After the wedding, I told George, one of my groomsmen, to give me the money for the minister. While picture taking was underway, I found my way to his office. I walked in, threw his envelope on the floor, and said: "Do not come to the reception unless you want me to knock you out."

I then turned and walked out the door. I did not want a man who tried to ruin one of the biggest and most memorable days of my life anywhere near the reception.

Regardless, the wedding was awesome, and the reception was a blast. It was held at the Juno Beach Yacht Club. They had a huge banquet room that spilled out to a balcony overlooking the coastline. There were two open bars and a DJ who entertained us with Motown and rock and roll. It was a perfect night, and my groomsmen pushed it over the top.

I didn't pick my groomsmen based solely on friendship; it was their positive attitudes and their zest for enjoying life. They included Pete Carroll and Jack Westbrook, who were coaches; Bo Dunn and George Jahn, who were teammates; and John Allen, my neighborhood friend who played in the greatest game ever after Hurricane Betsy. They were the life of the party as they took turns dancing with all the women. Watching them dance with my mom, Marti's mom, and Nana brought tears to my eyes. There were about 100 guests, and I think my groomsmen met them all. They were there to make it a fun and memorable day, and they succeeded.

* * *

Despite the culture shock and the fact that there were no corrective therapist jobs at the University, Marti quickly adapted to the situation. She found an interim job coaching the WSU cheerleaders, and I threw myself back into the 18-hour days. Heading into our first season, I was encouraged by the progress and the execution of our offense. At the same time, I was discouraged by the lack of talent on our defense.

When I started to get captured by the negative thoughts, I would refer back to my dad saying, "Don't worry about those things. Just worry about being a great coach." It would drive me to refocus my effort and make the offensive line the best it could be. Even though we averaged 25 points per game, the defense gave up 33 points per game, which caused us to finish dead last in the conference.

The saving grace was the family atmosphere that Coach Walden and his wife, Janice, created. They hosted post-game get-togethers almost every week. It was casual with food, drinks, and music. Win or lose, at the post-game gathering, no one was to talk about blame. Instead, we discussed what was needed to get better. Janice acted like it was her job to brighten the spirits after a loss and get everybody singing or dancing after a win.

Everyone was invited, even the kids. Coach Walden and Janice would host the recruits at their house as well, and the kids became our super recruiters. The kids wanted to know their positions and how fast they were; you could see the prospects' eyes light up when they talked about themselves. Coach Walden's kids were like well-trained spies, asking prospects questions that would reveal where their hearts and minds were and report back to the coaches.

Despite the losing season, I loved being a coach at WSU because the Waldens made it a true family culture. Beyond that, we were getting what we needed from the University.

Our second recruiting season was much better. Coach Walden got it done; we had an RV. It had a bathroom, kitchen, and a large seating area and dining table in the rear. It quickly turned into a party both to and from Spokane. We had the routine down. One of the coaches would drive while the student hosts and other coaches would review who we were picking up and plan to play cards or games. Once the prospects were on board, the coaches and hosts would assume their roles, turning it into a fun experience while gathering information on what was important to each recruit. We played Spades and Go Fish or Checkers and Backgammon while feeding them chips and finger sandwiches. Conversation was steady, and if we needed entertainment, I would tell a joke.

It became a tradition that the California recruiters, Coach Hughes, Coach Elliott, and I, would guard the curtains. Anytime a recruit put his hand on the curtain to peak outside, we slapped it, then said, "Pay attention to the card game." I was the official "curtain monitor."

When we got close to WSU, I would draw the curtains back and they, too, would see the beautiful campus. I was excited the RV trips were working.

We were midway through fall training camp. The feeling was electric because we could see the execution getting better. Finally, after missing seven consecutive practices due to incomplete course work, Spud Harris was back—our best defensive lineman. At 6'4" and 280 pounds, he was a force to be reckoned with.

Everyone loved his extroverted and congenial personality. His ability was sometimes overshadowed by his jovial and down-to-earth nature.

As Spud was going through a stretch routine with the team, players were hollering at him, "Great to have you back, Spud."

Coaches, including myself, walked over and congratulated him. It was the beginning of our second season, and everything was improving. The plan was falling into place.

We broke from stretching and hustled to our assigned areas for practicing position-specific drills. The offensive line and defensive line were close together. I glanced over, saw Spud, and smiled. He was standing in line for a defensive drill. I turned my head back to the offensive line, where I was about to start a stance and footwork drill. Then I heard a commotion, and as I looked back, I saw that it was Spud. He had collapsed and was lying on the ground. I assumed he had hyperventilated and gotten dizzy. Coaches and players started yelling for help.

In seconds, Mark Smaha, our head trainer, was kneeling next to him, evaluating him. Then I saw him grab his wrist and immediately put his fingers on his neck, checking his carotid artery.

"He has no pulse!" he screamed. Without hesitation, he started mouth-to-mouth resuscitation while another assistant trainer started cardio-pulmonary resuscitation.

Sirens were heard in the distance, and what was once a surreal moment was now reality—Spud was in trouble. The paramedics loaded him into the ambulance and drove off the field with sirens blaring. We made an effort to continue practice, but we were numbed by what we witnessed. Coach Walden ended practice.

Walking off the field, I looked over to where Spud was just lying. I hoped that he was going to be alright. The field was now deserted. The night air was cooling. I got a rush of goosebumps as I stood alone. I was scared for Spud, the team, and our future. The lights that once shined on our team were now being shut off. The sirens were gone. The quietness seemed to be amplified. I could only hear the thoughts bouncing around in my head. *How could this happen? Why?*

Within minutes, Greg Sykes, a defensive lineman, came out of Bohler Gym, where our football offices, locker room, weight room, and training room were located. He walked toward me with tears in his eyes.

"Spud died, Coach."

I was already trying to prepare for that statement. Now it was a reality. My eyes started to water. I closed them and dropped my head, just like when my father died, and pleaded with God to let this be a bad dream.

Losing someone you love is like feeling your soul, which once sat on a mountain top, falling into an abyss, where there is no light. I knew this hammer of pain. I knew the drill of agony. This wasn't the same as losing my father, but for his family, it was. I would get nauseous thinking about the pain his mom and dad were going through.

When you're on a team in a good culture, you can feel the pain of your teammates and coaches. It all becomes personal. I was able to help some of the players deal with Spud's death. The relationships we have to each other are at the core of our existence. It is those bonds that produce love, joy, and laughter. When the connection is broken, it produces pain, anger, and sorrow.

Looking at the faces of the coaches and team, I could see the uncertainty, the lack of faith, and the lack of understanding. For most of them, this was their first experience with death.

Coach Walden did his best to get the team back, but it was truly an impossible task. They never made a determination on what caused his death. The team was hurting, distracted, and left without one of their best players.

It was a season of heartache and learning that life can be so fragile.

* * *

That season, our defense gave up 33 points per game, and we finished ninth in the Pac-10 conference. The only highlights were that we beat UCLA for the first time in 21 years, and our younger players were gaining experience.

During the spring of our third season, Coach Walden promoted me to offensive coordinator. I was ecstatic. I wanted more responsibility, and he gave it to me. With the family culture and RV recruiting, the steady improvements were real. Each recruiting class brought a renewed enthusiasm. We had recovered from Spud's death, but thinking of him still left a hollow place in our hearts.

It was a Sunday afternoon in early May, and like usual, I was in my office grading film from practice. I had been working for about two and half hours when the phone rang.

It was Marti.

"Have you looked outside?" she asked, "You should see this thunderstorm."

Like I've never seen a thunderstorm before. It was annoying. "No, I'll be home in a few. I need to finish grading film." I hung up and returned to grading. I was just getting back into the flow when she called again.

"Pat, did you look outside?"

I was becoming irritated; I was in no mood to be bothered. "No, I'm trying to finish grading our scrimmage film."

"You need to look," she barked.

"Look, I know you get amorous during thunderstorms. I'll be home in thirty minutes," I shot back.

I could hear her seething through the phone line. "God-damn it, just pull up the blinds and look at it."

I sighed, signaling my frustration. "I will, but please let me finish my grading. See you in a few."

I hung up the phone and glanced at the window. The blinds were down, but there was no light seeping through. Curious, I walked to the window and pulled up the blinds. It was as dark as a windowless basement. There were large black/gray flakes falling. The streetlights were on. *What is going on?*

I picked up the phone and called Marti. "What the hell is that falling from the sky?"

"I don't know. It looked like a giant thunderstorm. There was weird lightning and then this stuff started falling."

"I am coming home now."

I instinctively covered my mouth and ran out to my car. It was like driving in the desert dust, only this was dark gray instead of brown. There was no one on the streets; visibility was almost zero. By the time I pulled up to the house, the ground was completely covered. This stuff was accumulating like blackened snow.

Could this be a nuclear event? I had no idea what was going on, but I was determined to find out. For the next hour, I was frantically checking the television and radio and calling friends for information. No one knew anything. Finally, we heard a news bulletin on an AM radio station: Mt. St. Helens on the Western side of Washington, two-hundred and fifty miles away, had erupted, producing a 70,000-foot ash cloud. It had literally blown its top.

I was beginning to think that the universe was against us. First, we had to overhaul a losing football program, then we had one of our top defensive players collapse and die at practice, and now we had a volcanic eruption.

In the coming days, the team experienced a bonding exercise as we all worked to clean up the ash off our field. We had brooms, shovels, and bags for the ash. We eventually cleaned it off, but due to the air quality, our spring practice was cut short. Despite all the setbacks, though, we were inching our way forward.

That fall season, we finished sixth in the conference. Although success is usually measured in wins, we could see the value of our hard work. Unlike the year before, every game was competitive. We had opportunities to win them all.

We felt we had all the factors in place to be successful as we entered our fourth season. Just as we were getting started, I received a tip-off phone call from a booster I befriended.

"Hey Pat, Sam Jankovich, Washington State's athletic director, is here in Spokane trying to collect money to get Jim Walden fired."

I was so livid, my blood was boiling as I hung up the phone. The athletic director was not only going behind our backs, but he was about to destroy all the progress we had made. I had been through this before at Miami. Everybody loses if they fire the head coach. My stake in the program was bigger now. We had convinced recruits to be part of building a winning football program. I wasn't going to accept this—we were too close.

I rushed to Coach Walden's office to report what I had heard. I could see the shock register on his face; it was clear he didn't know.

"Don't worry about it," he said, trying to act like he had it under control. "I think he's being petty. He's upset because I made a statement to a reporter that we would never go to the Rose Bowl until we played USC and UCLA in Pullman."

I could hear his concern, and it was more than troubling to me. My mind was racing, searching for a way to defuse the situation. Then a thought hit me. "Do you think Dr. Terrell knows?" Dr. Terrell, the University President, was an active part of our recruiting and was well known by our entire staff.

Jim shook his head. "I doubt it."

"Is it alright with you if I go up to see Dr. Terrell?" I asked. I wanted to know what we were up against.

Jim remained quiet for about 30 seconds. Then he smiled and gave me the go-ahead nod. "Pat, you can go because I trust you'll handle it properly."

I felt elevated because he was making me part of the solution. I hustled back to my office and set up an appointment for 2 p.m. with Dr. Terrell. I collected my thoughts, then went up the hill to the Administration Building. His secretary told me to take a seat, but before I could sit down, he yelled out, "Send Coach Ruel in."

I was wondering if I was crossing lines that were not supposed to be crossed. I knew it was a bit risky, but I was in combat mode.

"To what do I owe the pleasure of this visit?" he said, standing up and directing me to have a seat in front of his desk.

I went straight to the point. "Do you know that Sam Jankovich is trying to fire Coach Walden and was actively seeking donations?"

His forehead wrinkled as he looked at me. "No, I did not know that."

His admission emboldened me. "We need the full support of the University and Jankovich if we're going to make this season successful."

He nodded in agreement, then said, "I'll take care of this."

I got up, shook his hand, and proceeded to walk out. I stopped at his door, hoping that we had his full support. I turned toward him. "Can I tell you one more thing?" There was this tinge of doubt that was creeping in.

"Sure," he responded.

"There was this man back in the nineteen twenties who was asked, 'Are you for prohibition, or are you against it?' The man replied, 'Some of my friends are for it, and some of my friends are against it, and I am for my friends.'"

He looked at me in disbelief. "Pat, I will take care of this, you go back to work." I could hear the irritation in his voice.

I left his office thinking I should not have finished our meeting with a back-handed story about playing politics. On the other hand, his last statement made me feel that he had full control and was on our side.

The next day, Sam Jankovich called me to his office. I knew he was foaming at the mouth, but I wasn't concerned, as I knew Dr. Terrell was on our side. When I arrived, he wasted no time unleashing on me.

"What you did was disloyal," he fumed. "Don't you ever do that again." He was barking like a dog reclaiming his territory.

I stood in front of his desk, waiting for him to finish. He was angering me. I was being loyal to the University and our hard work. "What you did was disloyal—you forced me to go over your head. You took a newspaper headline and turned it into motivation to fire Jim. You should have talked to him. And besides, we hadn't beat UCLA in twenty-one years, and you got them to play on our campus, and we upset them. It's proof of what Jim was trying to say—those big games needed to be played here."

"You stay out of my business," Jankovich barked.

"I will, if you don't damage all the hard work we've done," I retorted as I turned and walked out of his office.

I knew there could be ramifications for battling Sam. Walking down the hallway, I was wondering if my dad's lesson when I was seven years old to stand up to the bully wasn't causing me problems. I didn't want to be the focus of a problem; I wanted to be the solution. I knew I was a good coach with a good attitude, but I was going to fight to defend our efforts.

* * *

It was a week before our opening game, and everything went quiet. I was waiting to hear some kind of resolution, but nothing came from what had transpired.

Then game day arrived. I was on the field focusing on pre-game preparations, when I noticed Sam walking around the field shaking all the coaches' hands. It was a clear sign Dr. Terrell had done his part. When he got to me, I raised my index finger like my mom used to do and shook it back and forth, signaling Sam that I would not shake his hand. I was still carrying the anger over his disloyal comment.

On Monday, after beating Montana State, Jim called me to his office. Sam apparently told him to reel me in.

"You're a grown man," he said as soon as I stepped into his office. "You don't need me to tell you what is right and wrong. Be cordial, but if you don't want to shake his hand, that's up to you."

Jim was pleased that this was behind us and that we could move on. We were opposites in a way. I appreciated his methodical and thoughtful approach and his ability to forgive and forget. I became so invested in my goal that I was unyielding when I knew what was right and tended to hold onto my fury.

Sam Jankovich was a hard-working athletic director who needed to read Dale Carnegie's book. He was about as tactful as a new puppy on brand new carpet; someone was always trying to clean up his shit. I became a bit of a thorn in his side because I stood up to him. I was wrong for not shaking his hand for the whole season. I look back on my actions as somewhere between principled and petty.

We had departmental meetings on Tuesday at 7 a.m. I hated them because I would rather use early mornings for game planning and film study. So these meetings drove me nuts. I would listen to reports on concession sales, updates on all the other sports, facility usage, new projects, and upcoming events. None of it was of my concern. I was particularly irritated during a meeting that took place before our UCLA game. It had already been going for 90 minutes when Sam laid into all the coaches and administrative personnel about long-distance phone calls.

"Anyone who calls you long distance will call you back if it's important, so there's no need to return those calls," he said forcefully. "Anything you have to say can be said in two to three minutes."

My arm quickly shot up like an excited third grader who had the answer.

"What is it, Pat?" Sam asked.

"Sam, if that were true, then this meeting would have been over a long time ago." Everyone laughed.

Sam responded, "I'll see you in my office."

More laughter ensued, but I was not laughing. This was my second trip in six weeks. Even though I didn't like how he treated people, I knew what I did was disrespectful. My deep-seated anger was disguised as humor.

I walked into his office and immediately said, "I apologize, Sam." I didn't take a seat.

Sam looked at me like he wanted to kill me. "You need to just listen and keep your fucking mouth shut," he said angrily.

Probably true, I thought, then proudly said, "Thanks for the advice, but we're five to zero, and I got to go." I quickly got up and hustled out of his office. I let go of the anger that day; it was serving no purpose. I was instantly happier.

Later that season, we were 8-1-1 and playing the University of Washington, our in-state rival, for the Apple Cup. It was the ultimate success story. A university located in the middle of the Palouse in Eastern Washington was now competing for the Pac-10's biggest prize, the Rose Bowl.

We headed over to Seattle. It was their home game. For three years, the offense was the stabilizing factor at WSU. Ironically, it was the defense that kept us in this game. Our offense had six turnovers, three fumbles, and three interceptions. We outgained them statistically with 21 first downs and 364 yards. But we tried too hard to make plays. We lost 23-10; it was heartbreaking. We had a good chance of being the Pac-10 representative in the Rose Bowl, but we fumbled it away. The University of Washington went to the Rose Bowl, and we accepted a bid to the Holiday Bowl in San Diego to play BYU and Jim McMahon. It would be WSU's first bowl game in 51 years.

I reflected as we prepared for BYU. We fought our way through the tragic death of Spud Harris, the Mt. St. Helens eruption, and an athletic director who let his ego get in the way. We had a university president who believed in us, an athletic director who worked extremely hard, a head coach who had built the culture needed to be successful, and assistant coaches that were dedicated and creative. The team had great character and played for each other. Together, we did it, and I was filled with gratitude.

The San Diego weather was perfect. Our families and team were having a blast. The Holiday Bowl committee had made it an awesome week. They lined up a tour of the aircraft carrier USS Kitty Hawk and an afternoon at Sea World followed by a banquet.

The banquet revealed that our 18- to 21-year-old players were playing BYU's 21- to 24-year-old players. It was the adults versus the kids. Most of the BYU players had completed their required Mormon missions. Quite a few were already married and had children. Despite the differences in age and maturity, it was one of the most exciting bowl games that season. Unfortunately, we lost the Holiday Bowl 38-36. Time ran out.

Regardless, we were filled with a wonderful sense of accomplishment. We had put WSU back on the map and were now ready for recruiting.

Our opponents would say, "If you go to WSU, you can see the end of the world from there."

We would tell them, "If you haven't seen it, you should come—it's beautiful."

CHAPTER 12

DEATH, ANGER, ACHIEVEMENT AND THEN CHAPTER

I had been given a 30-minute heads up that a coach at Texas A&M would be calling me, but I could still feel the rush of adrenaline when I heard the phone ring.

"Hi Pat, this is Jackie Sherrill," he said in low and gravely whisper. "Would you be interested in the offensive coordinator job at Texas A&M?"

We were finishing up a successful recruiting season and were basking in our achievements. Everyone was pumped up about our future. But the idea of coaching at Texas A&M was intriguing, as it had a national reputation.

"Yes," I replied, trying to contain my excitement. "But have you talked to Coach Walden?" I knew that getting permission was standard tradition.

"I will, but I wanted to make sure you were interested."

"I am, Coach." I quickly replied. I wanted to find out what they were offering. It was always nice to be wanted.

"I'll call you back," he said, whispering like it was a secret conversation.

A week later, I was at Texas A&M for an official interview. I was conflicted. The thought of leaving Washington State was going to be difficult. I had fully committed myself to its success, but there was a piece of me that was always looking for the next adventure.

The university was located in East Texas, just about 90 miles northeast of Houston. This place was as flat as a pancake. You could toss a bowling ball toward Mexico, and it wouldn't stop rolling 'til it hit the Rio Grande.

Everything about A&M told me that they were serious about their football. Kyle Field, their stadium, was huge and seated 72,000. It was usually sold out. They had long-standing traditions, one of which is calling their alumni "former students," which was to solidify their attachment to the university. I was given a quick drive-by tour of the campus before being deposited at the football offices, which were on the seventh floor of Rudder Tower, an 11-story high-rise. I felt more like it was an executive corporate office than a football office, which were usually located next to or in the stadium.

Entering Coach Sherrill's office, I was confident. Although I knew very little about him, other than his successful stint at the University of Pittsburgh, I knew I had a lot to offer. He greeted me with a firm handshake and motioned for me to take a seat. Then he got down to the business of the interview.

"Pat, tell me about your offense."

Like on the phone, he talked in a low voice. It was halfway between a normal tone and a whisper. It was like he was guarding classified material. I did a quick assessment of him. I put him in his mid-thirties, which was a few years older than me. He had a mop of dark brown hair and a square jaw. What struck me most was that his brown eyes were set deeper back and seemed to convey no emotion.

I spent the next few minutes listing the reasons our offense was so successful. I knew that our offenses were similar, and they were looking for an upgrade. We had gotten national recognition for the creative style and execution.

Midway through our discussion, he suddenly asked me about pass protection techniques for offensive linemen. He started describing the techniques he had used at Pittsburgh, and before I knew it, we were walking through techniques in his office. This threw up a red flag, as we spent the greater part of the hour on pass protection. It was only 20% of my offense.

After about an hour or so, Coach Sherrill locked his eyes on mine. "You're too young to be an offensive coordinator."

The statement puzzled me. I was told once before that I was too young. I was in no mood to defend myself. "You're too young to be a head coach," I shot back.

Coach Sherrill smiled, as though he was expecting that kind of answer. He shifted the conversation to my salary and benefits. I would be making $47,000, which was $12,000 more than WSU. He offered me the job, and I took it. I was enamored by the money and the facilities.

As soon as I got back to the hotel room, I called Marti to tell her. She congratulated me, but I could hear the ambivalence in her voice. She had quit her cheerleading coaching to take a job working in student activities and loved it. My quest for new challenges would disrupt her career once again.

I only had a few days to say my goodbyes at WSU and report back to A&M. I knew Coach Walden viewed his staff as part of his family, so I expected his disappointment, but the reactions of some of the other coaches caught me off guard. One coach said that I was all about myself, another said that

I was a liar, and then Steve Morton said, "He's not your type of guy, Pat."

I was worried because I trusted these guys, but I had already taken the job and chalked it up to jealousy. I was back at Texas A&M and settling into my new office when I got another surprise phone call. It was Gil Brandt, the VP of player personnel for the Dallas Cowboys.

I felt a rush of excitement, as he was one of the top NFL executives. He was nationally recognized for his success evaluating college athletes. After a brief hello, he got down to business.

"Coach Walden asked me to wait till after recruiting to talk to you about a position with the Dallas Cowboys. He didn't tell you?"

I was stunned. "He did not. I can't leave Texas A&M. I just signed a contract and I've been here for a week." Why would Coach Walden hold that information from me? We had a great relationship. I was so rattled, I didn't know what to think.

"So you're going to turn this opportunity down?" he asked.

I felt trapped; I had this huge opportunity, and I was sick about the fact that I was giving it up. But I felt that I needed to stick by my commitment to Texas A&M. Signing the contract was my bond, and although I could have broken it, it wasn't in me.

"I wish you would have called me a week ago," I managed. I waited for his response, but there was only silence. I realized he had hung up.

I shrugged off the whole Cowboy thing and went full throttle on being a Texas A&M Aggie. About a week into the job,

Coach Sherrill walked into my office and threw the Pittsburgh playbook on my desk.

"This is what we're doing—this is what I know," he announced.

I stared at him, dumbfounded. *What the fuck is going on?* I thought I had been recruited to put the WSU offense in because they were already running a form of it. I took a deep breath.

"Coach, I thought you wanted to run my offense," I said with dismay.

"You're an excellent coach—it doesn't matter what offense you run."

That was a total bullshit answer. My expertise was the offense that I ran for four years. I was being manipulated and deceived. I tried to stay calm as he walked out of my office, but I was pissed. He knew what he wanted from the start. I was too enamored by the facilities and the money, and I ignored what the coaches who had worked for him had told me.

I knew it was too late to do anything about my decision, so I picked up the Pittsburgh playbook and began studying. It was a pro-style offense. It made Dan Marino a top NFL prospect. I decided to fix my attitude and treat it as a growth experience. I could learn this as well.

The more I was around Coach Sherrill, the more I realized that I was working for someone with narcissistic tendencies; he was always trying to manipulate the truth. During our staff meetings, Coach Sherrill would tell us about what a great player he was at Alabama and expound on how he played four different positions. It was obvious that he was the most improved player after graduation. Besides, I only had to look at his ankles; they were fat. Athletes don't have fat ankles.

Knowing that he lied about his football career, I decided to have some fun one day and clip off a two-inch piece of 16mm film and tape it on the whiteboard in the offensive staff room. I wrote above it, *Coach Sherrill's College Highlight Film.* Then I polled the offense coaches for a yes or no vote as to whether he would laugh. Five voted no; I was the only one who voted yes.

When he walked into our offensive staff room and saw it on the board, he immediately became irate. "Who put that up there?" he demanded.

It was the reaction I had anticipated, and I bit the inside of my lip to keep a straight face. "I did, Coach. I was betting you would laugh and everybody else said you wouldn't."

"Take it down—it's not funny," he replied.

"Sorry, Coach. I thought you would laugh." I was wondering if I would get called into his office.

As he left the room, George Pugh, our tight end coach, said, "Pat, you're crazy."

It was just my way of dealing with someone I perceived as a narcissist.

A couple of months after my arrival, I started getting strong signals of NCAA violations. There were whispers about an alumni at a local bank that was helping athletes with the acquisition of cars. There was also talk about meetings in Houston and Dallas to raise money for recruiting slush funds. One day, while walking to Cain Hall, which was the athletic dorm and training table for athletes, I noticed a few students were pointing at the cars in the parking lot. They were saying "star player" or "role player" based on the newness of the cars. Those students were pretty much right on in their guessing game.

We actually printed out a cliff note guide to recruiting rules for the prospective athletes, handed them out on their visits, and then proceeded to break all those rules. Why does Texas A&M need to break NCAA rules? They have money, facilities and tradition. I was shocked but not surprised because the Southwest Conference had a reputation of bending the rules. It was difficult to be in that environment. This really bothered me at my core; I wasn't worried about my actions, but I was concerned I would be deemed guilty by association. However, my focus was my job as offensive coordinator, so I pushed the rule breaking out of my view.

For our first season, we finished 5-6. We beat the teams we were supposed to beat and lost to the teams that were better than us. The highlight was that we had learned the Pittsburgh offense. Our quarterback, Gary Kubiak, had the top quarterback rating in the conference. We were making progress. The problem was that every day I continued to be reminded of our indiscretions.

The following season, we were going to open with the University of California at Berkley. Coach Sherrill sent Tim Nunez, a graduate assistant, to Cal-Berkley, to spy on their practices. It was totally an illegal move by Coach Sherrill. What the fuck were we doing?

Tim dressed up as a jogger, a sun-bather, and a janitor as he roamed around the stadium watching the California practices. He was disguising himself to make sure he wouldn't get caught. He reported back, telling us what they were working on.

"The offense was working on throwing play-action post routes," he said. "And their defense was working on edge pressure blitzes."

As we prepared for the opener of our second season, we were now starting quite a few of the freshmen. We told the players that we had good info from a good source what this team would like to do. The California Bears threw a post route for a touchdown in the first quarter. So much for telling the players what to expect. We lost 19-17. When you cheat, it's never worth it. Even if we had won, it wouldn't have felt right.

Coach Sherrill took the saying, "If you ain't cheating, you ain't trying," to a whole new level.

Again, it was the assistant coaches who kept the attitude positive in a toxic environment. We looked for moments to laugh. During a game versus Arkansas State, Jim Helms, our running back coach, replaced our starter with a backup player, as we were ahead 31-0 in the fourth quarter and had the game won. The player fumbled the ball on his first carry, and they recovered. I was in the press box on the headset with Coach Helms, who was out on the field, when I heard the defensive coaches say that Coach Sherrill was looking for Coach Helms.

"Jim, Coach Sherrill is looking for you," I snickered.

"Where is he?" he asked.

I went into full announcer mode. "He's on the opposite forty-yard line, but he's walking your way. Jim, he's crossing the fifty-yard line. He's at the forty-five, at the forty, at the thirty-five."

I paused.

"Is he still coming?" Jim asked.

"Yes, and heeeee's... got you."

Having a perfect view from the press box, I watched Coach Sherrill put his hand on Jim's shoulder, turn him around, and berate him for putting that player in the game.

"Jim, tell him to stick a sock in it," I said, laughing into my microphone.

"Shut up," he barked.

Then Coach Sherrill chimed in angrily, "You talking to me?"

"No, I was talking to Pat."

Coach Sherrill grabbed his headset and put it on. "You got something to say, Pat?"

"Yes, I was just telling Jim not to put in players who fumble."

"You need to shut up and let me handle this." He knew I was playing a game with Jim.

I was chuckling with the other coaches in the press box. It was the type of devious fun I could have since I knew we'd already won the game. We finished 5-5-1. That was not good enough in Aggieland.

I was struggling; nothing felt right. Younger players were playing critical positions, we were violating NCAA rules, and we were being led by an egocentric liar. I would go home and sit on the couch after grinding out a 16-hour day and not say a word as I stared at the TV.

Marti, who was working in student activities at the time and enjoyed her job, was concerned for me. "Are you okay?" she would ask.

"Yes, I'm fine," I always responded, knowing full well I was not okay.

"What are you watching?"

I couldn't even answer because I wasn't engaged with anything, and Marti knew it. I was feeling nothing, but I was like a ticking time bomb. I was kicking myself for turning down the Cowboys.

The shit hit the fan in our training camp for season three. We were in a goal line scrimmage. We ran a play that scored. There was a pile of players in the end zone. I watched as Coach Bobby Roper, our defensive end coach, pulled Nate Steadman, one of my players, out of the pile. Then he drop-kicked him in the stomach.

I ran over and yelled at Coach Roper, "What the hell are you doing?" No one does that for any reason. I was furious.

Coach Roper shot me a defiant look. "He was hitting people after the play."

I suppressed my anger and decided to get to the bottom of this. It would all be on film. That night after dinner, I played it back. Nate did not hit anybody. I was ready to blow. I was so mad, I could feel the heat from my core running up my neck and into my face. I walked down to the defensive staff room and poked my head in the door.

I looked right at Coach Roper and said, "You need to apologize to Nate for that bullshit you did on the field."

"Fuck you," he shot back.

I closed the door and went to look for Coach Sherrill.

Nate Steadman was a member of the Fellowship of Christian Athletes. He would never subvert authority. He was 6'4" and 285 pounds of what every coach loves: a dedicated, hard-working athlete with a great attitude. I felt he needed someone to stand up for him, or nothing would be done about it.

Coach Sherrill was nowhere to be found. He apparently had slipped down to Houston for a secret rendezvous.

I needed to calm down. I went to my locker and put on running shorts. It was almost midnight. I called Marti and said I was staying at the facility that night, told her I was pissed about the scrimmage. She knew it was something else, but she respectfully decided to let me handle it.

I started running at 1:00 in the morning. I ran for two hours away from campus, then turned around and started running back. I was calming down. I didn't want to make a bad decision because of an over-emotional response.

Finally, I walked the last bit and arrived at the stadium at 6 a.m. I drank a bunch of water and rested for a bit. I was exhausted; I ran about twenty miles and hadn't slept for 24 hours.

Coaches started coming into the locker room. Jerry Pettibone, who was our wide receiver and led our chapter of the Fellowship of Christian Athletes, knew I was seething about the day before. I thought I had calmed down, but bringing all the actors back to the scene of a crime reignited me like a Roman candle that had taken a momentary pause.

"Are you okay?" he asked.

"No, Jerry, I'm not. I'm going to kick someone's ass."

"Damnit, Pat, stop this shit. Let it go."

"Jerry, you've never cussed in your life, don't start now."

Just then, Coach Sherrill appeared.

"Can I talk to you?" I asked. Instead of responding, he headed to the bathroom. I followed him and spoke to him while he was taking a shit. There was a sense of urgency on my part, and a lack of caring on his part. "I want what happened yesterday settled."

"Drop it. There's nothing that needs to be done," he said through the closed stall door.

As I walked out, I said, "I guess we have a head coach who doesn't want to solve the problem." It was loud enough for him and everyone else to hear. I wasn't dropping anything.

When Coach Roper walked into the locker room, I said, "I need to talk with you." I was trying to calm down and wanted to handle this cerebrally. I directed him to the hallway that was between our locker room and the stadium. We walked through the open door and I pulled it shut. The door automatically locked when it closed.

We turned and faced each other, and I did my best to extend an olive branch. "Listen," I said intently. "You really need to apologize to Nate and the offensive line." I was staring at his lips, hoping for the right words to come out of his mouth.

He looked at me and said, "Fuck you."

Like the playground when I was seven years old, I gave myself the go-ahead nod and punched him hard in the chest. His 6'2" athletic build fell against the wall and slid down to the floor, gasping for air. I had no sympathy; I was out of control. I was prepared for an all-out, knock-down fight.

"I want my glasses," he pleaded while trying to regain his breath. They had fallen off when I hit him. I took my foot and pushed them farther away.

"Not until I get an apology," I said with conviction.

Then suddenly the trainer and Coach Sherrill were pounding at the door. It was locked.

Coach Roper said, "We're going to get fired."

"I don't care. You kicked one of my players in the stomach. I'm not Jesus—I will not turn the other cheek."

The door flew open, and Coach Sherrill yelled, "You two go into the team room, now."

By now, I was committed to getting Nate's apology. "No coach is going to strike any of my players," I said as soon as we were seated.

Coach Sherrill relented and told Coach Roper to apologize. He and I walked down to the offensive line room. I was feeling some satisfaction about him apologizing, but I was evaluating my behavior, and I was embarrassed by my actions. I realized I was not happy working for Sherrill, and my frustrations were part of my problem.

Coach Roper stood in front of the room, looked straight at Nate, and apologized. Then he apologized to the offensive line and to me. It was a very sincere and remorseful apology. We shook hands, and I said, "Thanks, Bobby." I regretted hitting him.

At the staff meeting that night, Coach Sherrill said, "Keep your hands on your own players because we have coaches that are sensitive about it."

I looked him straight in the eye with a degree of disdain that could melt the artic.

A few days later, the defensive coordinator, RC Slocum, asked me to his office and enlightened me. "Pat, that was not Roper's intent—that was Coach Sherrill's intent. He told Bobby to create some animosity between the offense and defense, so that the scrimmage would be intense."

I instinctively knew it to be true. Too often, we bow and forego our principles to the unethical boss to keep our job. I went home and explained to Marti that I could no longer work for this asshole.

"Put the house for sale, we're getting out of here before the NCAA blows it up."

She was more than happy; she didn't like him from the start. Even though it was another move, she saw what it was doing to me.

When Jerry Pettibone got wind of what I was doing, he decided to leave as well. Within a week, he put his own house up for sale. Marti and Susy Pettibone were at a game function midway through the season when the wife of the director of football operations found out our homes were up for sale. She told her husband, and he told Coach Sherrill. The dam had been breached. That Monday, Coach Sherrill called Jerry to his office and began grilling him on the reason for selling his house. Jerry told him it was too big of a house, so they were downsizing. Jerry informed me of what he had said; he didn't want a confrontation.

I was called in next. I walked into his office thinking I was going to try and blow it off like Jerry. But the minute he opened his mouth, I knew it wasn't going to be good.

"You need to get control of your wife," he snarled. The asshole, after two-and-a-half years, still didn't know her name.

"I don't need to control my wife," I calmly said. "If you have a problem with Marti, I can give you her number."

"Are you saying you can't control your wife?"

My anger was pouring out of my body like sweat from a three-mile run on a hot and humid day. "No. Here's what I'm saying," I exclaimed as I slammed my hand on his desk, "I'm resigning—not at the end of the season, not next week, but right fucking now." I got up to walk out.

He yelled, "You'll never get another job!"

I got three steps out of his office with my blood at a full boil before turning around walking back in. "When I get through with the NCAA, you won't have a job either."

As I departed, I slammed his door so hard that it shook the walls of the seventh floor of Rudder Tower. Back in my office, I shut the door and sat down. Taking a deep breath, I noticed my right leg was shaking uncontrollably. My phone rang and I picked it up.

"Pat, he's at your door," Coach Helms whispered. He had a clear view to my office.

"Thanks, Jim." I hung up and heard a light *tap... tap... tap...* on my door. My leg had stopped shaking. "Come in," I said.

Coach Sherrill opened the door and sat down in front of my desk. He was obviously here to defuse the situation. I knew he was worried about that last statement I had made. "I like Pat Ruel," he said as he forced a smile. His emotionless, sunken-in eyes betrayed him. I did not respond. He repeated, "I like Pat Ruel."

Suddenly, I felt as if I was in charge. "Coach, I don't like you, but I will not quit the team during the season. I will resign afterward."

"Well, let's keep it quiet and concentrate on the team." When he said that, it was like a harbinger of deceit ringing a five-alarm fire. Never trust someone with narcissistic traits.

I called Jim Walden that night and explained the situation. He told me not to wait until the end of the season because he would just fire me and blame everything on me. But I was not convinced that this was the best idea. I needed another opinion. I decided that the perfect person to call was Lou Holtz.

As I waited for him to answer, I thought how ironic it was to be calling one snake to get advice on how to handle another snake. Holtz's answer was the same as Walden's. "You need to leak it to the press that you're resigning, otherwise he will fire you and blame everything on you."

Hmmmm... I had just gotten that same advice from someone I trusted.

I promised Coach Sherrill I would keep it quiet, but now things had changed. After I hung up with Holtz, I immediately called Harold Wheeler, a friend of mine who was coaching defensive backs at the University of Houston. I asked him to leak it to the press. He did, and I got calls from the press. I told them that Coach Sherrill and I were like oil and water; we didn't mix.

The following morning was the encore to the previous day's fireworks.

Coach Sherrill called me to his office, and by the time I arrived, he was foaming at the mouth. "What the hell is going on? We had a deal!" His anger was flowing like lava down the side of a volcano.

I shot him a confused look. "That's what I want to know— you told me one thing, then did another. You just can't be trusted."

"I didn't do it—I'll promise you that," he said in disbelief.

"I think you did, but we'll just have to deal with it and get the focus back on the team."

"That's right, but let's not talk to the press anymore about this."

Momentarily, it felt good to blame him for something I had done. It may be the most deceitful thing I have ever done in my life, but I now was in control of the termination.

The offensive line was the best. They told me how much they respected me, and then said, "Let's finish strong, Coach." They had great character. Good coaches don't coach for money; they coach to make a difference. Those relationships are priceless.

We finished the season by beating the number 17 ranked TCU 35-21 and number 13, Texas, 37-12. I was an instant celebrity, as the Aggie alumnus wanted to hear about beating TCU and Texas and my decision to leave. I spoke at several events. I never blamed Coach Sherrill. I said it was a personal decision.

While I was making the rounds on the speaking circuit, Jerry, who had applied to Northern Illinois's head coaching job, approached me about being his assistant head coach and offensive coordinator for the Huskies. I balked at first, because it seemed like a step down. I didn't want to commit to Jerry and have the same thing that happened with the Cowboys happen again. Then he explained that if he could tell NIU that I was coming, it would help him get the job. My heart got the best of me. I loved and respected Jerry and wanted to help him.

"Let's do this, Jerry," I said, but I was concerned that I was taking a step backward in my career as a coach.

CHAPTER 13

BACK TO A GREAT CULTURE

Jerry was nationally recognized as an excellent recruiter. He was personable and had a politeness about him that gave him instant credibility with parents. What we were about to find out was that recruiting at nationally recognized schools was a lot easier than at the second-tier schools.

Northern Illinois University was a public school located 60 miles west of Chicago, smack in the middle of the Corn Belt. I was picked up from the Chicago O'Hare airport by Bob Chmiel, the linebacker coach. Heading west on I-90, it was a WSU déjà vu moment. First it was city, then suburbs, then 30 miles of snow-covered cornfields. As we drove, Bob filled me in on NIU and stories of Lee Corso, the previous head coach. We finally reached the exit for NIU and entered DeKalb, a city of about 30,000 people which nearly doubled when the students showed up.

"Those are the happiest people in DeKalb," Bob said as he laughed, pointing to the cemetery just inside the city limits.

Well, that's not an auspicious start, I thought as I forced a laugh.

Our first recruiting weekend was in early January. We were under a winter storm warning. In the transition period, the coaches stayed at the Holmes Student Center, which doubled as a hotel as well. The typical recruiting weekend itinerary was to come in with the recruits on a Friday night or Saturday morning and leave Sunday afternoon. There were tours of facilities, meetings with position coaches, player hosts taking them out in the evenings, then a final meeting with the head coach.

It was a Sunday, and due to the weather, Jerry held the final meetings with the recruits in the Holmes Student Center. We were having a steady snow during that weekend. The temperature was 12 degrees with 20-mph winds and gusts up to 30 mph. I was saying goodbye to the recruits when one of the parents announced that none of their cars would start. I had a light coat, which wasn't good enough to be out there for any length of time. I ran up to my room and took the blanket off my bed, wrapping it around me. I secured a pair of jumper cables, and with no gloves and no hat, and started running back and forth from the Holmes Center, starting cars for the recruits' parents.

After starting four cars, my hands were a light blue color, my eyeballs felt frozen, and my cheeks were red and burned. Besides thinking about purchasing a bigger coat, hat, and gloves, I wondered if I had made the right decision. I sat down in the lobby trying to thaw out when Mr. Paterno, father of Chris Paterno, one of our recruits, came up to me.

"Hey, you need to start our car now," he said as he stood in front of me with a winter jacket, hoodie, and gloves on. I had been managing successfully until then.

"Your son isn't that good," I shot back, trying to be funny. "You can wait five minutes." I'd just broken every rule of the Dale Carnegie book.

Worse yet, Jerry had heard me and pulled me aside. "Pat, I know this is a tough situation, but let's try and ignore his rudeness and fight through it."

I knew what I said was wrong. I was letting the fact that I'd stepped down a notch accepting this job—as well as my frozen body—affect my attitude.

I agreed and went over to the Paternos to apologize.

"My son has something to tell you," Mr. Paterno announced.

Chris Paterno flashed me a smile. "I'm making a commitment to become a Northern Illinois Huskie," he said.

I shook their hands and congratulated them. I was relieved that my actions didn't result in a rejection. I finally got their car started while they waited in the lobby.

Heading to my room in the hotel that evening, I was reflecting on my first week at NIU. I had traded the mild temperatures of Texas, a 72,000-seat stadium, and executive type football offices for frozen, snow-covered corn fields, a 28,000-seat stadium, and 7' by 7' football offices that were more like small bat caves. But I was happier than I had been in three years. I'd also traded a narcissistic liar, who was breaking NCAA rules, for an honest, caring, and principled coach. We seemed to naturally hit it off.

Texas A&M taught me a valuable lesson. It's never the salaries, facilities, equipment, or the perks that make you happy. It's the people that run your organization and the people you work with that help cultivate and nurture your happiness.

Looking at NIU's schedule was an eye-opener. Most universities playing football will play their conference schedule and then schedule a few wins out of conference by playing schools with a lower classification. For example, Texas A&M playing Arkansas State, or Michigan playing Appalachian State.

But NIU's non-conference opponents were not Wisconsin Whitewater or Eastern Illinois. They were West Virginia, Miami, Florida, Iowa, Wisconsin, and Northwestern. All money games for the athletic department and certain failure for a winning season. Obviously, the athletic director thought money was more important than winning.

Even so, we all threw ourselves into recruiting the best players we could find. I was in Chicago at the tail end of our recruiting season, just before the signing period the first week in February. It started to snow heavily, and a high school coach warned me a blizzard was on its way. It was going to be too dangerous to take the 60-mile trip home in a winter storm. I was on Cicero Avenue and pulled into a Hilton Hotel; they were booked. Then I pulled into a Holiday Inn, and they were booked too. Finally, I spotted the Miami Motel. I drove up to the lobby area, which really wasn't a lobby—just a man standing behind the glass.

"Would you like a room for three hours, six hours, or the night?" he asked. I was a bit confused, but I informed him I would take it for the night. He asked for a credit card and driver's license, then gave me a key to room 108. I got back in my car and drove up to the front of my room.

This place was old and dirty. I opened up the door to see a bed that looked more like a hammock with its sagging middle. The carpet was a deep red. *Probably to hide blood stains*, I thought. I threw my stuff on the chair, turned on the TV, and went to the bathroom to wash up before bed. Then, turning off the water, I could hear moaning, sighing, and an occasional scream. *Where is that coming from?* I thought as I walked out of the bathroom. Then I saw—it was on the TV. It was an X-rated movie. I switched the channel, only to find the TV had only three channels dedicated to porn. I started to laugh to myself. I was in Chicago, in a blizzard, in a dirty hotel, with porn on, sitting on a bed that looked like an elephant had been sleeping in it. Was I about to be part of a crime scene? All the signs were there.

I kicked off my shoes and socks, only to realize that the deep red carpet felt like a grease spill. As I lied down, I started wondering if sleeping was a good idea. Then my hotel phone rang.

"Would you like a date?" the voice on the other end asked. I was stunned—I seemed to be in a brothel disguised as a motel.

"No, I don't want a date, I want to get some sleep. Besides, my back is sore."

Five minutes later, the phone rang again. This time a different girl said, "Would you like a massage for your sore back?"

"No, thank you."

I hung up the phone, put my pants, socks, and shoes back on, and took two chairs to barricade my door. Then I lied on the bed fully clothed and, with one eye open, fell asleep. It was the worst night of sleep ever.

In the morning, I picked up scholarship papers from the athletes who had committed to NIU while snowplows went about the task of cleaning the streets.

I was missing Marti more than ever, and we still hadn't sold our house in Texas. It was 1985, and the state was in the middle of an oil slump. It was draining us financially. I was looking for a cheap house, and I found one on the golf course of the Kishwaukee Country Club. It was an old ranch-style house built in the early 60s. It had seven different carpets and smelled like a kennel, as it was primarily a rental for ten years. It was a dark house on a heavily wooded lot. Think of any scary movie about an old house in the woods—I'd found it. I made an offer because of the location and because it was all we could afford.

Marti came up for a visit. She had offered her resignation for the end of the school year. I picked her up at Chicago O'Hare airport. I was trying to prepare her for the downgrade. She was doing great until we turned into the gravel driveway, then tears sprang to her eyes. She had left a house that was brand new, one that we designed when we first got to Texas A&M. It was a beautiful house with a sunken living room, huge windows, and a pounded copper canopy over the fireplace that ran up to the vaulted cedar ceiling. It felt like a ski lodge. It also had a large atrium that bordered the hallway and entrance to the living room. She had reason to cry over the loss, but I was determined to make it a nice place.

I told Marti, "Don't worry, I'll fix it."

I spent the nights of my first three months there remodeling the house. I tore out rugs only to find gorgeous hardwood floors underneath. I tore down a wall to make it more open. Then I literally took the entire back of the house off and put in sliding glass doors and a huge bay window, before adding a 1,400-square-foot deck with built-in seats. I painted the house a tan cream color, which brought much-needed contrast to the heavily wooded lot. And all of it opened up to a view of the golf course.

When Marti came back in June, she was ecstatic. I had kept my promise and turned a pet kennel into a stunning home on a golf course. She had received her master's at Texas A&M and quickly got a job at NIU in charge of student judicial. Once again, we were both launching into our new adventure.

As the assistant head coach and offensive coordinator, I was now responsible for monitoring academics and issuing discipline for breaking team rules or missing class. My main focus was to introduce the Washington State offense. Because of its prior success, I felt it would be a great fit, but it wasn't enough. Although we made some progress, the first season demonstrated our quarterbacks did not have the passing ability to effectively run it. We finished 4-7.

Going into the spring of our second season, we were reevaluating our players and techniques. Coach Pettibone, who had contacts at Arkansas State, Air Force, and Oklahoma, suggested that we go and study the wishbone offense. He said they were running it effectively and that it would be a good fit for our quarterback. I had no previous experience running that offense, so Coach sent me to those schools to investigate it. I was immediately hopeful, as many teams who were running it were at a talent disadvantage. It was a ball-control run offense with minimal passing. I turned the duties of the offensive line over to Coach Lawrence Cooley and took over coaching the quarterback position because I felt it was the most critical position in the wishbone.

The best news came just after recruit-signing day for the high school prospects: Marti was pregnant and due in late October. We were about to add one more member to the family. We were so professionally oriented that we didn't really consider having a baby. But when Marti told me, I was bubbling with joy.

Our second season kicked off much like the first. Despite the new wishbone offense, we were all rookies at running it, and it showed. On top of that, the early schedule contained these powerhouses: West Virginia, Wisconsin, Iowa, and Miami. The injuries from playing those teams were taking their toll, and now we were being forced to play our younger players.

In addition, I was attending Lamaze classes once a week so I could be part of our child's birth. Fitting those classes into a coach's schedule was next to impossible. They taught me how to help her breathe and told me she might say things that would upset me but to understand that it was just the pain talking.

We were getting ready to play Western Illinois, a team we could beat. It was a Monday in late September, and we were 0-4. Our experiment with the new offense was not moving as fast as we wanted.

Marti called the office at 5 p.m. "My water broke, and the doctor wants me to get to the hospital immediately."

Oh, my god—she's four weeks early! I was instantly worried. "I'm on my way," I assured her. Suddenly, football was taking a back seat.

I drove to her workplace on campus and picked her up. She was in a lot of pain. I was stopping at red lights, but when it was clear, I went through them, not waiting for the light to change. She was moaning and in discomfort.

I said, "Breathe, take deep breaths," resorting to my Lamaze training.

"Shut the fuck up and get me to the hospital," she replied.

"Remember, they said you might say things you don't mean." I was trying to keep it light.

She took a deep breath. "Pat, shut up."

When we arrived at Kishwaukee Hospital, they put Marti in a wheelchair and whisked her to a room with me in toe. One nurse was getting us situated when another nurse popped into the room. "Have you seen the film of an actual birth in the Lamaze class?" she asked.

"No, I think that's this week," I replied.

"I'll be right back." She ran out of room, and I could feel her sense of urgency.

I was trying to act calm and cool, but this unfamiliar territory was filling me with anxiety and anticipation. Another nurse came in and gave Marti an epidural.

When the nurse returned, she had a 16mm film projector and a film of the actual birth of a child. She said, "Here, you need to watch this."

You have got to be kidding me, I thought. *Marti is in pain and I'm a nervous wreck, and you want us to watch a film?* "Is this necessary?" I managed.

The nurse glared at me. "If you want to be there by her side during the birth, then yes, it is. We have had too many fathers faint in the O.R., and we are not going to take any chances."

I held Marti's hand as the nurse turned on the film. With a painful sigh, she said, "Really, we're going to watch this?" I could feel her frustration.

Just as the film was starting, the doctor appeared in the door. "The baby is breached—we're going to have to do a C-section. Her epidural did not take, so, Coach, you won't be allowed in the room with her. We might have to take her to Rockford Memorial Hospital in an ambulance."

Everything was happening so fast I could barely process it all. But for a brief moment, I thought about how ironic it would be that our daughter might be born in the same hospital as my father.

As quickly as they brought it up, they decided there was not enough time. They rolled her into the O.R., and I was left in the hallway pacing like a lion in a zoo before dinner. I peeked through the double doors to see doctors and nurses doing their jobs, when another nurse came up behind me.

"Mr. Ruel, we have a waiting lounge with a TV, and the Monday night game is on."

I was too wound up to watch a game. When I entered the lounge, there was a guy sitting on the couch. I asked him, "Is your wife having a baby?"

He said, "Hold on until after this play."

I waited anxiously for his answer. Finally, the play ended, and he turned to me. "Is this your first?" he asked.

"Yes," I replied. "And you?"

"We have two boys, and my wife is about to deliver triplets," he said as he shook his head in disbelief.

I looked at him with astonishment. How could he be so calm?

"Sit down. It's all out of your hands," he said.

I went back out in the hallway and peeked between the crack of the double doors. Marti was lying there, arms dangling over the side of the gurney, out cold. *Is she ok? Did they deliver the baby? What's going on?*

The same nurse that had just sent me to the waiting room scolded me, "I thought I told you to go to the waiting room."

"Well, I'm too excited to sit down." I felt like I was on drugs.

Then she smiled. "You're the father of a baby girl."

"What about my wife?"

"She's fine and is going to the recovery room. But you can come to the NICU and see your daughter through the glass."

I looked at her, confused. "What is a NICU?"

"It's where we take babies who are premature or need extra care."

We went to the NICU, and a nurse pointed out our daughter. She was absolutely beautiful, except for one thing: She was breeched, meaning her head was up instead of down. Since her ankles had been up near her ears in the womb, when the nurse in the NICU pulled her legs down, they shot right back to her ears like a spring-loaded door.

I looked at the nurse, and she looked at me. I was mouthing through the glass, "We need to fix that." She laughed, and I said, "No, seriously." Then I laughed.

We narrowed the names down to Kelly or Sabra, and we chose the name Sabra because it was unique.

The new addition to our family was the best gift ever. Our football team may have been 0-4, but for a moment, I felt undefeated. I had purchased two dozen cigars to celebrate Sabra's birth, and I thought I would break them out after our first win. Four weeks later, we were 0-8. However, some of the players that we lost to injury were finally back when we headed down to Bowling Green University in Ohio, who had a home game winning streak of 16.

During the game, our quarterback, Marshall Taylor, misread a play. I chastised him on the sideline. It was the tear that snuck out of his eye and rolled down his cheek that made me realize I needed to coach him, not criticize him. I spent the rest of the game whispering encouraging words in his ear and asking for his input. He took command and led our team to its first win, 16-8.

Finally, the cigars were lit. We celebrated the win and my daughter's birth. We did the unimaginable. The coaches and team were acting like we just won the National Championship. Guys were standing on chairs and benches, dancing, and smoking cigars. Sam Sample, our defensive line coach, objected to the cigar smoking. But Coach Pettibone, who stood 5'9" tall with a medium build and won the square jaw contest told Sam, "You need to relax and enjoy this special moment."

We all did.

At the end of our second season, Lawrence Cooley, the Offensive Line Coach, went to the University of Cincinnati—probably because I drove him crazy, micro-managing his teaching of the offensive line.

After teaching Marshall the basics of the new offense, I moved back to the offensive line. It was my natural position. I played it, understood it, and could help the players develop a toughness that would be vital to our success.

We hired a new quarterback coach, Jay Schaake, who played quarterback in high school. It always helps you teach when you have first-hand experience.

Mike Summers, our running back coach, was my graduate assistant at Texas A&M. He was totally serious and detailed about his coaching. I loved being able to rely on him.

At the start of our third season, I could finally see the execution of the wishbone developing right before my eyes. Marshall Taylor was the ideal quarterback. He was very intelligent and had good running skills, as well as a wonderful personality. He also happened to be black. Midway through the season, he was being taunted by Mr. Gust, the father of one of our offensive linemen.

"Get that nigger off the field," he yelled. It was evident that he wanted Pete Genatempo, our white backup quarterback, to be the starter.

I could hear his disgusting comments on the sideline. I had an internal rage, so I turned around, pointed at Mr. Gust, and told the players, "That bullshit behavior is unacceptable."

That night, I called David Gust's Dad. "If you ever say that again, I will call a time-out and come up in the stands to kick your ass." I expected an apology, but instead he challenged me.

"I would welcome you anytime," he replied.

I hung up the phone, knowing full well I may have to back up my promise. I thought about benching his son, but it wasn't his fault. Fortunately, it was the last of the derogatory comments that we would hear out of his mouth during a game.

We ended our third season 5-5-1, and we were one of the top rushing teams in the country at 295 yards per game. Marshall Taylor had become the "Wishbone Wizard." We averaged 28 points per game, and four of the games we lost were by a total of 12 points. Running the wishbone had accomplished what it was meant to, and like WSU and Texas A&M, we had resurrected the football program.

Even though NIU was not a big-time program, Coach Pettibone had put together a good staff who were good teachers. We didn't get captured by our schedule, our small stadium, or our lack of fans. We stayed focused on the goal of developing our players and our football program, and we accomplished what we had set out to do.

But my daughter Sabra was truly the highlight of the 1986 season. The amount of love in a parent for their newborn child is so deep and soul-grabbing. I loved holding her and teaching her. As she grew, she was becoming more animated, and I started looking for songs that I could play while I danced her around the living room.

During the spring entering our third season, Sabra was seven months old, and I found my favorite song to dance to with her: "My Special Angel," by the Vogues. This became a bit of tradition until she decided it was time to walk and dance on her own.

The joy she brought to us even in that year of frustration was incredible. Eventually, she would perform her own dance to "Caribbean Queen" by Billie Ocean. Watching her stand in front of the stereo in her diaper and bare feet, bopping up and down, was enough to make me forget any problem.

CHAPTER 14

JAYHAWK JOURNEY

Here we go again. It was January 1988, and given all the progress our team had made, I was excited to jump into recruiting. As if on cue, I received another phone call. This time, it was Glen Mason, who had just been named the new head coach at the University of Kansas. He offered me the offensive coordinator and offensive line job.

I knew our job wasn't quite done at NIU. I was conflicted. *Is this the right time to go?* Leaving NIU was not that difficult. It was leaving Jerry Pettibone and his culture that I was struggling with.

"You're the number one guy I want," Mason said, as if he knew I needed coaxing. Kansas played in the Big Eight Conference with Oklahoma, Nebraska, Colorado, Missouri, Oklahoma State, Iowa State, and Kansas State. It meant that I would end up back on a major stage—at least, that's what I thought.

Besides, I had a unique connection to Kansas. When I was thirteen years old, Gale Sayers, a running back for KU, was making national news. They called him the "Kansas Comet." The Chicago Bears drafted him in the first round, and he was the number four pick overall. My uncle, Rube Thorson, was President of the Chicago Stock Exchange and hired Gale

Sayers in the off-season. One day, he surprised me with a personally autographed photo of Gale that I proudly displayed in my room and showed to all my friends. *Maybe I could coach the next Gale Sayers.*

When I talked with Marti, she was all in. "Let's do it," she said with a broad smile. She put on her red ruby shoes and clicked her heels three times. She had been a corrective therapist, coach, student activities advisor, and student judicial administrator. She had her master's degree in administration and was now a mom looking for a new job in Kansas.

As soon as I set eyes on the university, I felt like I had found a rare diamond. Its natural beauty was breathtaking. The campus sat on a hill called Mt. Oread. It loomed 200 feet over the city. I marveled at the campus sitting atop its hill. It was an ideal setting for higher education.

As I began recruiting and showing the prospects around, I realized that the football program wasn't a diamond—it was a plain old rock. It didn't have an identity. For starters, the football offices were adjacent to Allen Fieldhouse, the basketball arena, and there were no designated meeting rooms for off-the-field teaching, and the weight room had last been updated in the 1960s.

The more I learned, the more alarmed I became. I was shocked to see a Division I program in total disarray. They had 85 players on the roster: 54 scholarships and 31 walk-ons. KU was allowed 95 on scholarship. *What the hell is going on?* I thought.

They had not won a conference game in two years, going 0-13-1. Student athletes were bailing out of the program. Who could blame them? No one likes losing, especially at that rate.

We were starting with an empty glass. So much for being back on a major stage.

Mason didn't seem as worried about the lousy facilities as he was about instilling a toughness in his team. Mason was about 6'1" with sandy brown hair and a fivehead. *That's a big forehead.* He looked more like an insurance executive than a drill sergeant, but he had the toughness role down to perfection. Mason played for the legendary Woody Hayes at Ohio State, who was iconic for his brash toughness. Whether he learned it from Coach Hayes or on his own, the one thing he was really good at was teaching grit. In his effort to instill a marine-like attitude, he trained the players by constantly challenging them and running them to exhaustion.

Off-season training centered around a super steep hill on campus called 14th Street. We would line up and run the hill by groups. Every other day, another player quit.

I often ran with the players to be at their side while they battled the physical strain, and on one occasion, as I was walking down the hill for my next trip up, Mason said, "I know I'm being an asshole."

"You're not being one, you are one," I replied as I smiled; he smiled back.

The biggest danger is assistant coaches trying to emulate the head coach's toughness. If it swings too far, the compassion and caring piece disappears, and you lose an ingredient that is critical to building a great culture. Most of our coaches stayed true to their principles of being human first. We were trying to be the balance to Mason's toughness, but it wasn't enough. Some of the players found it easier to quit because, after going 0-13-1 versus conference opponents the previous two years, there was no reward for their hard work.

Our meeting rooms for learning and teaching players were the absolute worst. At every other place I had coached, I had a classroom setting with desks, a whiteboard, and a film screen. Here, I had to meet in a racquetball court, complete with an echo. After two weeks, I was fed up. I took the offensive line to the equipment room in the indoor practice facility. Track, baseball, softball, and football all had their paraphernalia stacked in there. I moved the equipment around to give us space. There were folding chairs instead of a desk, and a portable chalk board instead of a whiteboard.

At every other place I had been before, we had at least 13-15 offensive linemen. Here, I had only nine players, so I put a sign on the door and called it "Club 9." I was creating our own identity: nine players who exemplified the ability to adapt and be resourceful. Club 9 was a wonderful group of young men. What they lacked in talent they made up for with effort and attitude. I guess we were lucky to have such a unique environment for learning...

With the 30 new scholarship players that we had signed, we went 1-10 our first year. It was the longest season ever. The beginning of this nightmare started with the University of Auburn. They gave us a taste of big-time football. Auburn was ranked sixth in the country. Their stadium was a grass field that would embarrass some of the top golf courses in the world. They scored at will.

It was 42-0 at halftime.

"Don't throw any more passes," Coach Mason yelled at me. An incomplete would stop the clock. Mason wanted the game over quickly.

Pat Dye, Auburn's head coach, was feeling our pain. "There's a big storm coming, and I'm going to let the clock run in the second half," he offered.

Mason nodded in agreement.

Auburn played its third team in the second half, and we lost 56-7. It was the fastest half ever played in college football. There was no storm; it was a mercy killing. We all appreciated Coach Dye's intention of not wanting to embarrass us. Our only victory that season was over our in-state rival, Kansas State, whose football program was as bad as ours. They called it the "Toilet Bowl." Pretty appropriate for two shitty teams.

There were 105 teams at that time in Division I. Our offense ranked 90th and our defense ranked 105th. We sucked.

The following year, we made progress: We went 4-7, with our offense moving up to 56th and our defense to 101st. We still sucked. We didn't have experienced players, so we needed to find every motivational tool we could to help us maintain a focus that could give us an edge. We beat Missouri 46-44 in the final game of the season. Mason gave the defense the game ball for not letting them tie the game on a two-point play.

What the hell? We score forty-six points to win, and defense gets the game ball? I thought Mason had lost his mind.

"Pat, they need some confidence," he later said. I totally disagreed with giving the defense the game ball for making one play, but I understood his concern.

By the third season, I started leaning on my psychology training. Midway through, we were preparing to play the Oklahoma State Cowboys, a team we had not beaten in 17 years.

"I've got an idea," I said to Mason. "We won't say their name all week. No coaches, players, or trainers will be allowed to say 'Oklahoma State' or 'Cowboys.' This week is all about us."

Mason liked it.

It was Friday, and we were in Stillwater for the game on Saturday. My job was to take the team to the movies on Friday night.

Standing in the parking lot with the team, we were waiting for the buses to arrive. I was getting pissed—they were ten minutes late already. Tim Allen, our director of football operations, had already called the bus company. They were on the way, but one of the buses had apparently broken down, and they took Oklahoma State to the movies first. When they finally pulled in, the team boarded, and I began to question the bus driver.

Then one of the players shouted, "Is everything okay, Coach?"

"Apparently the bus company thought they should take Oklahoma State to the movies first."

The team quickly replied as a group in a loud voice, "WHO?"

I was caught in my own scheme.

We beat OSU 31-30. After the game, Coach Mason congratulated the team: "Great win over Oklahoma State."

Again, the whole team shouted, "WHO?"

We all laughed. We had kept the focus on us.

Coach Mason recognized the power of motivation and introduced the team to the "Little Man." He was an imaginary figure that lived in their heads and constantly told them to do the easy wrong rather than the harder right. Coach was so into this form of motivation that he had a six-inch male doll in raggedy clothes that represented the Little Man at practices and meetings. He would remind the players that "the Little Man is always with you trying to fuck up your life." Then he would ask, "Anyone see the Little Man?"

The coaches and players would immediately look for him. He would be on the goal post, equipment bag, fence, under a desk, on the podium, hanging from the ceiling, or sitting in his own chair.

One day, Keith Loneker, our right tackle, walked into a meeting with the Little Man sitting on his shoulder. The team laughed hysterically. It was the original game of *Where's Waldo?* and we were playing it daily.

When Coach Mason introduced the Little Man, he gave the team examples of how the Little Man talked: "Don't go to class"; "Don't work hard"; "Take a break"; "Cheat on the test"; "One more drink."

He was a bad dude.

One day, I asked Coach Mason, "Where did the Little Man idea come from?"

"Pat, when I went running every morning, he would try to get me to quit. The better the shape I was in, the more it forced him to shut up. The worse the shape I was in, the louder he got."

"I know that guy." I snickered.

"You're damn right—everybody knows him."

"So, we're all trying to kick the Little Man's ass?" I asked.

"Every day," Mason replied. It was then that I realized his personal commitment to toughness and self-discipline.

By the time we kicked off our fourth season, our motivational tactics were having an impact. It was keeping the team focused. We were 5-5 entering our final game versus Missouri, and my dream came true. Our running back, Tony Sands, had earned the nickname Tuxedo Tony, as he always wore a tux to the stadium on game day. Tony was a 5'6" and 170-pound rolling ball of butcher knives. He ran with the fury of a cheetah chasing a gazelle. He was relentless.

I gave him the ball 58 times that day, and by halftime, he broke the Kansas rushing record. In the third quarter, he broke the Big Eight single game rushing record, and in the fourth quarter, he broke the NCAA single game rushing record. He rushed for 396 yards, a record that stood for eight years. We won 53-29, and his 58 carries is still an NCAA best.

After the game, some reporter suggested he should be a Heisman Trophy candidate.

"It would be the first time the trophy was bigger than the recipient," I responded. I was deflecting, like I usually did, but inside I was beaming with joy. After four years of trying to fill an empty glass, I was witnessing my own Gale Sayers.

We finished 6-5, and it was Kansas' first winning season in ten years. Our offense ranked 24th out of 107 teams, and our defense ranked 54th out of 107.

Just as we finished recruiting for our fifth season, I got a call from Bruce Coslett, the Head Coach at the NY Jets. I was recommended by Pete Carroll and Larry Beightol, who were on his staff. I was excited; he wanted me to be the tight end coach. I tentatively accepted, but Coach Mason had given me the title of assistant head coach and I had lots of responsibility, which I loved. I was in charge of discipline, working as a liaison with academics, and of course filling the coordinator and offensive line position.

I did my homework this time by calling a few guys that worked with Coach Coslett. They said he was a narcissist, that everything had to be his way. He was not a good people manager. *Nope*, I thought. *Been there, done that...* It wasn't about money or the NFL. I had learned my lesson.

You can't create a good culture with those kinds of guys. I'm not saying that you can't win, but it's a matter of being happy and excited about going to work. I knew I was in the position I wanted.

I called him back to decline his offer, and he unleashed on me.

"You told me you were coming, and now you've ruined my vacation."

CHAPTER 15

SUCCESS BECOMES US

I was so high on life that I was soaring as I sat on stage in my Santa suit playing the part for the two dozen kids waiting to meet me. It was Christmas Eve after wrapping up our 1995 season, going 9-2, and ranking 11th in the country.

We were in Honolulu for the Aloha Bowl, which was set to play on Christmas day. Most of our game planning was done before we left for the bowl game. I was feeling good about our practice organization and execution. As a result, we had a few afternoons to play tourist. The weather was a perfect 78 degrees with an ocean breeze. It was a nice reprieve from the frigid Kansas winter.

We spent the first day touring the Pearl Harbor Memorial, which was a deeply emotional experience. The *USS Arizona* lay at the bottom of the harbor and was the final resting place of 1,102 sailors and Marines; droplets of oil from the *Arizona* were still reaching the surface 54 years later. In the following days, we explored the island. We went to Hanauma Bay, where we snorkeled and fed beautiful tropical fish. Sabra, who was now nine, was totally enchanted. I was a veteran tourist, as we were there in 1992, and I knew all the good spots, including where to find the big waves on the north shore that were 20-30 feet high.

It had been a magical week. But the biggest gift of all was that Mason had recently accepted the University of Georgia head coaching job, which made me the heir apparent at KU.

I scanned the packed ballroom at the Sheraton Waikiki Hotel, taking in the faces of the coaches, players, and their families. I could feel the excitement of the evening, and thoughts of taking over the program and doing it my way were exhilarating. I had already talked with some of the other coaches about a position on my staff. For some, it would be a well-deserved promotion.

I returned my attention to the kids who were lined up to my right, ready to see Santa. The KU booster club had put a bunch of presents next to my chair on stage to give to them. I was mic'd up and ready to go. As the kids came up to me, I would hoist them on my lap, then ask their name and whether they had been good or bad.

One five-year-old boy, in particular, made us all laugh. "I've been good," he said, "but my dad has beer in the cooler in our room." He glanced out at the crowd, looking for his mom's approval.

"Is that bad?" I asked.

"My mom thinks so."

The audience burst into laughter.

"Well, no gifts for him, then."

Just then, Mason, who was on the front row, started giving me the "hurry up" sign, taking his hand with his index and middle finger together and revolving in a circular motion.

You've got to be kidding, I thought. *This night is for the children.*

I glared at him because, in reality, he wasn't even supposed to be here. Eight days earlier, he had been offered and taken the job at Georgia, returned to KU to apologize for his sudden departure, and announced that he would still be coaching the bowl game. He wasn't going to miss the fruits of his labor. The players and the coaches were all upset, as he had deserted KU.

While Mason was in Georgia, Bob Frederick, our athletic director, told me to handle a team meeting to answer questions they might want to ask. It was a horrible experience as I tried to explain why Mason wasn't telling them himself. The players were mad at him because they found out through the press. He always told them to stand up and be a man, but when it came down to his turn, he didn't do it. Neither did the athletic director; I guess no one wanted to be the bearer of bad news.

To add to the bizarreness, Mason had been calling Georgia recruits while all the rest of us were prepping the players for the game. It really pissed me off. Either you're in, or you're out.

I continued to glare at Mason. *What the hell is his problem?* It was *his* request that I was fulfilling. Just two days earlier at a staff meeting, Coach Mason said, "We need someone to play Santa at the Christmas Eve Party for all the families traveling to the game."

It was crickets—no response. So I raised my hand. "I'll do it."

"Great, Pat, you'll be an excellent Santa," he said, smiling, but I could see the distress on his face. Something was bothering him.

I wondered if playing Santa was beneath the expectations of what was desired as a head coach. I didn't care; I was going make this a fun week.

Mason continued the non-verbal signaling. I could see that the audience was aware of his antics. I'd had enough.

"Sorry, Coach Mason, this is Santa's night, so you just sit back and relax."

The crowd roared with laughter. When I was done, Mason requested that I come to his room immediately. If he thought he was going to chastise me for wanting the kids to enjoy the evening, he was dead wrong.

Still fully dressed as Santa, I knocked on his door.

"Take that hat and beard off," he demanded as soon as he opened the door. I didn't want to. I felt a certain amount of freedom and protection by keeping it on. As I complied anyway, he announced that he was in negotiation to get his job back. It was like my heart had just gotten yanked out and run over by a cement truck.

"Are you fucking joking?" Suddenly, the distress that I had seen all week was making sense.

"No, I'm not. There's a lot going on."

"Like what?" I felt like throwing up. I was supposed to meet with the Chancellor in about an hour to talk about the head coaching job.

"I have a custody problem." Mason explained that his divorce from his first wife and his marriage to a Lawrence dentist named Kate was going to result in a custody battle. Was he talking about his kids or her kids? At this point, I didn't care. My opportunity was gone.

My meeting with the chancellor was canceled. I went to my room and told Marti. She was upset but was taking the high road. She was trying to reduce my pain.

"There will be other opportunities," she assured me.

I shot her a "You don't understand" look and shook my head before responding. "I've invested so much in this one."

Marti had completed her doctorate the year before and was promoted to assistant vice chancellor. It was obvious that I already had a big fan in the administration. I had built-in support. But now, it clearly was not enough.

I felt like a man lost in the desert with no idea which direction to go. I started thinking about all the things I did to advance the University of Kansas football program. The offense, the discipline, the liaison to academics. I even thought about the 13 days I spent in a tent during fall camp.

When the season began, the players were bitching that the dorm had no air conditioning. Some of the complainers were the offensive linemen.

I quickly sympathized with them and offered, "Would you like me to sleep in a tent for fall camp so that I, too, can experience the no air conditioning dilemma?" I knew that my sacrifice would act as a motivational tool and keep them from verbalizing the negativity.

The harmony of ten offensive linemen barking, "Yes," in unison is something everyone should experience once in their lives. The sound of togetherness was undeniable.

I retrieved my camping tent from the garage and set up just off the field, next to the goal post. The press started to ask questions.

"Well, since my players have to deal with no air conditioning, I thought I would join them," I explained. Then, trying to inject some humor, I provided them a guest list.

My invitees included Marti, our daughter Sabra, Head Coach Glen Mason, Chancellor Gene Budig, President George Walker Bush Sr., and Meg Ryan. *Might as well make this fun,* I thought.

The next day, my guest list appeared in the Lawrence Journal World article about my living in a tent for fall camp.

Marti declined because there was no mirror or place to hang clothes. President Bush didn't have time, and Meg Ryan was cancelled by Marti, so that left me with Sabra, Coach, and Chancellor Budig. Sabra was by far the most fun and the most interesting, plus she stayed the night; Coach Mason and Chancellor Budig stayed for a couple hours each, then bolted home for their cushy beds.

I spent 13 days in the tent. I managed to fight through a bad rainstorm that flooded my tent and a couple of local women yelling through the fence at one in the morning that they wanted to be on the invite list (they had been drinking). Then there was the National Press from Oklahoma City, who said they were with ABC, who woke me up and interviewed me at midnight.

I was doing everything I could to help us be successful. The talk of no air conditioning died. I had earned the respect of the players.

So, after all that hard work, a piece of me literally died on that Christmas Eve night. By the time I woke up Christmas morning, I was determined not to get captured by the negativity.

That morning, Coach Mason called a full team meeting and announced to the coaches, team, trainers, and equipment personnel that he was coming back to be the Head Coach at KU. Nobody clapped, and no one cheered; there was a silence of shock. Mason had downgraded the KU football program indirectly in the press by praising Georgia and its commitment to its football program. It was a lot to process. Mason said he would make the official announcement after the game.

Mason was perplexed about why no one was excited. While riding the bus to the stadium, I could see he was deep in thought. Normally, I would ask him if he was okay, but for now, he was on his own. I was crushed last night, but today I had only one thought, and it was to kick UCLA's ass.

At the stadium, the press was running around asking about rumors of Mason coming back. One Big Eight conference reporter came to me during the pregame and asked, "Is it true that Mason is returning as the head coach?"

I shrugged, curbing my frustration. "I have no idea—go ask him."

When we went into the locker room after the pregame, Coach Mason came up to me and accused me of telling the press he was returning to KU.

I went off on him. "I have been totally loyal to you. I didn't say anything, so fuck you. Maybe you shouldn't have told the entire KU athletic personnel that you were returning before the game," I barked angrily before walking away.

I immediately started talking to players about their responsibility to finish strong and not to get captured by the bullshit. The game was all KU. We scored on our first possession. We were up 7-0. On our third possession, we were at mid-field, and it was third down and eight.

"What are you going to call?" Mason asked.

I wasn't really in the mood to answer him, but I did. "We're going to run the power play."

"You run the power play, and you're fired."

That was the wrong thing to say—I had studied the film. I was on the headset with Coach Dave Warner, our Quarterback coach.

"What's the call, Pat?" Coach Warner asked.

"You heard me. We're running the power." I knew it was a good call, but I was also in a combative mood with Coach Mason.

"Are you sure? I heard what Coach Mason said."

"Signal it in," I yelled. Coach Mason was glaring at me. I was trying to ignore him.

We signaled it in to Mark Williams, our quarterback. The ball was snapped. Mark handed it to June Henley, our running back, who ran 49 yards for a touchdown. Mason came charging at me with his hand high in the air, wanting a high-five. I shook my head and denied him.

By the third quarter, we were ahead 37-7. We went on to win 51-30. It gave us a 10-win season. Last time that had happened was nearly a century earlier, in 1905. We broke a lot of the offensive records, both at KU and the Aloha Bowl.

Coach Mason and I made amends after the game. When he asked me why no one reacted to his announcement, I decided to use an analogy that I knew he would understand.

I told him a story about a guy who dated a girl for seven years, and then one day he decided that there was a more attractive girl and dumped her for the new one. He explained that she had more brains and more beauty. Then somewhere he realized that he made a mistake. So, he ran back to the first girl—but she wasn't clapping.

* * *

Going into the spring after a historical season, I was internally devastated. I was 45 years old, and I was in a mid-life crisis. Over the next couple of months, I ran a half-marathon, parachuted out of an airplane at 13,000 feet, went whitewater rafting on class five rapids, bought $800 cowboy boots, and lost 20 pounds.

Marti knew I was swimming in the abyss. I was looking for anything to give my life meaning and to be happy, but there were days that spring I would be driving and, without explanation, tears would appear in my eyes and roll down my face. I had lost my desire to be a head coach, and Mason had lost the team. Our chemistry was gone. The next season, we finished 4-7.

Mason knew it was time to go. He got an offer to be the head coach at the University of Minnesota, and he took it. After a record-breaking offensive performance in the Aloha Bowl, I was a natural pick to be his successor. But this time was different; the magic of last year was gone. Although this was my second chance, there were some obstacles that I was going to have to hurdle.

At the beginning of our magical 1995 season, the athletic director's wife, Margie, made some comments in the stands that Mason should be fired if we didn't win seven games. Laird Noller, who was a prominent supporter, overheard the statement she made to all those sitting around her and reported it to Mason and me.

I asked Mason what he thought we should do.

"Nothing, let it go," he said.

"I think we should tell Bob. Maybe he doesn't know," I said.

"You can, if you want to."

Having a good culture was important to me. It seemed like I was the culture police. I walked down to Bob Frederick's office. When his secretary sent me in, it was cordial. Bob was a nice guy whose wife was active in his job. She was a helicopter wife.

"Bob, I just want to make sure you know that Margie was in the stands and announced after our win over Cincinnati that we should be fired if we don't win at least seven games."

His face turned red. *Oh fuck.* "You're a liar—she would never say that."

Obviously, I had struck a nerve. Who calls someone a liar without checking first? I took a deep breath, looking to diffuse the conversation. "Bob, I'm not trying to cause a problem, just fix one. We need everybody pulling the same direction."

Bob's face shifted from anger to concern, but he was not ready to acknowledge the reality. "Margie wouldn't do that."

"Okay, fine. I just thought you should know." I left thinking that I had at least addressed it.

I headed back to Mason's office and told him that he called me a liar. That lit a fire under him. Mason picked up the phone and called Laird Noller. My eyes were locked on Coach Mason as he repeated the conversation.

Then he hung up and said, "Laird will handle it. He lives a couple of houses from the Fredericks."

Laird's words had influence because he was a major donor to KU athletics and owned one of the most successful car dealerships in Kansas. He provided a lot of courtesy cars for the athletic department.

Shortly before lunch the next day, Bob Frederick called me to his office.

"Margie wants to meet with you," he announced the moment I arrived. Apparently, Laird Noller's conversation fixed everything.

"Sure, when?"

"She will meet you in the athletic alumni lounge at one p.m."

The room was a brand-new congregating spot and was built for alumni functions after basketball games. It was decked out with fancy couches, plush chairs, and a classic fireplace. It was a perfect spot to make amends.

When I arrived, we exchanged formalities, then she started firing bullets.

"How dare you get into my business? You need to worry about the team."

I looked at her, stunned—we were not on the same page. If she was a guy, I would have ripped her a new one. Instead, I forced a smile. "I'm worried about the team and the culture around it," I said, trying to soften the conversation.

She stared at me like a lioness ready to eat her prey. "What I say to others is none of your concern."

I almost let it go, but this was not the first time this type of thing had happened. She often over-extended herself with negative opinions across the athletic department. I decided right then that I was not having it.

"Look, Margie, to be honest, I don't think anyone in the athletic department likes you. So, if I were you, I would stay away from the athletic building and stay out of your husband's job." I could feel my voice rising and my anger flowing.

Margie started to tear up. "You shouldn't talk to me like that," she said. Her voice was cracking with emotion.

"Probably true, but it needed to be said, and your crying has no effect on me." I was wallowing in disgust because I made the mistake thinking she was there to apologize.

She was no longer responding, just sniffling like a five-year-old who got reprimanded for throwing her toys.

I rose to my feet and turned to leave. "Thanks for coming—glad we worked it out," I said, trying to toss a positive spin on it. I waited outside in the hallway and watched her leave, thinking she would run to her husband's office. She didn't. *Maybe we did solve the problem?*

But walking back to my office, I thought, *That might cost me.* I was told several times that some fights are not worth fighting. Choose your battles. My problem was that I had a hard time dealing with those who cancelled hope and decency for power. It was that playground message that my dad had taught me.

So here I was, mired in Mason's wake, a losing season, and the confrontation with the athletic director's wife. It was not exactly a momentum builder, but I was determined to give it my best shot.

I was to meet with the selection committee whose job was to offer their recommendation for head coach. The meeting was in two days. Thank God I had already done a future plan for Mason. I liked that he regularly valued my opinion. It gave me an edge. I just tweaked what I had done for him.

When I entered the committee meeting room, I gave them all a folder with a five-year plan for the KU football program. Academics, recruiting, discipline, scheduling, and a look at my staff recommendations. They were professional with their questions, except one person kept asking me about my brother, who had served a year in jail for transporting drugs. It was clear he had an agenda.

After the second time he brought it up, I said, "My brother and your brother are not being considered for this job, so let's leave them out of it." I chuckled, hoping to signal the room that I was not going to entertain questions with no relevance.

I was on cloud nine as I made the five-minute drive home. I was getting a lot of affirmative head nodding and could feel the positive energy in the room. I knew I had performed well.

When I pulled into the driveway, I couldn't wait to tell Marti. I called out to her as I entered the house.

"How did the interview go?" she asked while walking to greet me.

"It went really well. Everyone seemed to be very excited to hear my five-year plan." Finally, it seemed as though my dream of head coaching was going to be a reality. Marti and I hugged.

"I'm so excited—you deserve this," she said softly in my ear.

We ordered pizza, sat down, and talked about who I was going to keep on staff. I wanted to make sure I hired passionate coaches and enthusiastic recruiters.

"You and I will be in charge of recruiting quarterbacks," I joked with Sabra.

I got a few congratulating calls that night saying that my presentation was excellent; it was organized and passionate. I was excited beyond belief. Then, later in the evening, just before bed, I got a call from John Jefferson, who was on the selection committee, was previously part of the football staff, and was now part of the administration running Student Life Skills for all the athletes at KU.

John Jefferson played pro football for the San Diego Chargers and Green Bay Packers and was a great NFL receiver. He knew what the football program needed.

"Pat, Frederick decided to go out on his own and bypass the committee. Apparently, he had enough of Mason and those connected with him."

"He has no idea what he's doing. Mason's staff brought Kansas out of the Mariana Trench to a competitive program. Now he wants to look elsewhere? Putting KU in the top ten and winning two bowl games when they had not won a bowl game in thirty-one years was not enough?"

Marti was standing there as I got the latest update. It was over. The selection committee wasted my time and theirs.

The emotional rollercoaster of the last two years was exasperating. Marti and I both received accolades from the University community for our commitment to KU. Bob Frederick never said a word of support for the football program. Admittedly, in my effort to do things right, I stepped on a few toes, but always with the good intention of improving our program.

"He has always put football on the back burner," Marti said with anger. She looked at me for a response.

I took a deep breath and paused. I was going to take charge of my life, which seemed to be caught in a blender of bullshit.

"I'm done with Kansas and football."

CHAPTER 16

RECONNECTING WITH MY FAMILY

In a philosophy class in college, I recalled a famous philosopher, René Descartes, who said: "A thought cannot be separated from me, therefore, I exist." Or more famously, "I think, therefore I am." I was in a fight to give my life meaning.

I didn't think about failure or prepare for failure; I reacted to failure. After being shut out of two head coaching opportunities, I was lost and angry. I felt like I had given so much, and I was done being used. I was taking my life back. I could feel the words bouncing in my brain: *You got this. You got this. You got this.* Got what? I've been on sports teams my whole life. Where was my team now?

Then I realized that my family is my ultimate team. I had a year left on my contract. Rather than resign and lose that income, I forced them to fire me. Marti was still working as assistant vice chancellor. So, I began taking Sabra to school every day. We would listen to my 60s and 70s music and belt out the lyrics when one of our favorites, like "Return to Sender" by Elvis Presley or "La La Means I Love You" by the Delfonics, came on. Other times, I used the drive to review her homework or to teach her life lessons that my dad taught me.

One day while driving Sabra the mile and a half to Deerfield Elementary, I told her my dad used to say that 99% of all the problems you will incur are either directly or indirectly related to choices you make. I was teaching her, but in some ways, I was also re-teaching myself. You must own your problems and fix them. She looked at me with her intense blue eyes. I recognized that curious look; it was me listening to my dad. I knew she was processing, much like I did. I also knew that some of the lessons and advice would come rushing into her life years later.

I felt responsible for the culture that my family experienced. I didn't want them to see me struggling. I started looking for fun things to do. I was getting calls from coaches and friends asking me what my plans were going forward. I honestly didn't know.

"Marti hired me to be head coach of the family," I would tell them. "So, I am currently working on scheduling. We are opening with the Six Flags amusement park, the Kansas City Zoo, and tornado chasing."

I was in transition—but to what, I had no idea. In late January, I went into the Kansas football office to pick up my mail. The entire new staff was in the office. What in the hell were they doing? It was the height of recruiting, and no one was on the road. They should've been out selling Kansas to the prospects and the high school coaches. I could feel anger begin to surge through me. I would have had all of them on the road connecting with high school coaches and scouring the country for prospects. It looked like they had no idea what they were doing. I wanted to walk into the athletic director's office and tell him, "You just made a bad hire." Instead, I put my emotions back in the closet and headed home.

By the time early February rolled around, I had been in my self-imposed coaching exile for a month, and I was already getting edgy. I felt like we needed a vacation. It was tough being in the KU environment. I decided to take Marti, Sabra, and her friend Amanda skiing. We headed west to Steamboat Springs, Colorado. Driving through western Kansas, there were wheat fields, corn fields, and a few cattle farms. We decided to stay the night at a Holiday Inn in Denver. Before leaving, we got breakfast.

Amanda ordered a yogurt. We were all enjoying the morning meal when she announced in a loud voice, "There's fruit in the bottom of my cup!" It was like she had found buried treasure. Marti and I looked at each other and busted out laughing. Just like getting a new bike for Christmas, she seemed excited beyond belief. It was a pure moment of joy that reminded me of a child's innocence.

I looked back at Marti, still laughing. "We're not in Kansas anymore," I said, repeating a line from one of my favorite movies, *The Wizard of Oz*.

After arriving and renting all the necessary equipment, I stepped into my coaching role. Marti and I had learned to ski while at Washington State. Sabra and Amanda had never been before. I decided to start with the most critical part, how to get up if you fall. I flopped down on the snow to illustrate.

"Sabra and Amanda, watch me," I directed. "Put your skis on the downhill slope, bend your knees, and use your hands to position yourself back over your skis." I demonstrated it flawlessly.

On her second try, Sabra was able to stand up.

"I can't," Amanda said.

I shot a look at Sabra. "Show Amanda again."

Sabra repeated the up move.

I looked at Amanda, who was still on the ground. "Okay, Amanda, your turn."

"I can't," she said, burying her head into her knees.

I felt my impatience rising. "Yes, you can." My voice was now more forceful.

"I can't," she repeated.

Sabra interjected, "My dad doesn't like, 'I can't,' Amanda."

Marti, who had been quietly observing my coaching, jumped in. "Pat, put them both in ski school," she said, reminding me that I wasn't talking to a football player.

"Good idea."

I helped Amanda up and we headed over to ski school. It appeared that they had about fifteen kids enrolled. I skied over to the instructor and said, "It must be difficult to teach all these kids how to ski."

"Actually, they're a hundred times better than the adults." He shot me an "I got this" look.

"Why's that?" I asked.

"They listen and will mimic my movement. The adults have preconceived ideas of how it should be, and they don't listen," he said, smiling. "Be back here at noon to pick them up."

I was a little skeptical of his boastful language, but now Marti and I had three hours to ski by ourselves. Awesome.

After an hour on the slopes, we stopped to take a break. The snow was glistening in the rays of the sun. It was absolutely beautiful. Cold, but not too cold. This perfect day was revitalizing my worn-down soul. Within minutes, the ski school went by, and Sabra and Amanda were traversing down the mountain like they had been doing it for years.

Any doubt I had about the instructor's ability to teach kids vanished into the mountain air. When I picked them up at noon, they were no longer rookies and wanted to keep skiing. We had a quick lunch, and we were back on the slopes.

It made me think about coaching. Average teachers tell you what to do. Good teachers demonstrate how to do it. Great teachers inspire you to be special. He had obviously made a connection with all of them. They called him by name as if he was a family member. I regretted not telling him personally that he was a great coach.

Before leaving, we spent a day snowmobiling on the Continental Divide. We had a guide who went with us. The guide had Sabra and Amanda on his snowmobile. Marti and I were on our own, riding single. I began to show off with sharp turns at higher speeds until I crashed, rolling the snowmobile. Marti zoomed by me as I stood up. She must have been at full throttle. She made a wide turn and headed back toward me. I was amazed that she was that aggressive.

"Are you okay?" she asked.

"I'm fine, I just have to get my accident-waiting-to-happen back upright." I paused, then added, "You were driving really fast."

Marti grinned at me. "I've never had so much power between my legs."

"Wow, that hurts," I bellowed.

Marti laughed and replied, "Don't worry, I'm going home with you." I watched as she rocketed away, turning the throttle to max.

I could feel the joy of our time on the snow-covered mountains. It was like I was bubbling with delight from the inside out.

On the way home, I was doing 80 mph on Interstate 70. I was pulled over by a Kansas state trooper. He asked for my license. I had left it in my ski jacket in the back of the car. I retrieved my jacket, but the pocket zipper was open. My license, money, and credit cards were gone. I calmly explained to the officer that it was resting in a pile of snow on the Continental Divide.

"Promise me you'll slow it down," he said.

"I promise. And thank you."

I told Marti to drive, as I didn't trust that I could drive through western Kansas without speeding. Before pulling away, Marti turned and looked at me, and I could see the admiration in her eyes. "While you were talking with that State Trooper, I noticed how at peace you were. I would have thought getting pulled over and losing your wallet would have made you upset."

She made me realize I was coming out of the battle to find myself. The past two years had been a rollercoaster, but that ski vacation washed away my anxiety. It was like hitting the reset button.

* * *

We were back in Lawrence for two days when I got a call from Bill Perkins, who was the Head Coach at Gavilan Junior College. We had met a couple of times in recruiting and coaching clinics. I was always impressed with his people skills. He had this idea to revolutionize the college recruiting process and wanted me to be the CEO. It intrigued me, and as we talked, we began to exchange views on the structure of the company.

"I would like to use your connections and that coach's work ethic to help advance this business plan," Bill said. His voice always had a sincere quality about it.

"Well, lucky for you, I've always wanted to be a CEO, and I'm available."

This offer to start a business from the ground floor excited me. The company was called USAthlete, and its purpose was to build a database for college recruiters. In addition, it would expose the athletes to hundreds of Universities, which would result in scholarship opportunities, and those who didn't get scholarships would be put into a pool to be randomly selected to receive scholarship money from Coca-Cola or Nike, which would be the two exclusive advertisers on the website.

Within a week, we had set up our home offices and started designing brochures and posters to be sent to every high school in the nation. We were organized and had a plan. We were on the phone and emailing constantly. Like usual, I buried myself in the business. It felt good to have a purpose. But working alone in my office was quite a change from what I had been doing the last 21 years.

After four months of embracing USAthlete, I was starting to really miss coaching. The camaraderie of working with the coaches and teaching the players was something my soul craved. I thought it would be easy to make the transition from a coach to a businessman. But the daily tasks of data entry and contacting high school coaches by phone was becoming more and more unsatisfying. Besides, we were putting our own capital in the business, and it was going to take a lot more to attract companies like Coca-Cola or Nike.

Will I ever go back and do what I love doing? I'd think. I wanted to coach again. I called Bill and broke the news—he sounded relieved.

"I hate to waste an extraordinary idea, Pat, but I'm having the same issues. I have coached my whole life and don't really want to give it up." We both loved teaching and having an impact on young men's lives. USAthlete died that day.

* * *

Coaching changes don't happen until December and January. So, I needed some things to do.

It was late May on a Friday night. I was getting ready for bed when Marti, who was already in bed, said, "Eastern Kansas is in the tornado watch tomorrow." Marti religiously watched the Weather Channel before bed. She loved Jim Cantore, one of the main reporters.

"How is Jim doing?" I said, like he was part of the family.

Marti laughed. "He's doing great." Her voice echoed with excitement.

"Of course, he is. I've caught you and him together late at night more than once," I chuckled.

"Love you more," she giggled.

As Marti's pseudo-boyfriend predicted, a tornado touched down the next day. It was mid-afternoon when Marti alerted me to the news. "There is a tornado about twenty miles southwest of Lawrence. We should be ready to get in the basement."

"Let's go see it. I'll drive south and then get behind it." It was a chance to see Mother Nature's power. I was thrilled.

She looked at me with eyes as big as hockey pucks. "Pat, are you sure?"

"Absolutely. Let's go." I had witnessed a couple of hurricanes; it was time to see a tornado.

We got into our car. Sabra, who was ten years old, climbed into the back seat. We were all buckled in, and I headed south out of Lawrence to get behind the tornado. As we looked west, there was an ominous green sky. I turned right and headed west down a farm road. As we neared the storm, the rain started to gently splatter our windshield. I stopped the car at a farm road intersection, trying to contemplate my next move.

"What do you think?" Marti said a bit fearfully.

Just then, small hail started to dance on the car.

"Dad, Dad, Dad, Dad, Dad—" Sabra said, desperately trying to get my attention. I think she had a copyright on the repetitive Dad sentence.

"What is it, Sabra?" I finally answered, turning to look at her. She was absolutely adorable with her towhead, cute button nose, and beautiful blue eyes that always seemed to communicate joy. But now those eyes were communicating anxiety.

"This is a bad idea," she said. Her words triggered a return to reality. If I was going to do this, why would I drag my wife and daughter along? I should have done this on my own. Our daughter was displaying better judgement than her dad.

"Sabra, you're right, let's get out of here."

Marti quickly agreed, and I thought, *Am I still having residuals of my mid-life crisis?* I had always been a bit of an adrenalin junkie, but this was taking it too far. I drove south and away from the storm.

* * *

I went back to doing home projects. I needed something to occupy my time. I started writing an offensive line manual to help young coaches with the fundamentals and techniques. It wasn't enough, so I started looking for something else. I wanted something fun.

A few years earlier, when I attended a National Football Coaches convention in New Orleans, I went to a casino boat. I recognized Head Coach Barry Alvarez from Wisconsin. He had been playing craps. I had no idea how to play. He started teaching me the basics. I was fascinated by the odds and the table atmosphere.

It was a Tuesday afternoon in mid-august, and I decided I was going to go to a river boat casino in Kansas City about 45 minutes away. Once I got there, I started walking around, looking for a table that had good vibes. The table I picked seemed to be having fun. I took what I learned from Coach Alvarez and won over $300. When I drove the hour back to Lawrence, I thought, *That was easy.*

I gave Marti half of it. I continued to go every Tuesday and Thursday from 1-3 p.m. I had a two-hour time limit. I returned home and always gave Marti half of what I won.

After eight weeks, I said to Marti, "I'm worried that I'm getting addicted. Do you think I should quit?"

Marti looked at me like I was crazy. "I think you should think about adding a day."

She didn't just say that, did she? "You're not serious, are you?"

"I have over five thousand dollars of serious in the bank."

I wasn't expecting that answer. I did enjoy playing, and I played with discipline. Ten days after our discussion, I lost for the first time in the amount of $500. I had won 19 times in a row. The gambling was over. I don't like losing. I never went back.

A group of local businessmen had invited me to take part in a regular 9 a.m. Tuesday morning breakfast. When I showed up, I realized it was specifically for me. It was therapy for an out-of-work coach. I played handball with this group. It was like they had welcomed a stray wolf into their pack. With football season well underway and not being involved for the first time in twenty-one years, I needed that pack. They were a godsend.

Mid-November, I started networking more—I was becoming a bit anxious and concerned about my future. Finally, in early December, an opportunity came knocking.

It came from my former boss, Glen Mason.

"Pat, I fired Elliott Uzelac," Mason said as I picked up the phone.

"Why did you fire him?" I asked.

"I don't want to talk about it."

My curiosity was not going to let that go.

"I want to offer you a job with the same titles you held at KU."

After a year without coaching football, I was excited. I didn't always agree with his methods, but he valued my opinion. I was ready to get back to coaching. I was relieved that I was wanted and appreciated.

"Thank you, Mason. When do you want me there?"

"I'll get you a plane ticket for Friday so you can be involved in the recruiting weekend."

I hung up the phone, grateful for the opportunity, but determined to know why Coach Uzelac was fired. Several coaches now on his staff had worked at Kansas with me, so I made a couple of calls.

They all told me the same story. Coach Uzelac had lost his temper during the half-time of a game and slapped an offensive lineman across the face. He absolutely should have been fired for that. The verbal and physical abuse was acceptable back in the 60s and 70s; I know as a player that experienced it first-hand. But now it was 1997. Mason realized those abusive cultures were no longer acceptable.

When I told Marti about my new job, she was skeptical. "Are you sure this is what you want?" I knew her reservations were running parallel to mine.

"No, but I need to get back to what I love."

She knew I was hoping to find a new environment, but I had a fear of being left out.

I packed my bag, taking everything warm I could find. Minnesota in December is about fantasizing about the spring. Marti was going to take me to the airport. We got in the car and started heading east on Interstate 70 to Kansas City International Airport. The University of Minnesota had a ticket waiting for me. The car was quiet, and I was deep in thought. Was this really what I wanted?

Mason was brash, tactless, and selfish. But he knew how to build a football program with toughness and organization.

Marti broke the silence. "Are you having second thoughts?"

"You know what? Get off at the next exit—we're heading back home." It was suddenly clear to me; I wanted change. Minnesota was like starting an essay and realizing the first sentence was terrible, so I crumpled up the paper and threw it in the trash. I needed to start over.

I called Coach Mason as soon as I got home. "Mason, I'm not coming." I could feel his anger accelerating through the phone line.

"What are you talking about? I've already informed the press. You can't do this."

"Yes, I can. You did the same to Georgia," I replied. I was prepared to give him my reasons.

"It's not the same, Pat."

"It might not be, but I need to move in a different direction. It's not about you," I assured him. I hung up the phone, thinking that wasn't entirely true. It was his actions that ruined our team chemistry. His praise for how much better Georgia was than Kansas devastated our team and community.

What now? I thought. I saw that Tennessee needed an offensive line coach in the paper. I called Head Coach Phillip Fulmer and told him I was interested in the job. He explained to me that I would be splitting the offensive line duties with another coach. That was unacceptable to me, so I turned down his offer.

Turning down jobs when you don't have one is risky business. I was getting worried that looking for what I wanted would result in an empty hand.

Then I got a call from Nick Saban, the Head Coach at Michigan State. He had an offensive line job open and wanted me to come up to Michigan State for an interview. I accepted. I needed this one to work; I was running out of options. Mark Dantonio, who was an excellent coach at Kansas and had left, was now coaching defensive backs at MSU. It was obvious Mark had recommended me.

Arriving at Michigan State, I was prepared with a PowerPoint presentation on my philosophy and my teaching methods. Coach Saban ran the interview, questioning me constantly on why I did something a certain way. Coach Gary Tranquill, the offensive coordinator, shot me a few questions. Then, after 90 minutes, Coach Saban got up and left without saying a word.

I looked at Coach Tranquill with probing eyes.

"You got the job. Nick never stays that long unless he likes what he hears."

I continued to meet with the staff for a few minutes. There was a knock on the staffroom door; it was Nick's secretary. What Coach Tranquill said was reassuring, but I wanted to hear it from Coach Saban himself.

"Pat, Coach Saban would like to see you now." I left the staff room and headed across the hall to his office, which was very neat and orderly, a harbinger of his discipline.

I took a chair in front of his desk and looked at him expectantly.

"You did a good job. I'm offering you the position. Your salary will be a hundred and fifteen thousand, plus you get money from the summer camp and a courtesy car." His offer stunned me, as it was $30,000 more than I was making as the assistant head coach and offensive coordinator at KU.

"Great, Coach. I'm excited about this opportunity." I was not going to let this one go. "When do I want me back here?"

"Go home, get what you need, and get back here for a staff meeting on Monday."

I felt as if my soul had been illuminated. I was dancing on the inside and trying to act calm and cool on the outside. I didn't want to tell Marti on the phone. I was anxious to see her reaction in person.

Marti was waiting for me at the airport pick-up curb. As soon as I was in the car, it jumped out of me like a Jack-in-the-Box.

"I took the job."

She laughed. "I know, I talked with Coach Saban for twenty minutes."

Why is he calling my wife? "What did he say?"

"He knew my name. We talked about Michigan State. He conveyed there are job opportunities at the University and wanted me to make sure that you wouldn't pull the same act you did on Mason and not show up." Now it was obviously Marti's turn to act coy, and she was gleaming about her moment in the process.

I was immediately wondering how she became the main focus of my job. Then it hit me. "Well, now we know he's an excellent recruiter." I was impressed.

Marti seemed to be at peace leaving her job as assistant vice chancellor. After all that we went through in the last two years, she, too, was done and ready for the next adventure.

CHAPTER 17

MICHIGAN STATE

I was excited to be back in coaching. I didn't have the titles of offensive coordinator or assistant head coach, but I was doing what I truly loved: coaching the offensive line. With Michigan State Spartans in the Big 10 conference, I was on cloud nine. Marti and Sabra would have to stay in Lawrence, Kansas to finish the school year. Marti had already landed a research position at MSU, so we were all set.

I was escorted to Coach Saban's office by his secretary, Linda Selby, who had a wonderful disposition. I couldn't wait to get started. Coach Saban got down to business as soon as I entered his office. He had the player depth chart in his hand and was waving it back and forth as he started to go over each of the offensive linemen's athletic and personal qualities. Coach was known for his intensity and laser-like focus, and I was worried that I shouldn't interrupt, but I could not contain myself.

"It's better that I don't have any preconceived ideas of who they are—let me find out for myself," I interjected. I paused for a second, looking for affirmation. He looked at me intently, and I added, "I want the players that I coach to have a fresh start."

To my relief, he started nodding in agreement. "Good thought. I want to hear your evaluation when you're ready." I immediately felt that Coach valued my opinion.

I kicked off my first meeting with the offensive line by asking each player to stand up and tell me their name, where they were from, and what they were majoring in.

After hearing from several players, a young man stood up. "My name is Casey Jensen."

Before I could even acknowledge him, a couple of players spoke up. "No, it's Bunny Jensen." The room snickered like high school sophomores.

"Why is your nickname Bunny?" I asked, thinking it wasn't a good football nickname. The room was silent, waiting for Casey to answer.

"It's not a big deal, Coach." He clearly didn't want to talk about it, and I reluctantly moved on, but I was going to find out.

When we broke out of our meeting, I looked each player in the eyes. I could tell David Sucura was wanting to talk, so I pulled him aside. "Can you please tell me what that was about?" I asked. I sensed he was as concerned as I was about this nickname.

"Coach, there was this girl who had dated several of the freshmen players, and her name was Bunny. When Casey came in as a freshman, he fell in love with her and was with her constantly, so we started calling him Bunny."

The story caught me off guard. Casey was now a junior— this had been going on for two years? I was concerned it was damaging his self-image, so the next day I made an announcement to the coaching staff and to the players.

"No one gets to call him Bunny anymore." Some of them scoffed at my request, but I was unrelenting. "His name is Casey," I said with determination.

Casey appeared worried that I might be making his problem worse, but I knew it was critical to change this moniker. Coach Saban was aware of what I was trying to do but was unsure it would help. Many of the players and coaches viewed him as soft. I viewed him as a young man who needed self-confidence, and he wasn't going to get it with people calling him Bunny.

Coach Saban, who stood only 5'8", was like a hand grenade with the pin already pulled. He never smiled much around the office or on the practice field; he was all business. He had worked for Bill Belichick, who carried the same traits. He was the master of his philosophy: Know what to do, know how to do it, and know why it was important to do it that way. At first, he seemed to be missing the human qualities that would give him strong connections with his players and coaches. But as it turned out, he did have a charismatic side. It was like seeing two totally different people.

After two weeks on the job, I was walking down the hall in the football complex when I spotted Coach walking toward me.

"Hi, Coach," I said.

He walked by as if I didn't exist. The same thing happened a couple of days later. That lack of acknowledgement by him irked me, and I decided that I would turn the tables on him. The following day, I walked by him and didn't even look at him. Within minutes, I was called to his office.

"What is your problem?" he barked as soon as he saw me.

I looked at him with a deliberate face of confusion, coyly voiceless.

"You walked by me and didn't acknowledge me. What is that about?"

It was time for me to fess up. "Coach, I said hi to you a couple of times this week, and you didn't acknowledge me." I knew full well I was jogging on thin ice.

"Pat, I was thinking about things." He spoke in a tone that signaled he was in charge.

"So was I, Coach."

"Go back to work," he said, flashing me a smile. His reaction was so unexpected that it seemed like I suddenly had a connection to this no-nonsense coach.

That spring, Coach Saban taught the staff situational football. First down, third down, and red zone philosophies. The third down blitz packages that Coach brought from his pro football experience with the Cleveland Browns was expansive. I was totally engaged and enamored with it all. It was a part of the game that I did not have experience with because so few teams in college used that wide of a range of blitzes, which attack across the entire offensive system.

By the time we started the 1998 season, I felt well-prepared and ready to go. The amazing part was that Casey Jensen was starting at right tackle. Casey—no longer Bunny. He had transformed into a competitive football player. One of the great joys in coaching is to help a young man find his self-confidence and to develop him into an achieving athlete.

We were ranked 23rd in preseason polls and proceeded to lose our first two games. Then we played the 10th ranked Notre Dame team at home in Spartan Stadium. We didn't act like an 0-2 team, as we beat them 45-23. We lost to Michigan, our instate rival, the following week. We were on a rollercoaster.

It came to a head when we lost to Minnesota, 18-19, on the road. The next week, we were playing Northwestern at home. I knew I had to get them refocused.

"If we don't beat Northwestern, I'm going to dress up in full gear, take all of you to the blocking chute, and kick all of your asses," I announced to my players. They seemed to think it was funny, but I was serious. I knew we were a good team that was underperforming.

We won 29-5. I announced to the players after the game that they were fortunate not to have experienced me, fully dressed in football gear, kicking their butts. They laughed. If we had lost to Northwestern and I had got my butt kicked, that might have driven me back to private business.

The following Monday, we were preparing to play the Ohio State Buckeyes on the road. The players interrupted my meeting with a challenge of their own.

"Coach, we're playing number one, Ohio State, this week," Jason Strayhorn, the starting center, said. "And when we beat them, you have to put on full pads and take us on in the chute so we can kick your ass." They chuckled like teenagers talking about their first kiss.

As the offensive line stood there, waiting for my response, I looked at all their faces. I was loving the idea that they were issuing a challenge back. I was elated that they were motivated. "I accept the challenge." I was ready to do whatever was necessary to give us a chance.

The game was nationally televised, as we were the only team left to possibly derail their quest to play for the National

Championship. Ohio State was undefeated and at home, a tough combination to beat. After a good week of practice, we headed to Columbus, Ohio.

The Buckeyes led the Spartans 17-6 at half-time. We only managed two field goals. Going into the fourth quarter, we trailed Ohio State 24-18. The door was open to knock off the number one team in the nation. The game was close, and the Buckeyes were worried. Their confidence was being torn away as our defense shut them out and our offense scored ten points in the final 15 minutes of the game. We won 28-24.

It was quieter than a church on Tuesday morning as 93,595 Buckeye fans stood in disbelief. The celebration for the Spartans had started, and the players didn't wait until we got to the locker room—they began taunting me about going one-on-one with them.

"Oh, my god, Coach, you're going to get your ass kicked!" David Sucura announced.

"We'll see who kicks whose ass," I said brashly. I knew that a 47-, almost 48-year-old coach was in deep shit. There was no way I could tell Marti what was going on because she would have objected.

The following week, the offensive linemen kept asking, "When are we going to go one-on-one with you?"

I was determined not to let them see me scared, but inside I knew my 235 pounds was no contest versus their 290-320 pounds. I told them, "Tuesday before our final game against Penn State." I put it off a week, rationalizing that if I were to get hurt, there would only be one game left.

The day of reckoning had finally arrived. I went to see Bob Knickerbocker, who was in charge of equipment. "Bob, I need shoulder pads and a helmet."

He smiled at me. He had already pulled them. "Here you go, Coach. Check and make sure the helmet fits properly, and I'll call a priest."

"Ha-ha," I said, knowing that I might not need a priest, but a nurse, doctor, or trainer for sure. I zipped a jacket over the pads and walked out to the field, toward the blocking chute. The offensive line was waiting for me.

I yelled, "Who's first?"

Jason Strayhorn, the only senior, said, "I am, Coach."

Jason was 6'2", about 290 pounds, and exceptionally strong.

I lined up in front of him. "Whenever you're ready."

Jason fired out on me. I tried to lift him to take away some of his power. The result was me on my back with Jason on top. I just got pancaked. The players were laughing.

I scrambled to my feet. "Next," I said, and took a deep breath. It was important to me that they knew I was tough and could take it.

Shaun Mason, 6'5" and 290 pounds, buried me again. I realized that I had seven players to go—I might not make it.

"Next," I yelled.

Casey Jensen, who was 6'7" and 290 pounds, dropped me. *Et tu, Casey?* The players were no longer laughing and now asking if I was okay. I was determined to keep going.

David Sucura exploded out of his stance, and I caught him like a baseball catcher, only this ball weighed 285 pounds. He actually tried to keep me from going down on the ground again. My middle finger got caught in his helmet and dislocated at a

45-degree angle. Without screaming, I proudly held it up and pulled it back in place. It took every part of me not to show my pain.

"Next," I announced. I was slowly becoming meat, getting tenderized for the grill.

Matt Bonita was next. He was 6'7" and 272 pounds. He went easy on me, which I desperately needed. He knocked me back about ten yards, but I stayed on my feet.

The players started pleading. "You've had enough, Coach!"

"You're right. Greg will be the last one," I said. I was wondering if I could even coach practice. Greg Robinson-Randall was 6'5" and 328 pounds. I lined up over him and looked him in the eye.

"It would be a damn shame if you're the only one I beat."

I was planning to jump out of the way, but I mistimed my move and became a butterfly on the grill of an 18-wheeler. I thought of our daughter when we went tornado chasing... *This was a bad idea.*

I coached that practice, and I went home to shower. I didn't want anyone to see my bruised body. My legs had minor scrapes, my finger was twice its normal size, and my chest and abdomen was a light blue, dark blue, purplish, and blackish painting signed, "Love, the offensive line."

The challenge of doing something no one else thought you could do is immensely satisfying. Beating the number one team in the country when we were 27-point underdogs was a euphoric moment.

This was why I loved coaching. The tribal nature—being a part of something much bigger than myself. The team. The journey. The sacrifice. The achievement and the eternal bonds. What's not to love?

* * *

Coach Saban kicked off our off-season program by surprising me with the newly vacated assistant head coach position. I was honored. I appreciated Coach Saban's recognition, but it was about to become an issue.

Two weeks into my new position, I received an urgent call on Sunday from Reggie Mitchell, our running back coach. "Pat, is it okay if I miss Monday's staff meeting? I think my wife, Andrea, broke her ankle on a sprinkler today, and we're going to the hospital in the morning."

I could hear the apprehension in his voice. "I hope Andrea's okay, Reggie, but the permission to miss a staff meeting will have to come from Coach Saban."

I heard the deep sigh. "Damn, I was hoping you could do it." He knew he was dealing with a possible landmine.

"Reggie, it's the off-season; he'll excuse you." When we hung up, I knew Coach Saban would understand.

Within 30 minutes, I received another call. This time it was from Bill Miller, our defensive coordinator. He was in the process of moving his family from Miami to East Lansing, and his wife was dealing with some vandalism.

"Pat, I need to go back to Miami and help Lisa—she's struggling. I can leave tonight and be back Monday night."

I appreciated that they thought I had the power to excuse them. Thinking about it, I would rather call me, too, but unfortunately, it wasn't my decision. "You need to call Coach," I stressed. *Oh my, two staff members missing? This meeting could be a firework show.*

The following morning, we all entered the staff room for our 9 a.m. meeting. It was a classic board room with a big mahogany table, whiteboards, and a depth chart board behind the head coach's chair. We were engaged in small talk until Coach walked in, then everybody straightened up, and it became very clear that there were two empty chairs.

Coach Saban settled into his chair and started the meeting. "Let me be perfectly clear. We have guys on this staff who don't know how to win—they don't know what it takes. You're either committed or you're not. You think winning is easy—it isn't. I know it's tough. I wasn't even there when we adopted our kids. We better learn what it takes. Isn't that right, Pat?"

What the fuck? Are you serious? I could feel flames rising through my core. I stood up in anger. Standing up was a mistake. It was like I was alpha dogging the head coach.

"Coach, first of all, you excused them, and that doesn't make anyone less committed to winning." It was as if there was no one in the room. Our eyes locked on each other, his scathing look matched by my seething one. "It's the off-season, and it's the only time we can attend to our families because in-season is very difficult—they're virtually on their own."

His lips were pursed, and his eyes were stabbing me; the only thing missing was smoke coming out of his ears. I could tell this was not going well. You don't do that to the head coach—I should have known better—but it was too late.

Coach Saban raised his notebook over his head and slammed it on the table. "This fucking meeting is over." He stood out of his chair and left.

After a moment of stunned silence, the defensive coaches started to chastise me.

"Thanks, Pat, for ruining our day," Bill Sheridan, our linebacker coach, snarled. I understood why he was pissed; Coach Saban spent most of his days with the defense.

Gary, our offensive coordinator, said, "Pat, that was good that you defended them, but you know Linda Selby is going to knock on that door and tell you to go to Nick's office."

I was already starting to sweat, and as if on cue, there was a rap on the door. Coach Saban's secretary popped her head in. "Coach Ruel, Nick wants you in his office, now." That was really quick. I took a deep breath.

I was already planning to throw myself on the mercy of Saban's court. I should have never stood up, and I should have requested a sidebar like good lawyers do. I was like a fallen branch, and I could hear the woodchipper grinding away. I was wondering if I was going to be fired as I walked to his office.

His door was open, and as my eyes met his, he calmly raised his finger and said, "Close the door." Not a particularly good sign. I closed it and sat down in the chair in front of his desk. The verbal assault ensued.

"You disloyal motherfucker. I made you the assistant head coach to support me!"

My mind searched for a reasonable answer during his three-second pause.

"What you did was bullshit, and I am goddamn pissed. You call that supporting me?"

"Coach, you gave me that position to tell you the truth."

"No, I want your support," he yelled.

"Coach, I'm sorry, but-"

He interrupted me before I could finish; he was on fire, and I was the kindling. He kept barking like a guard dog protecting his territory. "I'm trying to build a championship program. You think this is easy? It's not, and I'm tired of excuses. I won't have it. What you did was disloyal. Do you have anything to say?"

Like usual, I reached for some humor to diffuse the situation. "Yes, I do. You ever watch Perry Mason?" I knew this was a stretch, but I needed some counterpoints.

"What the hell does he have to do with this?"

"Coach, he always prepped his witnesses before he put them on the stand." It was the only defense I had for my actions. It really wasn't about what I said as much as how I did it.

"Get out of my office."

I got up, went straight to my office, and called Marti. I was scared for my job. When she answered, my first words were, "I think I'm going to be fired."

"Why?" I could hear the concern in her voice. I recited the incident in detail.

Marti, as usual, was calm and put on her analytical hat. "Well, you should have asked him to go in the hallway for a side counsel, or you could have let it go and supported him, but that's not you, is it?" I could hear her thinking, *We've been through this before.*

"I don't know, Marti, but what I do know is that it was a nuclear event."

When I entered the football facility the following morning, I braced myself for aftershocks or a pink slip. I hoped to make it to my office without encountering Coach Saban, but halfway there, he intercepted me. I searched his face for a signal of what was to come.

"Pat, I know you offensive coaches know how to handle four strong pressures in the run game and pass protection, but what I want to know is your thoughts on four weak versus the run and pass protection. Will you keep me advised?" I was caught off guard by his sudden congeniality.

"Sure, Coach." I was still spinning with confusion as I walked into the offensive staff room.

Gary Tranquill, our offensive coordinator, flashed me a smile. "You still got a job?"

"I guess so. He acted like nothing happened."

Gary offered me a knowing nod. "Pat, I guarantee he went home and explained the whole thing to Terry, his wife, and it was verbatim. He is totally honest with her. She is his confidante and sounding board, and he trusts her opinions. So, you should thank her that you're still here." The offensive staff broke out in laughter.

I was still confused by the whole encounter. "How do you know this?" I asked.

"I was with him at the Cleveland Browns. Terry is his go-to when things upset him."

"How come you never told me?" I countered.

"Because you made it a whole year without pissing him off."

Coach Saban was honest to a fault. He never sugarcoated anything. He would be unable to hold a job at Hallmark or Krispy Kreme. But I gained a new appreciation for him that day because although he could be angered, he never fed that anger.

I learned a lot about football under him, for which I am very grateful, though at times his manic drive to be successful took its toll on our family lives. In the off-season, we would go on the road recruiting all week. Then we would come back for a staff meeting on Saturday and discuss the prospects we found. After doing some evaluations, a guest coach from the NFL or a successful salesmen would teach us football or selling. Then we would go home, pack, and be back on the road on Sunday. It was a grind.

One memorable visit was from Coach John Fox, who at the time was an excellent defensive coordinator for the New York Giants. He specialized in the bear defense, which was getting a lot of recognition around the football world. It was the same defense that made Buddy Ryan famous when he was with the Chicago Bears.

John had been coaching us up for about two hours. It was 1:30 p.m. when Coach Saban left the room to check on the pizzas he had ordered.

"You guys do this every Saturday during spring recruiting?" John asked. We all nodded like children who were in time-out.

John shook his head. "I think we should get you guys home." When Coach Saban re-entered the staff room, John said, "I'm amazed at all the questions your staff asked, and I'm worn out. Let's call it a day."

Coach nodded. The staff thanked Coach Fox, not only for the knowledge he imparted on us, but for rescuing an afternoon with our families.

By the time spring training wrapped up, we all knew we had a good team. The mostly young players from the year before were now more mature and experienced.

Going into the 1999 season, I decided to kick things off with a challenge and not wait for mid-season. I was all in on this one because it would not involve me getting mauled.

"If we win our first five games, you guys can shave my head." I made this bet because our sixth game was against Michigan, our in-state rival. I thought being undefeated and at home would be the key ingredient for beating Michigan.

The players were already planning the hair cutting event in their heads. "You're going to look awesome bald," David Sucura taunted as the rest of the players began to cheer in agreement.

We beat Oregon and Eastern Michigan at home and 24th ranked Notre Dame on the road. We were 3-0. The offensive line and some of the other positions started making buzzing sounds after the game, indicating that they were closing in on the bet. It made me laugh, but the reality of the situation was starting to sink in as I looked into a mirror and wondered, *What will I look like bald?*

Marti thought it was foolish, but I knew that teams that sacrifice for each other become tribal. It is a powerful chemistry that exemplifies unity.

We beat Illinois on the road, and the buzzing sounds by the players got louder. Next, we were playing Iowa at home, and we were now ranked 14th. We beat them 49-3. Our team was 5-0, and the scene in the locker room was a momentary celebration that turned into cheering over shaving my head. They put a chair in the middle of the room. I took a seat, and the cutting began; they each took turns buzzing my hair off. It was like basketball when they cut down the net after a championship win. All the linemen took part. They even brought out the shaving cream and razor. When they finished, my head was like a large cue ball, white and smooth.

They started to go after my mustache, but I stopped them—it wasn't part of the bet. "Back off, boys, the mustache stays," I announced.

Coach Saban seized on the opportunity in the Monday morning staff meeting and asked, "Who's next?"

It was crickets for about 30 seconds. Then Mark Dantonio, our defensive back coach, blurted out, "I'll do it."

The guy who recommended me to Coach Saban was now next. Michigan had a number three ranking. We beat them 34-31. It felt good to have a bald-headed partner.

We played 20th ranked Purdue and Drew Brees on the road next. Coach Saban was worried that the team was getting full of themselves, and he talked to them in a negative tone. "You guys are 6-0, and you can't handle success. If you think that you're going to go to Purdue and magically win, well, you're not—you'll probably go down there and play like shit."

This seemed to be the theme of the week. I never understood why he suddenly thought a reverse of the course we were on was necessary. I sensed that Coach Saban was trying to avoid the mistakes of last year's team, which was an erratic ride. This wasn't that team, and his negative psychology backfired.

We got crushed 52-28. We looked like a tired team. Then another loss to 16th ranked Wisconsin on the road, 40-10.

Coach Saban grabbed the team before we fell off the cliff. He was talking in a more affirmative voice, and I hoped it would get us back on track. Our next game was against 20th ranked Ohio State. They were not as good as the year before, but formidable nonetheless.

My brother, Mike, who was living in California, called me to say he was flying in for the game. "Pat, I need eight tickets."

The game was sold out, and he wanted eight tickets? He obviously had no clue of the magnitude of that request. Regardless, I managed to pull some strings and secured eight tickets on the forty-yard line. They were two sets of four each, on different rows but together. I thought he would be thrilled, but when I shared the news, he was upset.

"I need eight tickets on the same row." His demand was fucking ridiculous.

"Are you kidding me, Mike? These tickets are together. Front and back."

He continued to push. "I need eight on the same row, Pat."

This seemed like a pointless request, and I had better things to do. I was irked that he would be demanding a special seat arrangement, but I gave the request to Nick's secretary, who rightfully sneered at the idea, and she performed a miracle and found eight seats in the upper deck.

The game started, and our defense, which had given up 52 points to Purdue and 40 points to Wisconsin in successive weeks, was now dominating the Buckeyes. We beat them 23-7.

After the game, Mike's wife, Deana, came looking for me. "Pat, you should have seen what happened in the stands." She got my attention.

"What happened?"

"Mike would stand up and yell, 'That's another Spartan first down,' then someone behind us yelled, 'Hey, buddy, why don't you sit down and shut up?'"

Mike had by far the worse temper of my six brothers. "Oh no, what happened?"

"Mike jumped up and yelled, 'My brother is the assistant head coach and offensive line coach for the Spartans, and I will yell all I want.'" I imagined a boxing contest was the main event on the upper deck.

"What happened, Deana?"

She started to laugh. "It went eerily quiet for about ten seconds, then, someone else yelled, 'He must not think much of you to put you up here with us.'"

I joined her laughter. I guess the eight seats in a row in the Ohio State section was just what the doctor ordered.

We finished the season 9-2, ranked tenth in the country.

The Citrus Bowl extended us an invitation to play the Florida Gators in Orlando. Coach Saban wanted us out on the road recruiting immediately before we started practicing for the bowl game.

I was at Cerritos Junior College in Norwalk, California inquiring about a couple of offensive line prospects when a student trainer asked me, "Are you going to Louisiana State with Coach Saban?"

"What are you talking about?" I stared at him in disbelief. It was like I stepped on a landmine and was afraid to lift my foot.

"It was in the paper that his wife was in Baton Rouge looking at homes."

I continued to stare. Was it possible that Saban did this without me knowing? No fucking way. I knew it couldn't be true. Then my Nokia cell phone started ringing, and I realized something was happening.

I called the office. "Linda, what's going on?" I felt uncertain and was becoming anxious. I felt like a lost dog trying to find my way home. Everyone seemed to know more about what was happening than I did.

"Pat, I'm not at liberty to say. You should call Coach Saban."

I didn't want to call him—I wanted verification first. I called Mark Dantonio. He informed me that Saban had been talking about LSU with a staff member who had previously worked there.

I guess it's true. I continued recruiting that day, but I felt like a coach without a team.

That night, I finally called Coach Saban, who held his cards close to his chest. The conversation was one sentence: "We'll talk when you get back here."

I was evaluating the tone of his voice and his words carefully. It sounded like I was ok. But what did ok mean? Yes, I was going to LSU, or no, I'd be fine looking for another job?

On the flight back to Detroit, I was mystified. *Why is this such a big secret when the newspapers already know?*

When I arrived home, I told Marti what was going on, and she made it clear that she wasn't thrilled about living in Baton Rouge, Louisiana. "Pat, they don't have good public schools." I knew that wasn't the only reason. She loved her job and was moving up the ladder into student affairs, and now I was going to uproot her again.

"We can put her in a private school," I countered sheepishly. "I don't even know if I've been invited yet."

Two hours later, I headed to Coach Saban's house per his request. As soon as he opened the door, I launched in. "Why wasn't I in the loop on this?"

His eyes conveyed a bit of remorse. "You don't understand that too many people involved can sabotage a deal." His words stung. After all I had done to help us win, didn't he trust me?

"Why are you leaving?" I asked as I followed him to his recreation room.

We stood there like friends at a cocktail party. "This is good opportunity," he said.

"Well, it pissed me off to be on the road selling Michigan State and getting asked by a student trainer if I was going to LSU. Stopping at schools the rest of the day was like being a five-year-old lost at the fair."

My bitching was falling on deaf ears. Coach was a "Don't tell me about the labor pain, just deliver the baby" kind of guy. As usual, he was focused on the task at hand.

"I'm offering you the offensive line job or the tight end job with the title of assistant head coach."

I expected an offer, but I was relieved to hear the words. Suddenly, all the tension and stress from my day was gone. I knew Marti would not be thrilled, but she was a master at improvising and adjusting.

I flashed Coach a smile. "Thanks, coach." I accepted the offensive line job.

CHAPTER 18

WHAT IS NEXT?

The first line of the Michigan State fight song reads, "On the banks of the Red Cedar, there is a school that's known to all." The battle on that river was about to begin. MSU was back on the national stage in the world of college football, and the Michigan State president, M. Peter McPherson, was determined to keep it that way.

The morning after Saban offered me the job, my phone started ringing off the hook. The first call came from Morris Watts, our offensive coordinator, who had thrown his hat into the ring.

"Do you know what's going on?" he asked.

"No, I'm in the dark right now," I replied, wanting somebody to tell me something.

"I'm out, and it looks like if we can hold the staff together, they might give the job to Bobby."

"How do you know this?" I asked. I was a little shocked that Bobby was already being talked about.

"Joel Ferguson on the Board of Trustees seems to be heavily involved." Ferguson was a well-known powerbroker at MSU, and in politics. So, I trusted his source.

"What is Clarence Underwood saying?" I asked. He was our athletic director.

"I think he's supporting Bobby a hundred percent." I could hear the disappointment in his voice.

"President McPherson has called a meeting with the staff today at eleven a.m. At his office," he added before hanging up the phone.

Within a half-hour, the phone rang again. This time it was Coach Williams.

"Pat, I just interviewed for the Eastern Michigan head coaching job, but now it looks like I have a shot at this one. They called me and told me to hang tight. So don't get on the plane just yet."

I could feel his excitement rising, too. "You know there's a meeting with President McPherson?"

"Yes, I do."

"Okay, I will see you there."

A couple hours later, I was sitting with the staff in McPherson's board room. It was huge with a corporate feel to it. Bobby wasn't there. *Is this a red flag? Where is he?*

When President McPherson entered the room, it went eerily quiet. We all stared at him with anticipation. McPherson looked like your typical college professor: decorative gray hair around his ears, a full gray mustache, and a forehead that ran as far as the eyes could see. When he spoke, he sounded like a politician, talking but revealing nothing. He expressed an appreciation of our hard work and that he would like to maintain some continuity, but he offered no definitive answers. "Hold fast and stay true." It was a mantra of the Navy Seals. It was a phrase they used in the stormy seas, meaning to grab onto something and maintain the compass heading.

I went home with my head spinning. I didn't know what was happening. But what I did know was that I felt like a jerk for always asking Marti to sacrifice her job. Standing in front of Saban, it had been easy to say yes, but now standing in front of Marti and President McPherson, it was making me think twice. The pressure was mounting. Coach Saban had given me and the three other coaches he siphoned from MSU 24 hours to get our things together and board a private plane he was sending. He wanted us on the recruiting trail immediately.

I spent the day agonizing over my decision. Finally, I made up my mind. It was 11 p.m., and I called Mark Dantonio, who was one of the four heading to LSU.

"I've decided not to go," I announced as soon as he answered. "Marti is concerned about the public schools in Baton Rouge, plus she likes her job here." I was also thinking about the unique group of offensive linemen that I loved for their competitive nature.

For a couple of seconds, there was silence, and I could hear him thinking. "I don't know if Bobby will get the job," he finally replied.

I knew what he was implying; I was rolling the dice. But turning down a job when I don't have one—I had done that before. I always had confidence I was a good coach. I was part of taking two struggling programs, Washington State and Kansas, to bowl games. I wasn't afraid. On top of that, I knew Joel Ferguson felt it was time to have a black head coach at his alma mater, so he was pushing hard for Bobby Williams. The Spartans had a beautiful history of being one of the first schools to integrate college football. I knew Joel to be a strong influencer at MSU. I thought Bobby would have a good chance because President McPherson wanted to maintain some continuity after going 9-2 and finishing in the top ten.

"I know there's a chance I could end up with nothing," I admitted. "Who knew that winning could cause such turmoil?"

"No kidding. I'm unsure what to do, but I'll figure it out," Mark said. I could hear the stress in his voice. They say that copper wire was invented when two lawyers tried to pick up the same penny off the sidewalk. Mark was that penny.

The private plane landed at Lansing the next morning, and no one showed. Somewhere in the middle of the night, the other three coaches also decided not to go.

That afternoon, I received a heated call from Coach Saban. "You orchestrated this whole thing," he fumed into the phone.

What the fuck? I was honored that he thought I had that kind of influence, but that was not the case. "Coach, I didn't orchestrate this in any way," I stressed. There was part of me that felt a bit guilty, as he had hired me and promoted me, but like him, I was going to do what was best for my family.

I could feel his wrath as he continued to vent. "I sent a plane up there, and you don't have the courtesy to call and discuss this?"

He was right; I should have, but calling Coach late at night to deliver bad news would be like sticking a coat hanger into an electrical wall socket. I also delayed telling him because there was 10% of me that was not on board yet. I thought no communication could buy me some valuable time.

By the end of the day, it was national news. It had nothing to do with him being a bully or demanding, which was how the media portrayed it. Coach Saban had a knack for finding strong personalities and knowledgeable coaches. It didn't matter to him whether you were coming from a job, or you were out of coaching and looking to get back in. He wanted coaches who were committed and willing to work day and night if necessary. If you were committed, you were at the table. If you weren't, you were on the menu.

He chose four coaches who had conviction and believed in him. It was his gift, but this time it backfired on him.

Shortly after I hung up with Coach Saban, I received a call from President McPherson's secretary asking me to come to his office. I was feeling a lot more confident about my decision as I headed over to see him. All the signs to maintain the staff and hire Bobby were pointing in the right direction.

When I entered his office, he wasted no time.

"We're going to announce Coach Williams as the head coach, and I would like you to promise to stay and help him be successful."

A rush of excitement entered my body, and the apprehension was ushered out. I stuck out my hand and shook his. "I'm proud of what we accomplished, and I'm excited for the opportunity to remain here and help Bobby."

The battle at the Red Cedar River was won by Michigan State that day. If they had taken a week to decide on a head coach, the plane to Baton Rouge would have had four coaches on it.

* * *

I had always admired Bobby and was excited to be his assistant head coach.

We immersed ourselves in recruiting and preparing for the Citrus Bowl. We arrived in Orlando the day after Christmas. It was a perfect setting for bowl games. We would practice, meet, and go to bowl functions at Disney World, Sea World, and Universal Studios. It was a great environment for the coaches' kids and me.

It was December 31, 1999, the night before the game. We had a beautiful room at the Peabody Hotel, and we were going to witness all the firework shows from our balcony. Marti kept asking me about Y2K. It stood for the year 2000 in the computer world. There was talk that computers would not be able to transition, and the systems would collapse.

"Don't worry about it, Marti," I said, pausing for a moment. "We have a perfect view for all the firework shows in Orlando—we don't need no stinking computers." For me, it was always about enjoying the present.

We watched several firework shows, and it was breathtaking. When it was over, I jumped into bed like a young boy the night before Christmas; I could hardly wait for game day.

In the locker room shortly before the pregame, players were anxiously sitting at their lockers. The battle of the Southeastern Conference versus the Big Ten was about to begin. We could hear the Florida players chanting from their locker room, which was next to ours. Our team was sitting quietly, listening to the Gators in a frenzy. The doorway of the coaches' dressing room was open, and I stood there myself, listening like the players. I felt it was a bad vibe, so I turned to Coach Williams, who was reviewing the substitution charts.

"Coach, you might want to talk to the team."

"I'll address them right before we go out, but if you want, you can talk to them now. Go ahead." I loved the fact that Coach Williams had that confidence in me.

I went to the wall where I could hear the Florida Gators cheering.

"Listen up," I yelled. All the players looked up at me. I could tell they wanted some emotional food, and I was about to deliver. "You think chanting and cheering wins games? It doesn't. What wins is preparation and a belief in each other. It's knowing the guy next to you has your back. It's an emotional bond that cannot be broken. Let me tell you what I think: We are a team of destiny. We are meant to be here. It is our time, it is our game, and we will show the SEC how we play football in the Big Ten. So, fuck all that chanting and cheering."

The team started to bang on their lockers; it sounded much like a drum beat before battle. The Florida Gators were now wondering what all the banging was about. Now we were emotionally charged. There's something so primitive about preparing for a contest with 95 players. The truth is, whether it's singing, chanting, or beating a drum, it's a powerful stimulant. It removes an individual's anxiety and replaces it with unity and purpose.

The game was close for the entire contest. The score was 20-21 at halftime, with Florida having the advantage. It was nearing the end of the game. We were tied 34-34. Our kicker, Paul Edinger, who ironically was from Lakeland, Florida, finished off the Gators with a field goal, and so with no time left, we were 37-34. It was MSU's first bowl win in ten years. Coach Williams was well liked by all the players and was an excellent coach and recruiter. He had a smile that could light up a room, but on this day, that smile lit up the stadium.

* * *

We just finished recruiting in early February. Everything had settled down, and we were working on off-season. That's when I received a call from the Detroit Lions' assistant head coach, Gary Moeller, who wanted to know if I was interested in interviewing for the offensive line job. I was now at a crossroad. Just four weeks earlier, I had shaken hands with President McPherson, promising I would stay, but coaching in the NFL was the perceived pinnacle of my profession. It had eluded me twice before. But because this was an offensive line job with a bonus being that Marti could keep her job, and Sabra could continue her education at the same school, it felt like this was the time. It was meant to be.

I told Coach Williams, and he gave me the green light to interview. But I knew the harder conversation would eventually be President McPherson. My mind continued to grapple with the situation as I drove the next day to the Pontiac Silverdome. Marti was already giving me the side-eye.

What will I do if they offer me the job? I was bound by a verbal agreement. *Do I really want to leave the players I've grown so close to?* They were like sons to me. *Should I let another chance for pro football go by? Will I get another chance later? Will the Pentagon* (Marti) *declare war?* I wanted to stop that bantering going on in my head.

When I arrived at the Pontiac Silverdome, I took a deep breath and cleared my mind. I sat there in the parking lot reviewing my preparatory notes. It was basically my philosophy on teaching the fundamentals of the run game and pass game. I included common problems and solutions. I was ready.

When I entered the football office, I was ten minutes early. John Miscagna, who was the tight end coach, gave me a quick tour of the facilities and then we funneled into the staff room where Head Coach Bobby Ross and the offensive staff were sitting. They wasted no time. They put me on the whiteboard and started firing questions at me. I loved the engagement with the coaches; they were sincere and open about issues they had and were asking for my opinion.

After a while, there was a knock on the door. Some guy stepped in, leaned over, and whispered something to Coach Ross.

"Fuck, that really pisses me off. I'll be back in five minutes," he said as he left the room. The staff and I made small talk until Coach Ross returned. When he opened the door, he sat down and shook his head. "Men, I hope you will accept my apology for that language."

Wow, a head coach apologizing to his staff for using vulgar language? It was an unveiling of this man's character. I was blown away by his sincerity.

Coach Ross left and said he would send for me. His staff began telling me how wonderful and respectful Coach Ross was. Then they assured me that I was going to get the job. I felt great for that moment, but still unsure it was the right thing to do.

A few minutes later, his secretary poked her head into the staff room and said, "Coach Ruel, Coach Ross would like to see you now."

I was feeling a bit nervous, but when I entered his office, his smile and his eyes were beaming with happiness. "Pat, how much did you make at Michigan State?"

"About a hundred and fifteen thousand."

"I just got approval to give you a three-year contract. Two hundred thirty thousand the first year, two forty the second year, two fifty the third year." He paused, and I thought, *Holy moly*. He continued, "I'm doing this because the NFL is a volatile business. Don't tell the other coaches yet because I'm trying to do it for all of them." Then Coach Ross proceeded to tell me that Mr. Ford, who owned the Lions, had bonuses for a winning season, getting into playoffs, and Christmas. He even provided a turkey for Thanksgiving.

Oh my god... I felt like I had won the lotto. I wanted to jump across his desk and hug him, but I forced my game face.

"Do you accept the offer?"

"Yes, but I need to tell my wife and MSU. So it's a tentative acceptance, but I am absolutely coming."

Coach Ross laughed and said, "I totally understand, and we're happy to have you with us."

I was excited beyond belief. My adrenaline was in overdrive, and I missed my exit on the way home. Now came the hard part: breaking a promise I made to President McPherson, telling Coach Williams, telling Marti, and telling my players.

When I arrived home, I told Marti first.

"They want me to sign a three-year contract, and they doubled my salary. What do you think?"

"You can't turn that down."

"I know, I didn't." I laughed, and she punched me in the arm.

Next was Coach Williams.

I called Bobby, and he was happy for me. I was momentarily sad, as he was so genuine and caring. I hated the thought of leaving someone I respected so much.

Now it was time to do the hardest one, the man I made a verbal promise to, the man whose hand I shook. When I called President McPherson's office, his secretary said he had already left for the MSU basketball game.

I drove my car to the football office, parked, and headed over to the Jack Breslin Student Events Center where the Spartan Basketball played their home games. I was thinking, *What am I going to do if McPherson says no?* I chastised myself for making that promise, but it was part of the deal to get Coach Williams the job. My stomach was churning, and my brain was telling me it would work out okay. When I entered the arena, the game was in progress.

I started scanning the seats at mid-court. He should be there. Then I spotted him. That runaway forehead made it easy. Our eyes locked on each other. When he smiled at me, I returned it with a smile of my own. I walked up to his row, and he must have sensed I needed to talk, because he immediately rose and walked toward me. For whatever reason, his smile stopped my queasiness. Meeting on the stairway, he put his hand on my shoulder and said, "Let's go somewhere a bit quieter."

As we approached the lobby, he said, "What's the problem?"

He had good intuition. I took a deep breath and proceeded. "President McPherson, the Detroit Lions called me and asked me to interview for the offensive line job. Coach Williams gave me permission, and the Lions offered me a three-year contract."

The smile disappeared, and his face was stern; I was worried. "What's your salary?" he asked.

"It's two hundred thirty thousand the first year and goes up each year."

His eyes widened. "We can't match that, and you can't turn that down."

"What about my promise to you?"

"I would never deny you an opportunity like that. You're free to go, but we're going to miss you." I could tell he was disappointed.

"Thank you. I loved my time here." I shook his hand. It was easy to understand why he was a well-respected president of the University. He was thoughtful, engaging, and had a big-picture perspective.

I was happy to get all that over with, but my heart now shifted to my players. I hadn't told them yet, and I felt like a traitor for asking them to be committed to our goals at MSU and then leaving.

That night was like a full-court basketball game in my head. One team was running down and slam dunking for the NFL, and the other team was shooting beautiful three-point shots for the Spartans. I couldn't sleep. I had made my decision, but it came with a cost.

I went to the off-season workout early the following morning. I gathered the offensive line together on the turf of the indoor practice facility. The minute I made eye contact with them, my eyes began to fill with liquid emotion—the connection I had with them was coming to the surface. I tried to explain to them my decision to leave. The pain in my heart was enormous. Looking into the eyes of the ten young men, I saw that they were fighting the same fight, tears rolling down their cheeks. As men, we had always been told to hold back our emotions. But we shared too much together, and it was time to share our moment of sadness and vulnerability.

When I walked away, I turned and looked back at the group of young men who made coaching so much fun for me. I was lucky and grateful to have coached such a unique team.

CHAPTER 19

NFL, HERE I COME!

My grandfather, Bampa, a devout Catholic, wanted me to play football at the University of Notre Dame and become a doctor. Instead, I played football at the University of Miami and became an NFL coach.

I'm an NFL coach! I'm an NFL coach! The thought was bouncing in my head like a rubber ball with endless energy as I headed to the Pontiac Silverdome for my first day on the job. Managing an athlete's academics or initiating discipline for bad behavior was a thing of the past. I made it to the pinnacle of the football coaching world, and I couldn't wait to get started.

I spent a few moments getting my office organized before our 9 a.m. offensive staff meeting. The staff meeting room was only a first down (10 yards) from my office. The meeting room looked rather ordinary, but it was all business with whiteboards covering every wall. My eyes quickly locked on a depth chart which ranked players by position.

The coaches and I were all sitting at the staffroom table quietly when Coach Ross walked in and said, "Pat, today is about protections, so let's get you on the board talking about protecting the quarterback."

I was the meat in that stew. I took my spot at the board with a marker in hand and began reviewing five-man, six-man, and seven-man protections and their problem areas in front of the staff. We discussed the merits and the weaknesses of each protection.

Coach Bobby Ross, who sat at the front of the table, looked quite ordinary with his 5'9" frame, graying brown hair, and dress style that yelled fourth grade. He looked like he was dangling in the fifties. But when he talked, his passion and caring was evident. He was engaging and knowledgeable, with a resume to prove it. He had played quarterback at the Virginia Military Institute, guided Georgia Tech to a National Championship in 1990, and then led the San Diego Chargers to a Super Bowl in 1994.

He consistently asked about the techniques that I would be responsible for teaching. I explained each in detail, which made his eyes sparkle like he was looking at a brand-new car.

Sylvester Croom, our offensive coordinator, was asking the kind of questions that told me he knew a lot about offensive line play. It was a joy to be around so much football knowledge and experience.

Halfway through the meeting, Coach Ross excused himself to make a couple of calls and told us to sit tight.

That's when Frank Falks, our running back coach, announced, "I can't wait to be through with the NFL and go coach high school football."

Did I just hear that correctly?

As if on cue, Coach Croom chimed in, "Me too. They've ruined this game."

It was time for me to interject. "What in hell are you guys talking about?" I was stupefied. I felt like my dream was about to be crushed.

"Pat, you'll move every two or three years to a different city. The owners often let the press dictate their moves. The days of Tom Landry and John Wooden are gone," Coach Croom said with conviction.

I knew what he was referring to: The days of giving coaches time to build a winning program were gone. Landry suffered through six losing seasons before the Dallas Cowboys became America's team and won two Super Bowls, and John Wooden, the famed UCLA Basketball coach, coached 27 years at UCLA before he won ten national championships in his final 12 years.

Frank jumped in. "Besides, you won't be a part of your neighborhood barbecues because you won't be there long enough." He giggled like a child telling a secret with his hand up to his mouth, guiding his words to me.

I could feel myself becoming irritated. "Why didn't you tell me this in my interview?"

"Because you still believe in Santa Claus, and we didn't want to be the ones to tell you," Frank said, and they all laughed. I was the new guy, and they were breaking me in to the ways of pro football. I wasn't too worried about what they said; I hoped they were exaggerating.

I was immersing myself into my job and was mapping out our run game when rumors started flying around our office and in the media that Barry Sanders, who retired after the 1998 season, would possibly return. He was only 1,457 yards away from Walter Payton's career rushing title. The rush of excitement that I was feeling was overwhelming. The opportunity to block for one of the most talented running backs ever to play the game had me on cloud nine. But two weeks after my arrival, Barry Sanders squelched that rumor. Can't miss what you never had.

We spent January, February, and March designing football strategies in the morning, evaluating college players, and preparing for the draft in the afternoon.

The NFL draft. Wow. I was now part of it. It's a unique moment for the NFL to have the nation's attention on football in April. Everyone was interested in who their team would pick, and now I was a cog in the draft wheel. The scouts gave each coach a list of players to study. We would give them a grade and between the scouts' grade and coaches' grade, we would then rank them based on need and best availability. It was so much different than college, where I was the scout and the coach. I started evaluating my offensive line personnel to get a vision of what I needed. I gave the staff and scouts my recommendation: I needed a left tackle.

The draft was approaching, and management was secretive about who they would pick in the first round. The secrecy of what each team is thinking is vital for a successful draft. I felt like I was part of a cabal, only I was clueless about which direction we were heading.

On draft day, the draft room was like the stock market floor with people walking in and out with information on sheets of paper that had been accumulated on each of the draftable players. The extensive background checks left very little that we didn't know about a person's character. If a player ended up being a bad character, it was because we chose to ignore it, not because we didn't know. The buzz intensified as we got closer to our pick. The anticipation was building fast, and the energy in the room was electric.

"The Lions are on the clock," they finally announced. We had 15 minutes to decide. The anticipation was nerve-racking—for the club, and especially for the draft eligible players.

It was a consensus that we needed an offensive lineman. We drafted Stockar McDougle, an offensive tackle from Oklahoma with the 20th pick, in the first round. Stockar was 6'6", 340 pounds, and exceptionally strong and powerful. I had given him a top grade. We called him, and to hear his excitement was inspiring. We had just initiated a young player's dream to play in the NFL. It was a magical moment.

As we neared the end of the three-day draft, we started working on free agents. We added Casey Jensen, a center guard from Michigan State. That's right; the young man they called "Bunny" had just become a Detroit Lion. I was all set and couldn't wait to meet with them as a group.

For my first meeting with my offensive line in the off-season, I wanted to cover my philosophy. It was very simple: footwork, fundamentals, and finish. Footwork put you in the right place at the right time, fundamentals was putting you in good leverage positions, and finish would tell the team what type of competitor you were. It was important to me that they knew what the focus of my philosophy was.

The offensive line classroom was the same setup as high school or college: 20 plus desks, a bulletin board, whiteboards for play diagrams, and a list of installs for the day. I was organized and enthusiastic.

I immediately announced, "Ray Roberts and Mike Compton—you are the veterans, and I want you on the front row for your leadership." They looked at me calmly and shook their heads in refusal.

"What's the problem?" I asked. In college, they would have run up to the front row.

"We've been sitting in these seats for four years—we're staying here," Mike said. Was I being tested right out of the blocks? I was pissed. I glanced at all of them. The look on their faces said, "Your move, Coach."

I turned my back on the group and stared at the whiteboard. I didn't want to lose it in my first meeting. Like my dad said, "Before you get angry, take a deep breath and count to ten." They all knew I was processing my anger.

When I turned around, I walked slowly back to where Ray and Mike were sitting. Their heads all turned and watched me like lions scouting their next meal.

"This is now the front of the room," I barked. Then I said, "Now, no one has to change their seat—just turn your desk around, and I'll have them put a whiteboard here."

The young players laughed, and then Ray said, "Wow, really?"

"Yes, really," I replied. College athletes are not paid, and they ran to the front of the room. Now that these players were being paid, they had million-dollar opinions.

Mike said, "Coach Ruel, we'll move."

Ray followed with, "That was a good one, Coach."

I was proud of myself for finding a solution and not creating a problem. In the next couple of weeks, Mike started calling me "college boy" because I was energetic in my coaching. I didn't mind, as I viewed it as a compliment for my style. As we completed OTAs (organized training activity), it was clear we were going to have a good nucleus of players.

Upon completion of our OTAs, we all broke for summer vacation. It was a five-week break. The players would continue to train on their own. Marti, Sabra, and I headed to Florida to experience Disney World and see Marti's parents and my mom, only this time, the vacation was carte blanche, as I was no longer counting dimes. It was a great time to reconnect with family and recharge for the long NFL season which would hit full force in late July.

With the opening of training camp, our strength coach, Bert Hill, said, "There is a phrase that they say about the NFL training camp, Pat. Every day is a holiday because we're always playing (practice), every night is a Saturday night because we're always watching movies (practice film), every meal is a banquet (more food than you can imagine), and every woman is a ten (because you rarely see a woman at training camp)." In the days to come, all of that was verified.

Fall training camp was about physical and mental toughness. It was intense and combative. Rookies trying to make the team were trying too hard, and veterans would snap them back into place. We practiced twice a day. After dinner, we met with players, reviewed the practice film, and did the next day's install. Then, later, the offensive coaches met with Coach Ross to evaluate the day's practice.

At the end of the film evaluation, we all opened our playbooks, which were four inches thick.

"We're going to meet every night and make corrections," Coach Ross announced. "On our first night, Pat will read, and John Misciagna will red mark any mistakes."

These sessions would start at 10:30 p.m. and go to well past midnight.

I read.

Coach Ross said, "Shouldn't that have a comma?"

"Yes, Coach," I replied, and Coach Misciagna red inked it.

We changed the wording on some pages and fixed play diagrams on other pages. After about one week of this, at about 12:30 a.m., I blurted out, "How long have you been doing this, Coach Ross?"

"As long as I can remember, Pat." He flashed me a smile.

"And you still haven't got it right?" I said, laughing.

Coach Ross's smile was gone; he knew I was questioning his method. The other coaches looked at me with astonishment. Like I always do, I was trying to make a point by resorting to humor. It didn't work.

"Pat, this is for me. I want to know everything about our offense, so it's good learning for me. That should be your goal, too."

That was like a dagger in my heart. He politely put me back into place, and I continued to read. His sincerity and attention to detail was who he was.

* * *

Cutting players to get to the 53-man roster was tough. You could see the heartbreak in their eyes. So many childhood dreams of playing in the NFL were crushed as we neared the opening of the season. I said goodbye to Casey Jensen and others. "Come to the office and bring your playbook," was the phrase that all the players prayed they wouldn't hear. It was brutal and emotional. I hated that day.

When the season started, James Stewart, who we signed in free agency from Jacksonville, took over the running back position. I was so pumped up to coach at this level. Professional football was a mix of those who wanted to be the best and were constantly mastering their trade and others who were called JAGs (Just Another Guy) because they lacked the passion to be special. My job was to inspire them to be more. I often said, "Never doubt your abilities, always critique your effort."

We started our season with wins over New Orleans and Washington. Next up was Tampa Bay at home. We gave up seven quarterback sacks. Three were by Warren Sapp, one of the top defensive linemen in the NFL. I was boiling on the sideline as we looked out of sync; it's my job to keep the quarterback clean. We lost 31-10. Studying the game film, I knew I could fix some things. But something else was bothering me: Our quarterback, Charlie Batch, did not make any effort to throw the ball away. He took the sacks and consistently put us in long yardage situations.

This had Coach Croom, our play caller in difficult scenarios, calling plays for second down and 19 or third and 15. I hoped that Coach Jim Zorn, his quarterback coach, was addressing this issue.

The next week, we played Green Bay. We were 3-2 at home, and Charlie Batch ran a play-action boot pass on first down. He was outside the pocket and couldn't locate his receivers. He backed up and took a 9-yard loss. We ended up punting the ball.

I walked over to Charlie and yelled, "Throw the fucking ball away!"

Charlie Sanders, an All-Pro tight end who had been a scout and was now assistant director of pro personnel, grabbed me forcefully and said, "I'll come see you on Monday. Just let it go, Pat."

I was puzzled as to why a basic management skill by a professional quarterback was so hard to execute.

That Monday was a good one. We beat Green Bay 31-24, and we were now 4-2. Charlie Sanders stepped into my office and closed the door. It's never good when they close the door without you telling them to.

I couldn't wait to hear this; my mind raced to my confrontation on the sideline. "What's going on?" I inquired.

"Pat, there's an incentive clause in Batch's contract that gives him a significant bonus if he has a 65% completion percentage, so he's not going to throw the ball away."

"You're fucking joking, aren't you?" This was pro football, but right now it felt like I was back with my junior high buddies on the 15th fairway at the Biltmore. I suddenly realized that the front office was incentivizing contracts without taking account of its effect on winning the game.

What am I going to do about this? I wondered.

When Charlie Sanders left, I had decided I was going to go see Tom Lewand, the executive vice president of the Lions.

I was strolling down to his office, thinking that maybe I shouldn't push this; I had a history of confronting things when I deemed the action wrong—it had often gone sideways. I wondered if it was going too far. When I arrived, his secretary told me to go on in. I stepped into the doorway. I looked directly at Tom, and he looked at me. It was an awkward ten seconds.

"What can I do for you, Pat?" Tom asked.

Is this the right move? To call out management for their stupid incentives? "I've never seen your office, so I thought I would drop by and say hello." I was suddenly in retreat mode. My bold move just turned into soft-serve ice cream.

I didn't know enough about all the inner workings of the front office to even know who I should talk too. My gut was saying, *Don't do it, Pat.* I walked out almost as quickly as I walked in. I proceeded to Coach Zorn's office, and he assured me he had been addressing it.

* * *

It was time to play Tampa Bay for the second time, as they were in our conference. I went into Coach Croom's office and said, "I want to take Tampa Bay's Warren Sapp totally out of the game. I want to run right at him until he can no longer stand up." It was my intention to exhaust Sapp to the point that he had no energy to rush the quarterback. I was still seething from Sapp's first game performance.

Coach Croom liked the idea.

"You better get your boys ready for a barroom brawl, then."

"You got it, Sly." All the coaches called him Sly.

The game started, and we ran the ball for 170 yards—most of it was at Warren Sapp. He actually left the game in the fourth quarter, as he was exhausted by our relentless attack. Mission accomplished—we won 28-14.

As we neared the end of the season, Charlie Batch improved. But the Detroit fans were brutal. Batch attempted to run and was hit hard. He laid motionless on the turf and the Detroit fans cheered. When the medical staff finally got him to his feet, the fans booed. It was a disgusting display of a lack of sportsmanship.

My thoughts jumped back to earlier in the season when Sabra, who was 14 years old, asked, "Dad, can I go see a movie with some friends?"

"What's the name of the movie?" I asked, like a responsible parent.

"It's called *Road Trip*." I grabbed the newspaper and proceeded to look it up. It was R rated.

"Sorry, but you're not going—it has an R rating." I thought she knew better than to ask me about that, but maybe she thought she would give it a shot.

Sabra hoisted her hands to her hips, looked at me with disappointment, and said, "Dad, your games are R rated."

It was true: The Detroit fans were often just plain vulgar. It was okay for a discerning adult, but not the best place for young kids. It's tough for kids who have a parent who's a coach. They have to listen to people calling for their dad or mom to be fired, or slinging whatever other derogatory remarks. It was even worse for them at school, when teachers would call on them and ask what happened on Sunday. College football had a more innocent feel to it, and the fans were a bit more loyal to their team. NFL coaches' kids get a valuable lesson about dealing with criticism.

There was trouble brewing. With seven games to go, Coach Ross announced that he was stepping down because of health issues, but it was the opinion of the coaches that after two and half years of dealing with Bill Keenist, our public relations director, he was worn down. Keenist was constantly meddling with players in a negative fashion. He would tell players that they're not using them correctly, or that they should be playing more, and he was consistently criticizing the coaches. It was like having your own home-grown antagonist on staff. Coach Ross gave everything he had to make the Detroit Lions successful, only to be constantly undermined by Keenist. He had finally had enough.

Gary Moeller, our assistant head coach, took over. He had served as the University of Michigan's head coach from 1990-1994. He had won three Big 10 titles in five years with Michigan. He had the experience and the passion to do a great job.

It was December 24, the day before Christmas. The final game of the season was against the Chicago Bears, who we had beaten on the road and were now playing at home. We were 9-6 and assured a playoff spot if we won. We led 17-13 in the fourth quarter, and we had the ball and were driving.

Coach Croom called a time-out and talked with quarterback Stoney Case, who took over for the injured Charlie Batch. He told him that we were in field goal range, so he shouldn't take a sack and throw it away if the receiver wasn't open. Stoney threw it, and it was intercepted and returned for a 61-yard touchdown for the Bears. They led 20-17. We responded. We drove down and kicked a field goal to notch it up 20-20. With

1:56 remaining in the game, the Bears drove down to our 38-yard line, and that's when Michigan State's Paul Edinger, who was now the Bear's kicker, jogged on the field.

Paul kicked a field goal the year before at the end of regulation, which gave MSU a 37-34 victory over Florida. He was now lining up to kick a 54-yard field goal at the end of the game. I thought, *Lord, please don't let this happen*. When he kicked it, everything seemed to slow down, and the ball was spinning end over end as if it was in a time warp. It finally went over the goal post. My heart sank, as we were no longer looking at playoffs or bonus compensation—our season was over. We lost 23-20. How ironic that the same player who had given me a memorable win over Florida a year earlier was the one to knock us out of the playoffs.

There was no time to rest. Coach Moeller told us to hop on a plane to the East-West college all-star practices in San Francisco to help the scouts with evaluations. We were there two days when we received word to come back to Detroit ASAP. The Lions had hired Matt Millen, a TV sports announcer, as the new general manager, and we were to report back immediately. Matt was a player at Penn State and played pro football with the Raiders, the 49ers, and the Redskins (now called the Commanders).

The Lions wrote up losing incentives, and now they were hiring a talking head with no experience to be the general manager. *What the fuck?* Even a dilettante would know not to hire a TV personality to run an organization. We all wondered if it was Bill Keenist who had used his influence with Bill Ford Jr.

None of us were worried about our jobs because Bill Ford Sr., the owner, liked Coach Moeller so much that he had given him a two-year extension. Plus, I had two years left as well.

Upon returning, it was clear that Millen wanted to clean house. He was acting like a dictator and talking like one. He fired Gary Moeller, despite the two-year extension. Only four of us survived the first round of firings. I was one of them. But I wanted out, too, as I could see and feel the dysfunctionality. It was a lousy culture in the management area, and that was leaking into the coaching area.

Matt summoned me to his office. I placed a quick call to Marti to give her a heads-up that I was going to force my firing. She knew I was unhappy with the organization and wanted out, but she also knew the reality: I was under contract for two more years. I headed to his office, both nervous and excited to get it over with. The culture with Matt Millen, in less than a week, took a horrible turn toward complete dysfunctionality. I knew from talking with administrative employees that he had no idea how to manage people.

I stepped into his huge office, which featured an oak desk big enough to seat eight for dinner. He sat behind it like a king on his throne and waited for me to take a seat. There was no smiling, no cordiality, no handshake.

"You guys are sitting on a Super Bowl team and don't even know it," he bellowed.

"How would you know that? You've never coached a day in your life," I shot back, then added, "We did a great job coaching—we barely missed the playoffs, but that's a long way from the Super Bowl."

"How come you haven't come down to see me?" He glared back at me with his dark eyes. His black hair and square jaw gave him the football look, but like a locomotive off its track, he didn't know what he was doing.

"Well, you were a TV announcer, and now you're a general manager. I was actually waiting for a head coach." *Hopefully it won't be Alex Trebeck*, I thought.

"How come you've already boxed up your office?"

I was a bit perplexed when he failed to respond to my comments. He kept rattling off questions but seemed to ignore my antagonistic responses. "It's called preparation, Matt. You should be preparing as well—you have no experience for this job." Oh, how easy it was for me to talk boldly when I had two years left on my contract.

"You can leave my office, but you're to report for work until I decide on your future." That infuriated me so much that I wanted to punch him in the face, but that for sure would be a $500,000 act of stupidity.

I got up and walked out the same way I entered: no smiling, no cordiality, no handshake.

The next day, the four remaining coaches were surprised when we each found an addendum to our contract on our desk, waiting for signatures. It basically said that we could be fired and the contract terminated if we accepted a call from another team or made a call to another team. In effect, he now was making it impossible for us to answer or use our phones.

I didn't need a lawyer to tell me not to sign that bullshit, but I thought I should go down to see the new guy they hired as senior vice president of business operations and general counsel to get his opinion. His name was Kevin Warren.

I called his office and said, "Do you have a moment to speak with me?"

"Come on down, Coach," Kevin said.

I grabbed the addendum to my contract, and I took it down with me. Unsigned. When I walked into his office, I went right to the point. "Did you write this up?"

"Why are you asking, Pat?"

"Because only a fool would sign this. Would you sign this?" I asked, knowing I was about to find out the true character of Kevin Warren. Would he tell me the truth?

"I'm not allowed to say, Pat."

"Okay, you don't say anything. You never said anything. Just nod your head yes or no: Would you sign this?" I asked.

He smiled at me like we were brothers, and then carefully moved his head from side to side.

It was all I needed to know. "Thank you," I said as I turned to leave. "Kevin, you're good man." I knew I'd just met a man of principle.

Jobs were closing, and I stayed off the phone even though I didn't sign it.

Two week later, the Lions hired Marty Mornhinweg as the new head coach. Marty and I knew each other because I was at the University of Kansas and he was at the University of Missouri, one of our main rivals. The games against each other were offensive shoot-outs, as neither team played good defense.

They interviewed candidates for my job while I sat in my office, refusing to answer my phone. The Lions owed me $500,000, and I wasn't going to lose it.

Coach Mornhinweg popped his head into my office and said, "Pat, I'd like to interview you tomorrow morning." I felt Marty was a good coach but was gambling his career on Matt Millen. I wanted to do the interview because I wanted to show them that I was prepared and good at my job.

The next morning, I was grilled by Marty for about 40 minutes. We knew and respected each other. I could tell Marty liked the interview. He said he was going to talk with Matt.

I stifled my laugh. "Good luck with that. I don't think he likes me."

"What do you mean?"

"I said he was a TV announcer and had no experience for the general manager job."

"That's true, but I don't think you should have told him. I'll be back." Now it was his turn to laugh. When Marty returned, he confirmed what I knew was coming. "I think you did piss him off—he'll only let you coach the tight end position."

I wanted out, but the fact that Millen was telling the head coach who he could hire and who he couldn't was even more disturbing. *Good luck with that, Marty.*

It was mid-February, and the jobs in the NFL had run out. Matt had held me for five weeks. I was tired of being his hostage. Maybe that was Matt's plan from the beginning.

"So, I'm fired? I really don't need to be here anymore."

Marty nodded his head with regret and we shook hands. As I drove away, there was a sense of relief that I would not be part of the Lions' experiment with a TV announcer. I didn't necessarily want a three-year contract, but now I was so thankful for Coach Ross' insistence, because he said it was a volatile profession.

It looked like those coaches who teased me in my first meeting were right. They said I would be moving every two years; how about one year and a winning season to boot? Welcome to the NFL.

CHAPTER 20

MONEY AND NO JOB

My instincts were always commented on by my dad, wife, and friends. I could feel negative energy better than most. I had it as a young boy; I was always the one who got away before the shit hit the fan and was often the one who stumbled onto gold.

After my father died in the plane crash, I had gone to the Bahamas with Marti. She was my girlfriend at the time. We stayed at Paradise Island Casino and Resort. It was my first time playing Blackjack. Call it beginner's luck—I won $200. I was so excited. I cashed out, grabbed Marti, and headed to our room. It was then that I realized I had a five-dollar chip still in my pocket.

"I want to spend this," I said to Marti.

"Hold it 'til tomorrow," she replied.

"Nope, something is telling me to go to that roulette wheel and make a bet."

"Okay, let's do it," she said with reluctance.

I approached the wheel, leaned in, and put it on 16, my father's birthday—August 16th. I waited for the dealer to release the ball. When he did, I had a sudden premonition that I should have put it on 27. I reached over and moved it to Red 27.

"What are you doing? You're going to be mad if it lands on sixteen," Marti said in disbelief.

"Just relax." I stared at the ball as it finally fell, bounced around, then found its resting place.

"Red 27," the dealer barked out.

Marti screamed, "You won! You won!"

I smiled and winked at her like I knew what I was doing. In reality, I don't know why I moved it to 27. My hand reached across the table and pushed it as if someone from another dimension was helping me.

I cashed out my winnings: $175 on a five-dollar bet.

"You have such good instincts," Marti said. But this time, it felt more like divine intervention.

What I realized was there was nothing divine about the Detroit Lions, and my instincts were screaming, "Run." With Keenist, the culture was deteriorating. Now that Millen was thrown in, the franchise was doomed to be put on a respirator. That's what my gut told me. I was glad to escape, but I had no idea where my future was headed.

The NFL and college coaching jobs were gone, and I needed something to do. I quickly turned my focus onto our house. When I was hired by the Lions, we moved to a house that would be an easy commute for both of us. It was located in Farmington Hills. Marti would continue with her job as director of student services. I was about to become a painter, wallpaper remover, plumber, landscaper, electrician, and pain in the ass. I directed all of my motivation into remodeling the house, which drove Marti crazy.

It was mid-March when I got a call from Matt Millen, the general manager, that I had already erased from my mind.

"Pat, I have a really good deal for you," he said, acting like a shill selling swamp land.

"What is it, Matt?" I was sure he could hear the mistrust in my voice.

"We'll give you cash, thirty percent on the dollar."

I laughed as though I'd been offered a ride on the Titanic.

"You owe me almost five hundred thousand, and you're going to give me a hundred sixty-five?"

"It's cash in your hand right now."

I had heard enough. I was shocked that he called and even more stunned by his offer. "Hey, Matt," I fumed, "I'm not Johnny off the Pickle Boat. Don't ever call me again with that bullshit." And then I hung up on him.

Marti, who was standing nearby, shot me a look of frustration. "You just killed yourself from ever working in the NFL again." She didn't like it when I talked disrespectfully.

"Millen is not a reference, he's a bullshitter," I shot back.

I returned to my remodeling project, and I was getting close to the finish line. The wallpaper was gone and the interior of the house was painted. I pulled out all the rugs, ordered the new ones, and hired an independent rug installer.

By mid-April, the house was finished. That's when I got a call from Larry Beightol, who I worked with at Arkansas. He was now the offensive line coach for the Green Bay Packers.

"Pat, I was talking with Mike Sherman, our head coach, about hiring you to work with me. He wants you to call him."

I was astounded that a job opportunity was presenting itself, even if it meant a demotion. I wanted to be back in the game because coaching was what I loved doing. I was processing all this, and what kept flashing in my head was, *Get back on a team, then worry about the cons later.*

There's an intrinsic trait that many of us seem to have, and it's that we desire to be part of a team. I know I have this because I gave up the lonely sport of swimming for football. The constant communication and camaraderie of football was special, and I craved it.

I told Marti, and she was excited because she didn't want any more projects in the house. I called Coach Sherman, as directed, and expected the interview process to be set up. He surprised me when he said, "There's no need to interview. I just want your loyalty and commitment to me."

I assured him I would give him those things. I was filled with gratitude that he wanted me to be part of the Green Bay Packers.

I was back on a team, but I was leaving my other team... my family. Sabra would remain in school, and Marti would continue with her job at Michigan State. It was tough leaving Marti and Sabra behind, but I was thinking this would be a temporary assignment.

I was to report just after the draft in early May. I had a few days to get organized, and I was on my way.

Bampa, my grandfather, was born in Green Bay. He would constantly hint that maybe I would play for them someday. If only he could have witnessed his grandson as a Packers coach.

I drove to Green Bay and rented a New-York-style apartment that sat above an architectural firm. The people of Green Bay are all on the Packers team—they own the team. It's the only fan-owned, non-profit team in professional sports. The culture is built by the fans and maintained by the administration and coaches.

My first task in Green Bay was to determine how I was going to be compensated. The Packers had made me an offer, but I told them I was under contract with the Lions, and I was more interested in having them pay the greater part of my salary as punishment for treating me so poorly. I just wanted a small salary and benefits, and then I'd let the Detroit contract cover the rest. They were happy to oblige, and I threw myself into my new role as assistant offensive line coach.

I was excited to get started. Coach Beightol (Beck) had taught me a lot while at Arkansas. I jumped into learning new terminology. We were in OTAs (organized training activities) and started coaching the players and getting them ready for the next season.

The culture was so different, as everyone was working with a team attitude and the front office was well run by Bob Harlan, the chairman/CEO and president. I could feel the magic of the Green Bay franchise. The fans were loyal to their team as a mother is loyal to her family. It is the uniqueness of that relationship that sets it apart from any professional sports team.

It was late July, and training camp was underway. We were in the middle of a practice when Mike Flannigan, our center, said, "Hey, Coach, there's a hot chick with your name on a sign next to the fence."

The players always liked to play jokes, and I wasn't going to fall for it. I refused to look. "Paying attention to practice would be a good idea," I retorted.

Just then, our left tackle, Chad Clifton, said, "Coach, you have to give me her number."

"Good try, Chad." Their efforts were making me think I should peak, but I didn't.

Within a few minutes, Brett Favre came over and said, "Hey, Pat, who is the babe with your name on a sign?"

That's it—I finally turned to see the babe. She was a frail woman in her eighties with blue-gray hair and a dress that looked like a garden of flowers. She was holding a sign that was almost as big as her, and on it was my name, Golden Pat Ruel, in green block letters. She looked happy and excited as she flashed me a smile. I acknowledged her, then went back to coaching. After practice, I immediately went over to her and introduced myself.

"My name is Margaret Vishnevsky," she said. "I'm your third cousin, and I have your genealogy tree for you."

I was completely engrossed as she took me through my family tree. I was 50 years old, and I had no idea about my family background.

"Your great grandfather was John Ruel, who came to America from Sligo, Ireland with his girlfriend, Mary Golden, in the eighteen-seventies," she explained. "They were giving away land in Wisconsin as part of the Homestead Act. They eventually married and named their first child Golden Ruel."

"So that's how I got my name."

I knew it was a family name because they said I was Golden Pat Ruel the Third. I had no idea of the origins. Now I knew how my name came about. It was exciting to know my lineage. How amazing that I took a job in Green Bay, where my grandfather was born, and met Margaret, who revealed my family history. I was so grateful to have met her. It was like I had found treasure. Before we parted ways, she gave me some pictures of my relatives in Sligo.

When I joined the players at lunch an hour later, they had their mocking shoes on: "How many tickets does your girlfriend need?"

I laughed. "She told me about my family tree all the way back to the eighteen hundreds in Ireland, and she also gave me pictures from Ireland of people I was related to but have never met." Their mocking turned to envy, as some of the players were starting to talk about their family background and how little they knew.

* * *

We opened the 2001 season with the Detroit Lions, and we beat them 28-6. The taste of revenge was bittersweet. I enjoyed the fourth quarter like a child eating an ice cream cone on hot day. It tasted so good, and I was wearing it. After the game, though, I felt bad for the players in that culture. I had escaped, and they were still trapped there.

Next up was the New York Giants. It was a Tuesday night, on the players' day off. I was evaluating the Giants defense when, down the hall, Head of Security Jerry Parins yelled, "Coach Ruel, a plane just hit the World Trade Center."

"It was probably a pilot who passed out or had a heart attack," I shouted back.

"You should see this," Jerry responded. His voice was anxious, which was not like him.

"I'll come down in a minute." Walking the 20 feet to his office, I thought, *I really don't have time for this.* As I entered, he pointed to the TV. I was puzzled about why a plane would hit a building unless it was compromised and no longer airworthy. I had been trained as a pilot by my dad and a personal instructor, and I knew it was part of a pilot's code to always set a plane down away from people.

"I need to go back to work," I declared and headed back to my office. I sat down and was looking at the Giants defensive fronts, coverages, and pressures (blitz package).

"Coach Ruel, another plane just hit the other tower!" he bellowed.

This time, I jumped out of my seat and away from my desk. I ran down to see a second building engulfed in smoke. "This looks intentional, Jerry."

"No kidding. This is bad situation." I was wondering who was attacking our country. My thoughts immediately went to my family. Suddenly, I was regretting going to Green Bay. I called Marti and told her what she already knew. I was concerned about us being apart and not being able to protect them.

"We don't know what's going on, but if it gets worse, I want you and Sabra to drive to Green Bay." I said my goodbyes to Marti and immediately dialed my good friend, Jeff Marron, who worked in Manhattan near the World Trade Center. He had inquired about getting tickets for the Giants game, but now my concern was for his well-being.

"Jeff, this is Pat," I said, relieved that he answered the phone. I could hear people running and talking in the background.

"Everyone is trying to get out of the city. I'm walking with thousands of people trying to get out of here."

"I just wanted to make sure you were okay."

"I am, and I need to get back to my family."

I was in the serenity of Green Bay, while he was in the middle of a crisis. I could feel the panic in his voice as I envisioned him fighting to get back to his family.

I was so concerned about my call with Jeff that I immediately called Marti back.

"Hey, I don't want you to wait," I blurted as soon as I heard her voice. "Get what you need together. All air travel has been shut down, so start plans to drive to Green Bay now. I want you to leave first thing tomorrow."

The next day, Marti and Sabra finally arrived in Green Bay after an eight-hour drive. I was feeling much better now that we were together. All was good for now, but I feared our world would never be the same.

The NFL cancelled all the games that week and moved them to the end of the season. We all regrouped as a team and put our focus back on our games. The fans' love for their Packers and their country was evident as we marched through the schedule and beat the Giants in the last game to finish 12-4. We beat the 49ers in the wild card and then lost to the St. Louis Rams, who went on to the Super Bowl and lost to the New England Patriots.

After the playoffs, Bob Harlan walked into my office and handed me a bonus check for participation in the playoffs.

"Pat, I'm supposed to send this to the Lions to offset your contract, but after seeing what they are doing to you, I think you need some leverage," he explained.

Shortly after the season started, the Detroit Lions stopped paying me; I had heard through my lawyer that they were pissed that I went to a team in the same conference and about the deal I made with my salary in my effort to stick it to them. I was guilty of antagonizing Matt Millen, which may have been his motivation, but they had violated my contract.

I reached out to shake Bob's hand. "Thank you, Mr. Harlan, I appreciate your caring." It was so evident that the culture and character at Green Bay was superior to that of Detroit.

The leverage worked, because in February the Lions started paying me again. I received a lump sum for the back pay and a demand that I turn over my playoff money.

I decided I would play the Lions' game. I called my attorney and said, "Tell them they can have their money in six months, the same amount of time that they refused to pay me."

My relationship with the Lions' Matt Millen was cold as a Green Bay winter, which I was now looking to escape. I was quietly looking for another opportunity to oversee the offensive line. I loved what I was doing, but I wanted more responsibility.

Out of the blue, I received a call from the Cowboys' head coach, Dave Campo, who wanted me to interview for their offensive job. I flew to Dallas and was taken to Coach Campo's house. I was immediately taken back by how modest his house was, being a NFL head coach. It seemed to reflect his down-to-earth personality. I instantly liked him. Jerry Jones, the owner of the Cowboys, sat in on my interview. He was arrogant and charismatic. The interview lasted about an hour.

Then Jerry Jones asked me to ride over with him to his office in the football facility. While in the car, he asked, "What would you do if you had nothing—no money and no job?"

Was he looking for a creative solution, or was this a trick question? "Maybe you should tell me first so that I understand the purpose of the question?" I proposed.

He smiled at me like he knew I would refer back to him. "I would borrow some money from a friend to buy a really good suit, then I would get an expensive briefcase, and I would walk in and sell myself." He spoke with this unbelievable air of confidence that made me wonder how much of it was real.

"What's in the briefcase, Mr. Jones?"

"Nothing, Pat. It's about perception."

I laughed. "Okay, I get it, very clever." I was thinking that the next time a man in a fancy suit and expensive briefcase tried to sell me something, I was going to ask him to open his briefcase.

When we got to his office, he asked, "What do you want?"

I was prepared for this question. "A three-year contract would protect my daughter Sabra's high school career, and I don't need to be the highest paid. Somewhere in the middle is okay." I was not as interested in the amount of compensation as I was about ensuring my daughter could enjoy her high school experience. I think my priorities caught him off guard because he stared at me for about 15 seconds without speaking.

"I don't fire really good assistant coaches—I fire head coaches and coordinators." He smiled and I laughed, knowing he missed my point. On top of that, I was concerned that he didn't even have an offensive coordinator yet.

It was time for me to ask, "Don't you think you should hire an offensive coordinator first?"

"We will, and your hiring will be subject to his approval, but we like you."

"Who are you talking to?" I asked.

"We are in negotiation with Bruce Coslett." Oh, boy—the guy who was head coach of the NY Jets, who I accepted an offer from then turned down and ruined his vacation. *That Bruce Coslett.*

"Okay, so I'm on hold till you get a coordinator?"

"Yes, but it will happen in the next day or two." I was not too optimistic that this would work out if they hired Coslett.

Coach Campo called me as I was headed back to the airport. "Can you call Coslett and iron things out?" he asked. I could hear from the tone in his voice that he wanted me on his staff. But all I could think of was how Coslett lost it on the phone with me.

"No, I think he should get someone else," I replied. My instincts were telling me to let this go.

* * *

I threw myself back into my job with the Packers. We entered the off-season with a good feeling about our team. Mike Sherman, our head coach, was organized and cerebral. He was built like an offensive lineman: big-boned and thick. His sandy blonde hair gave him a boyish look. He always seemed to be worried that coaches or players would take advantage of his laid-back approach.

On one occasion, he became upset when a couple of coaches returned from their lunch time workout ten minutes late. The next morning, we all found a memo on our desks that stated we only got an hour of activity at lunch, and we could not go home until 5 p.m.

We worked 70-80 hours a week during the season, and now he was making sure no one cheated on our out-of-season hours. *Who does he think isn't doing their work?* The assistant coaches laughed, as it seemed he wanted to micromanage our every minute.

Our tight end coach, Jeff Jagodzinski, threw some humor on it. When 5 p.m. came, he would turn up the volume on his speakers and sound a factory whistle, signaling we were now free to go home. Oddly, most of the coaches didn't leave until six or seven.

Despite his quirks, Coach Sherman was good at team building. One day near the end of our off-season training, he announced to the team, "We're not practicing today. We're going bowling." We loaded the buses, and we drove right by the bowling alley and continued out of town to a paintball facility. We were all excited. Immediately, the teams were set: offense versus defense.

Those who had sweatshirts on were naturally protected from the sting of being shot because of the thickness of the material. Some players had just their workout T-shirts. I jumped into the middle of the action. I wasn't going to miss out on the fun. I put myself in a position to ambush some defensive players. When my location was discovered, the defensive line charged me and shot me many times at close range. They were getting a big laugh out of watching me squirm like a disoriented snake on the ground. By the time we boarded the bus, I was covered in welts, but I loved every minute of it.

As we drove back to the football facility, I sat next to Kabeer Gbaja-Biamila, a defensive end who was a pass rush specialist.

"Let's see your wounds, Coach," he insisted.

I lifted my shirt to reveal my battle scars.

Kabeer said, "Coach, look at us," as he raised his shirt as well. "If this was a real war, we would be dead." I was taken aback by his sincere observation. He then added, "I don't want to fight in a war." It was an uneasy and contemplative moment. I admired his introspection.

Regardless of our serious moment, it was a fun day.

* * *

Expectations for the upcoming season were high as we kicked off our training camp in 2002 in late July. We were in an offensive meeting. I sat in the back of the room. Tom Rossley, our offensive coordinator, was reviewing install, and we all had our playbooks open. Brett Favre, who was sitting next to me on the aisle, handed me his open playbook. Tucked inside was a New York Times crossword puzzle.

"Pat, what is six down?" he whispered.

"Brett, you might want to pay attention," I whispered back.

"Pat, I've run the same offense for ten years. I probably know it better than the coaches," he replied with a bit of mockery. He had a point. Not only did he know it, but he also executed it daily.

We finished 12-4 for the second season in a row. This time, we were knocked out in the first round of the playoffs in Green Bay by Atlanta, 27-7. It was a pathetic ending to a great season.

With the season over, it was time for me to move on. I was feeling anxious about my future. I needed to get my family back together.

I went to the Senior Bowl in Mobile, Alabama to evaluate talent for the Packers, but while there, I was looking for an offensive line job and networking. I ran into Dave Campo. Jerry Jones had fired him, Coslett, and most of the staff.

Dave said, "You're lucky, Pat. I just went through hell dealing with Coslett."

I believe that was Jerry's hire, not Dave Campo's. That's what's wrong with professional sports. Often, there are owners who meddle without understanding the chemistry, the culture, and the team's needs.

While at the Senior Bowl, I let it be known that I was interested in the Buffalo Bills offensive line job. It didn't take long for them to contact me. They immediately set up an interview. I sat down with Greg Williams, who was the Buffalo head coach. He was very engaging. It turned out he grew up in Kansas City, Missouri and had followed my career at the University of Kansas.

After our talk, he turned me over to Kevin Gilbride, the offensive coordinator. I could tell Kevin was intelligent and had a natural way about himself. He was asking lots of football questions, but in the later part of my interview, he focused on player management. He created example problem situations between coaches and players and wanted me to tell him how I would handle it. My answers revolved around relationship and recruiting.

He must have liked what he heard, because later that day Kevin called and said, "We liked your interview, and we're offering you the job."

I was feeling like I could levitate. My being suddenly felt electric. I'd gotten what I wanted. "I'm so excited and looking forward to being part of the Buffalo Bills. Thanks, Kevin."

It was as if the stars were lining up in my favor. Shortly after I returned to Green Bay to pack up my belongings, the NFL called and wanted to arbitrate the contract dispute with the Lions. I was still holding onto my payoff check for bargaining power and was more than happy to get that ordeal over with, but it looked like a Tyrannosaurus Rex (NFL) on one side, hungry Lions on the other, and me standing in the middle.

I refused to sign an arbitration agreement as another way of maintaining some leverage. When my lawyer reviewed all of Millen's antics with the NFL arbitrator, he chastised the Lions and sided with us. They told me to give Detroit ten thousand dollars of the fifty thousand earned in playoff money.

"Pay your lawyer and keep the rest," he advised.

I will always be indebted to the NFL for treating me fairly and understanding what Millen put me through.

I was shuffling off to Buffalo.

CHAPTER 21

YOU CAN'T CAPTURE ME

The Buffalo Bills was my third NFL team in four years. Wow, I felt a bit like I was on an NFL cruise! Our ship was on the move. Marti had given up discussing the next move; she knew that ships in the harbor were safe, but that's not what ships were designed for.

After two years of being apart, I was determined to do whatever I could to get our family back together. We bought a 5,000-square-foot house that sat on three quarters of an acre. It was a suburb of Buffalo, New York called Orchard Park. It was an upscale neighborhood with beautifully landscaped yards. Ours bumped up to a forest which often entertained us with deer. It was five miles from the stadium and football offices because my biggest concern was to be close to work. The 16- to 18-hour days should never include 30-minute commutes.

I hoped that the house would lure Marti to find a job in Buffalo. But over the years, I had asked her to give up several high-powered positions, including the assistant vice chancellor job at Kansas. I knew that we didn't need the extra money from her salary. Her concern was that she couldn't keep quitting jobs.

"It's not the right way to build a resume," she stressed.

When my dad died at 49, I'd always had a fear of what would happen if I died—would my family be okay? I had encouraged Marti to get her master's and then her doctorate. My motivation was that she would have a career and the ability to carry on without me. Besides, what I loved about her was the fact that she had no borders; she was an intelligent and independent woman, though it sometimes felt like a catch-22 situation. We gave up everyday companionship to ensure our family's future, which caused a strain on our relationship.

She quickly wanted to see if it was feasible to keep her job at Michigan State. She got out a map. It was 320 miles. She determined that it was all major highway and, driving 70 mph, she could cut through Canada and make it in five hours. She loved her job. She would leave at 4 a.m. on Monday and return on Friday just in time for dinner. That wasn't what I had pictured, but I understood. We were working hard to protect our future, but, in retrospect, living in the moment might have been a bit more fun.

Sabra, who was now 16, stayed with me and was enrolled at Orchard Park High School. I secured a two-year contract to make sure she would finish there. After several moves, Sabra had to adjust and make new friends. We had moved quite a bit in my younger years, and she seemed to adjust as easily as I had. It caused her to grow up fast. Sabra was mature way beyond her age.

Buffalo was a blue-collar town where gray skies prevailed, and sunshine was like finding a rare gem. The highlight was the Niagara Falls, but the best view was from the Canadian side.

As always, I was anxious to get started with my new job. Head Coach Gregg Williams gave Kevin Gilbride, the offensive coordinator, the opportunity to choose his offensive line coach. I was glad he picked me; we seemed to have a natural connection. He reminded me of my dad, in that he was very intelligent and a big-picture thinker.

On my first day at the office, I finally asked the question that I had been pondering since my interview: "Who were you talking about when you asked all those player management questions?"

"I was talking about a really good player, Ruben Brown." I knew he was All-Pro and played left guard.

"What's his issue?" I asked.

Kevin sighed. I could hear the exasperation in his voice. "He's an emotional player. He can be very disruptive by questioning play calls and arguing with coaches. We need him to be more team-oriented. Even players are not happy with him."

I knew I was the right guy for the job because I was good at developing connections with people. "I'll recruit him," I assured Kevin. "I'll take him to lunch and dinner and help him understand his role and leadership capabilities. He needs to trust me and realize that we have his best interest in mind."

"That sounds good," Kevin replied.

That's exactly what I did. Ruben and I connected really well, but it was off-season, and there was no pressure.

Buffalo the year before, under Kevin Gilbride's direction, had broken most of the offensive records set by the Buffalo Super Bowl teams in the early 90s. I was supercharged to get started and to be part of the next step for this high-powered offense, but trouble was on the horizon.

After going 8-8 the year before, Tom Donohoe, the general manager, wanted to strengthen the defense. The defense was the team's weakness. His answer was to use offensive players in trades to beef up the defense. The off-season was slowly becoming a dismantling of the offense. We eventually lost four starters through trades and free agency.

I was shocked at the strategy, so I walked into Kevin's office and said, "You and Saddam Hussein are in the same boat—they're taking away your weapons of mass destruction." I laughed, and Kevin shook his head.

We both knew that you don't destroy the strongest part of your team to fix the weakest part. They traded Peerless Price, an All-Pro receiver who had 1,252 yards and nine touchdowns with Buffalo, to Atlanta for a first-round pick.

When draft day came, we were excited to see who the first-round pick would be. We all knew that they would be the key to the re-strengthening of our offense. Buffalo's GM, Tom Donohoe, chose Willis McGahee, a running back from the University of Miami. I wondered if he had consulted the head coach. It was a controversial pick because McGahee had a total knee reconstruction from an injury in the Fiesta Bowl in his final collegiate game. He was slated for rounds four or five by most of the teams because of a 12- to 16-month rehabilitation.

When the announcement was made, Dan Neal, our tight end coach, leaned forward and whispered in my ear, "We just got fired." I was trying to process what he said, and like a giant light bulb had suddenly illuminated, I understood. The first-round draft picks are reserved for touchdown makers or touchdown stoppers, not injured players in rehab.

Bill Parcels, the famous coach of the New York Giants, once said in an interview, "If they want you to cook the dinner, at least they ought to let you shop for some of the groceries." It was another example of how things don't function properly when the management and the coaches are in different universes.

The fans were pumped up going into 2003 because it appeared the problem on defense was solved. We beat the Super Bowl champs, the New England Patriots, 31-0 in our opener. We were able to patch up our offense, but things quickly turned ugly when we lost Eric Moulds, our remaining All-Pro receiver, and Travis Henry, our best running back, to injuries. We now had Drew Bledsoe, a quarterback who had poor mobility but was an extraordinary passer, with no receivers and no running back. It reminded me of my first year at Kansas, when our players were slow and slower. We were now a gun without ammo.

I had made it a habit to jog to the stadium when we played home games. We were 2-1, and the fans cheered me as I jogged through the tailgaters. When we hit mid-season, we were 4-4, and the tailgaters were throwing chicken bones at me. I went one more week, and that time it was potato salad, half-eaten bratwursts, and more chicken bones. I feared what was next—a beer bottle, hot coals, or a hub cap. I started leaving five hours before the game to bypass the hit-the-coach game.

Our defense was playing well, but we were losing games. The injuries and the decision to replace four starters with a first rounder who had to go to rehab for 16 months virtually devastated our record-breaking offense.

Despite the losses, everyone was praising me for the job I did with Ruben Brown, because his attitude seemed much better, and he was being a better teammate. But when we reached the spot where we were mathematically out of the playoffs, it all began to unravel. It started when Ruben attacked

Kevin Gilbride on his radio show, calling for him to be fired. I wasn't aware of it, but it was verified by administrative and player personnel.

I called him to my office. "Why would you do that?" I asked. I thought he was better, but this was a bad sign.

"Whose side are you on?" he shot back.

"Rube, there are no sides. We're all on the same team." I looked at him with pleading eyes. He was clearly angry. "Let's talk about this more after practice," I offered.

He stood up abruptly. "I'm through talking." His anger was heating up. I knew his behavior pattern. He would carry this anger all day. I was thinking I might need to handle him with kid gloves.

At the offensive line meeting, I announced I wanted us to hurry out to the practice field to review some pressures.

Ruben barked, "Why do we have to hurry for you?"

Oh boy, here we go. "Rube, because we want to be prepared, and we want to beat the Dolphins."

"Fuck you. I'm not going to listen to your bullshit." Rube had lost control of his emotions.

I was about to lose mine. I started walking back to his table. When I got face-to-face with him, our eyes were locked on each other. "You're going to do as I ask for the team."

Rube stood up and flipped the table. Playbooks and pencils went flying everywhere. I was about to make a bad mistake, and thank God, the players knew it. I stepped closer to him, and we were nose-to-nose when the rest of the offensive line grabbed both of us. I was hoping they were holding him good, because I knew it would mean a trip to Buffalo General

Hospital for me. I was no match for his 6'3", 300-pound, 30-year-old, six-time All-Pro frame.

Trey Teague, one of my favorite players, said, "Coach, I don't think you want any of that. You're a thirty-point underdog." His humor dropped the temperature in the room and somewhat diffused the situation.

I didn't want any fallout from this, so I announced, "What happens in this room stays in this room."

The offensive line nodded in agreement. Just then, Sam Adams, a defensive lineman, blurted out from across the hall, "We heard the whole thing, Pat." The defensive line room broke out in laughter.

I sensed more trouble brewing, as Rube was pissed and sulking. When we got to pass rush period, Rube laid on the ground, refusing to take his turn. I was going to let it go, but his disrespect for the team—and then me—in the meeting room was more than I could take.

"Get off the damn ground, and get off this field." I was in no mood to placate his behavior.

"Fuck you, Pat," he yelled as he started to leave the field.

"That's beautiful, Rube," I called after him. "Just keep walking and get off the fucking field."

He continued his rant all the way into the locker room, and once there, he continued his raving. The whole team could hear it because the indoor practice facility magnified the sound, but at that point no one really cared.

As we went to team period, several players came up to me and praised me.

"Coach, that needed to be done. You're the only coach in three years that was willing to confront him."

It was then that I realized just how much of a virus he had become. They hired me to handle him so that he wouldn't be disruptive. I failed because I didn't have the vision to see how much losing affected him, how he internalized his pain, and how his emotional outbursts were toxic. He had become a raging Buffalo.

When you're coaching a landmine, it's key to disarm it and not set it off. The explosion that day was the talk of the team. We were not focused on our game. I recommended that we not play him, but I was ignored until he showed up late for practice the next week, and Coach Williams had also had enough. We left his disruptive behavior at home.

Before our final game, there was talk that Gregg Williams would be fired. It infuriated me that he was another victim of lousy decisions by management. Gregg was an excellent head coach and developed a good culture, but the dismantling of the offense followed by injuries proved to be our downfall.

I hated the dysfunctionality of pro football. We had owners who continually offered their sacred opinions, general managers whose opinions were not in line with the head coach, player personnel who thought the players were not being used correctly, and a lot of people who never played the game and didn't understand the importance of having a team attitude and a good culture. When it's all working together, it's a beautiful thing, but when it's not, there is no joy in Uglyville.

Uglyville was magnified in our last game versus the New England Patriots. There was a verbal altercation between Coach Krumrie and Sam Adams, his defensive tackle. Sam was due a million-dollar bonus if he participated in a certain percentage of plays for the year. He needed about ten plays to get his bonus. Management wanted him out. We were losing 31-0, the same score we beat them by in our first game of the season. Sam, who was a run defender and not used in pass rush situations, refused get off the field. Coach Williams had to go on the field to get him. Imagine if we were in a tight ball game and a player refused to come out because of a million-dollar bonus. It always seemed that losing organizations lacked vision when making their decisions.

The loss to New England resulted in a dismal 6-10 record. The following morning, I walked into Coach Williams's office and offered myself up as a sacrificial lamb. I hoped that in doing so, it might save his job.

"Fire me and blame it all on me." I was sincere, but in the same realm, I wanted out because it seemed as though Gregg had no control over his destiny. We were like a sailboat with no wind, just floating aimlessly in a vast ocean.

Gregg looked at me in disbelief as he leaned back in his chair. "No way. Why would I do that?"

"It might save you and the staff from getting fired," I replied. It was uncomfortably quiet as I stood there and he sat at his desk. "Gregg, I have another year left on my contract. I'll be fine, and I have good references. I'll survive."

With a face that revealed his dismay and defiance, Gregg leaned forward. "I said, I'm not doing that."

I appreciated his integrity, but it was time to say what I really wanted to say. "Gregg, this place is dysfunctional. Drafting a severely injured player in the first round? What the fuck?"

Gregg nodded affirmation. "I know, and I was so pissed that day that I wanted to fight somebody." It was just as I thought; no coach would do that to his team.

The next day, they fired Coach Williams and the staff.

I realized that the NFL was not as pure as I thought. Coaches were often at the mercy of administrative decisions which had nothing to do with winning or building a good culture. On the other hand, coaches were often their own worst enemies, as we made bad decisions as a result of the high-stakes pressure or the inability to maintain our core principals. In any case, the end result was failure. I witnessed it firsthand with the Detroit Lions, and now the Buffalo Bills.

* * *

I was now a stay-at-home dad. Marti continued commuting back and forth. I was very proud of her and the sacrifices she made. She was a wonderful mother as well. Sabra was a straight-A student.

"You should make a C in one of your classes. Then I would know for sure that I'm your dad," I told her. We laughed. She had my sense of humor, and she was very intelligent, like her mom.

We grew closer as we worked out together and had wonderful father-daughter talks. She was articulate, a clear thinker, and had the social skills of a seasoned adult.

Once again, I was a coach without a football team. I began reflecting about how much time and effort goes into a professional football season. It had been our open week that fell on Halloween, which seemed to exemplify what it was to be a pro coach. Because of my profession, I never celebrated or took part in Labor Day, Halloween, or December 5th, my birthday. Christmas and Thanksgiving were four-hour breaks.

But as luck would have it, Halloween had fallen on our bye week that season. I went all out. I put up Halloween decorations and had speakers in the bushes playing sounds of crickets, owls, and squeaky doors. I put on a scary mask and had plenty of candy on hand. As the trick-or-treaters came by, I was having a bit of fun. One of my neighbors came by with his young son, who had a football and wanted me to autograph it.

His father said, "Don't ask Coach to sign your ball—he won't be here long enough." I thought his dad was an asshole for saying that.

The young boy pulled back the ball with a sad face and said, "Thank you for the candy."

"You're welcome." I extended my hand and shook his son's hand, then reached to shake his father's hand, but he didn't extend his.

"Like I said," he began as he turned to leave, "You won't be here long enough."

I was right—he was an asshole. At that moment, I felt like I didn't exist. I wasn't a friend or a neighbor, just a passerby.

Five minutes later, the doorbell rang again. It was the same father. *I bet he wants to shake my hand and apologize*, I thought. I took off my mask and opened the door.

He said, "My son really wanted your autograph."

I smiled, and said, "No problem."

He handed me the football and a pen to sign. I signed it and handed it back. He didn't say thank you, just turned and walked away.

I came to Buffalo a stranger and would leave a stranger.

CHAPTER 22

SHUFFLING OUT OF BUFFALO

Those Detroit Lions coaches were right about being an NFL coach. It meant moving every two years to a different city, not knowing your neighbors, and not being part of the community. I had something to add: Don't unpack.

"There's nothing to remodel in this house," Marti said as she reflected on the last time I was fired. She was correct. The biggest project was its three-quarters of an acre yard that needed constant attention. Although, if it was covered in snow—which was December through March—I was free from the manicuring and landscaping.

I laughed. "I know. I'm going to work on my offensive line manual, workout, and watch Sabra play volleyball." I was ready for family time and more one-on-one time with Sabra. I saw so much of me in her.

When Sabra was four years old, I was flipping through the channels with the remote when she announced, "Look, Dad, punchers." I wondered where she got the term "punchers."

"No, Sabra, those are wrestlers." *Fake wrestlers,* I thought. "You want me to teach you how to wrestle?" I asked.

She didn't say a word, just gave me the go-ahead nod. I sat down on the living room floor. I told her to get on the other side of the room. "When I put my hands up, you run and jump on me," I instructed. I looked at her adorable face. I loved her curiosity.

"You ready?" I threw my hands up, and she charged me like a young cub going after her first meal. I caught her, raised her over my head, and then quickly brought her down, gently setting her on the carpet. She started crying, as the suddenness of the act had startled her.

I leaned over, seeing her tears, and said, "Don't ever let your opponent know you're hurt."

Marti yelled from the kitchen, "Don't be rough with her! She's a girl, and she doesn't understand a word of what you said."

I picked her up, comforted her, and said, "Daddy didn't mean to make you cry. We'll try wrestling again when you get older."

Less than a month went by before Sabra asked, "Can we wrestle now?"

"Of course, we can," I replied. Only this time I wasn't going to upset her. I sat down on the floor, and she got on the other side of the room. I raised my hands, and she charged me without any hesitation and jumped onto me. As I caught her, my back slammed into the pointed corner of our coffee table.

I was suddenly gasping and moaning for air. I laid there in momentary agony.

Sabra put her hand on my shoulder and locked her eyes on mine. "Dad, never let your opponent know you're hurt."

"Did you hear that?" I called out to Marti, still gasping for air.

Amazed, she responded, "Yes, I did… and are you okay?"

"Yes, I am," I replied. I was a proud daddy whose back hurt and whose breathing was back to normal. It was a football lesson I had taught my daughter and of which she, in turn, reminded me. Although a bit inappropriate, it demonstrated to me how remarkable those young brains can be.

I was looking forward to being more involved in her life. I wanted to be a mentor and advisor like my dad was to me. This was a perfect time for Sabra and me to have those father-daughter talks that centered around her academics, volleyball, life lessons, and sometimes boys. The adversity of getting fired turned into a beautiful opportunity to be a great father.

It was early March and Sabra had returned from school with a look of sadness.

"Are you okay?" I asked.

"We have a new volleyball coach," she said, "And he demoted me to second team. Dad, I was a starter all last year." I could see and feel her anguish.

"So, what are you going to do?"

"You need to talk to him."

That was not the answer I was hoping for. I looked at our beautiful 17-year-old daughter, who was wanting to be tall like her dad but was 5'6", like her mom. She had beautiful blonde hair and blue eyes and a smile that was so genuine. Only that smile had disappeared. It was time for me to pass on a life lesson my dad taught me.

"No, I won't talk to your coach. You need to show him why you should be a starter by doing your drills better than anyone and exhibiting great effort. Go be a great competitor. I have complete confidence that you're capable of doing that."

That was not the answer she was hoping for, but I could see in her eyes she trusted me. Each day, I would look at her face when she got home from school to determine her state of mind. She had the look that said, "I'm on a mission."

Then, about ten days from the time we had our talk, Sabra stepped into my home office with a smile that shined bright like a spiritual light illuminating from her inner soul. I knew before she said anything she had won her job back.

"Dad, guess what?" she started.

"You got a boyfriend?" I asked.

"No boyfriend."

"I know you're not running away from home because you have a car and the best parents ever."

She smiled. "I'm back as the starter on the volleyball team."

"Oh my god! I don't have to talk to the coach! How could you possibly have done this without me?" I loved teasing her because she could fire back with something witty.

Like always, she didn't disappoint. "It was easy," she laughed. "I got advice from an out-of-work coach."

I smiled back. "I'm so proud of you." I wondered if what I felt that moment was the same thing my dad felt when I made him proud. Such a wonderful emotion.

I started to take Sabra to the Buffalo Athletic Club to help her get physically stronger, but it turned into a disaster in mid-April when I decided to show my daughter just how strong her dad was getting. While demonstrating my strength gains, I tore the labrum in both shoulders and the rotator cuff in my right shoulder. I realized soon after that I could no longer lift with my arms and shoulders.

Instead, I went to the leg press machine to show Sabra how much I could press. I put 480 pounds on the leg press and proceeded to sprain my right knee. I went home a physical wreck. The NFL had a term for my current situation; I was on the PUP list (physically unable to perform). I needed my shoulders surgically fixed. I couldn't raise my arms above my chest. My knee would mend in time.

With two damaged shoulders and a sprained knee, my workouts grinded to a halt. Instead, I threw myself into rehab.

It was late April, and the NFL draft was getting underway. I thought it was necessary to study the offensive line picks because I could be coaching them in a year. I called coaches, trying to keep up with the trends and the possible job openings. Shortly after the draft, I received a call from Kevin Gilbride, the offensive coordinator for the Buffalo Bills, who was now the quarterback coach for the New York Giants.

"Pat, Coach Flaherty, our line coach, has cancer, and we need you to fill in until he gets well. You don't need to formally interview because I told Coach Coughlin all about you. He wants to meet with you."

"When?" I asked. I had my mind set on being Sabra's mentor and attending her games; I wasn't interested in a job offer. But since it was Kevin, I was willing to explore it.

"As soon as you can. We'll set up travel arrangements."

"Thanks, Kevin. Give me two days," I replied before hanging up the phone.

I was in a state of ambivalence. I wanted to be with my family, support my daughter, and watch her compete. I really wanted to be part of her senior year.

When I arrived at the New York Giants facility, Kevin brought me in to visit with the offensive staff. They asked me some questions about places I had coached at and basically welcomed me.

Coach Coughlin, the New York Giants head coach, opened the door and asked me to come to his office. I followed him, but I had already made up my mind: I wasn't going to join them. I was still getting paid by the Buffalo Bills—I didn't need a job.

Coach Coughlin looked deep in thought as he took his place in a chair behind his desk. Coach was an average-looking man whose graying hair was thinning, much like a light snow that only covered half the yard. He wore eyeglasses that gave him a very studious look.

"We need you now, and you should expect to be here through the preseason until Coach Flaherty gets cleared to coach again. We'll pay you one-hundred thousand dollars for five months," he said, as if it was already a done deal.

I sat there not saying a word. I wasn't interested in money.

When I didn't respond, he raised his offer. "I'll tell you what—we'll boost that to one hundred and fifty thousand and give you a six-hundred-dollar car allowance."

I sat there thinking, *Why am I here? I don't want this.*

Coach Coughlin could see that my face offered no clues. It was a pure poker face. I didn't react to anything he said. After another moment of silence, he blurted out, "We'll pay you two hundred thousand dollars, plus ten thousand in moving expenses."

At this point, I was amazed that he never asked me what I wanted.

I remained silent, then he barked, "We'll pay you two hundred and fifty thousand. I'm not paying you coordinators' money."

I just sat there.

With a heavy air of frustration, he finally said, "What do you want?"

I had suddenly changed my mind. I wanted a contract for one year, so it counted toward my pension. The money from Buffalo would be replaced by the money from the Giants, and the difference would be that I would now get a year added to my pension.

"I want what you offered, and I need this year to count toward my NFL pension."

He snapped out of his chair quickly and announced, "I'll be right back."

While he was gone, I thought about what I just learned in the art of negotiation: *Keep your mouth shut.*

"You are all set," he said as he returned. We shook hands and he spoke again, "Go home, get what you need, and be back here on Monday."

I was elated that I was back to coaching, but a piece of me will always regret that I made that choice. I never got to see Sabra play her senior year. My dad was present for all my home games. Coaching is seven days a week, 14 to 18 hours a day during the season, which leaves so little time for family and friends. I considered myself lucky, as I was doing what I loved. The final piece of my decision was that it would be easier to get a job coming from employment as opposed to being unemployed.

When I returned to the NY Giants that Monday, we immediately began to meet with players and the draft picks. We were preparing them for OTAs—the equivalent to spring practice in college.

Coach Coughlin was the purest football coach I had ever met. Football was his job, his passion, and his life. He was immersed so deep into his job that it made me feel that I was just a pawn on a chessboard, waiting for his next demand. He ran the organization in a military style.

On the first day of OTAs in June, I was out on the field talking to the players during the team stretch. It was my time to remind, motivate, and converse with the players. When I was a player, I loved when coaches would come by and remind us of our goal for the day or motivate us to have a great practice.

Coach Coughlin walked up to me and said, "What are you doing out here?" Before I could answer, he pointed to the sideline where all the other coaches were standing and said, "Don't talk to the players. Get on the sideline."

I looked at the sideline and saw all the coaches were snickering. I was a rookie on the staff and didn't know Coughlin's rule of not conversing with players during stretching. In a weak moment of defiance, I walked off the field, pointing at players and saying, "I'm not talking to you, and I'm not talking to you." The players laughed—they knew the drill.

What a strange requirement, I thought.

A few days later, I was at my desk evaluating practice film. Coach Coughlin walked into my office. I could tell by the look on his face that this was not a cordial or fact-seeking appearance.

"What is that on your shirt?" he asked, motioning to the logo. I was wearing a collared golf shirt with a Great Waters emblem on it.

"That's a golf course at the Reynolds Plantation in Georgia," I said. I had bought it while on a golf outing the last summer.

"Do you think you're on vacation?" he asked.

"No, sir." This seemed quite trivial to me. I wasn't doing media interviews—I was just sitting in my office evaluating the offensive line.

"Then take it off and wear a plain white shirt or a New York Giants shirt."

I shot him a look of bewilderment as I started my trek to the coach's locker room. No one had ever objected to what I wore. I wanted to tell Coach Coughlin that what I wore had no effect on our ability to score, block, catch, or tackle, but I deemed it a losing position to argue with him. After all, he was the head coach.

As soon as OTAs ended in late June, I headed back to Buffalo, where I picked up my family and headed to Florida. Marti's parents and my mom still lived there, and we divided our time between family visits and Orlando, Sabra's and my favorite place. When we went on vacation, Marti was the only adult on site.

We did all the theme parks and stayed at the Marriott World Center. It had a huge pool, water slides, waterfalls, and a hot tub. NFL coaches' summer vacations last a whole month. I usually tried to forget football, but by the third week, I would be chomping at the bit to get back to it.

Returning to New York, I was looking forward to the 2004 football season. After our preseason games, I realized Coach

Coughlin not only hated losing, but he was going to find some-one to blame. An old coach once said, "Be tough on them when you win, and love them up when you lose." It made sense to me because no one likes losing, and there was no point in piling on harsh criticisms when the players and coaches were already feeling bad. Coach Coughlin delivered the harsh critiques win or lose. I hated watching another coach or player getting ver-bally chastised in front of his peers.

We were playing well, were 4-1 to start, and were healthy. It was the week of October 17th when we reached the bye week of our season (open week).

I went back to Buffalo to spend a few days with my family. I was looking forward to seeing Sabra play volleyball, but the day I arrived, she came home from school with a cast on her right hand.

"When did this happen?" I asked.

"Two days ago. I dove for a ball and broke my third metacar-pal." I could see her sadness. "I'll miss the whole season, Dad."

"Is it painful?" I was about to initiate a possible solution.

"Not really," she admitted.

My times of playing through pain were dancing in my brain. My senior year in college, I played with a separated shoulder, getting anesthesia shots before game and at halftime. That would never be allowed in today's athletic environment. But back then, it was my choice.

I was looking at Sabra, trying to read her state of mind. "How bad do you want to play?" I wanted her to make the decision that I was about to suggest.

"I did everything to prepare for my senior year, and it's all over now," she said sadly.

I offered my solution. "We can cut your cast off, and you'll have to learn to play through the pain. All great athletes must learn how to be comfortable being uncomfortable. It's what separates the good ones from the truly great ones."

She looked at me with uncertainty. "Mom's going to be mad," she said. "And what if it doesn't heal right?"

"They'll re-break it and recast it, and you can let me explain it to Mom," I said. I paused for a minute to let my proposition sink in. "So, it's your call: Do you want to play your senior year, or do you want to be a hand model?" I was encouraging her, but I could tell she was already moving that direction.

She opened the kitchen silverware drawer, looking for a cutting tool.

My eyes went to the wood block on our counter that held a slew of knives. "Hold on, we were sold these Cutco knives and scissors because they could cut a penny, so I'm sure we can cut off a cast." We laughed.

The cast came off, and she looked as though she had been set free to chase her dream. When Marti came home, I explained it to her. She mildly objected, but realized it was what competitors did: They were undeterred by setbacks, resilient and unwavering.

Before I headed back to New York and Marti began her commute to Detroit, I got a call from her coach, the one I was supposed to talk to when he demoted her. "Mr. Ruel, this is Sabra's volleyball coach. Did you know she cut off her cast?" I could hear the incredulity in his voice.

"Yes, I helped her, and she wants to play."

I could feel his smile across the air waves. "That's awesome. Thanks, Coach. We really need her."

"Just keep an eye on her, and if it's bothering her too much, rest her," I replied as my fatherly instincts kicked in.

I was extremely proud of my daughter for showing a will to compete, which required both physical and mental toughness. This was more than just a life lesson; it was the day I knew our daughter would be a success at whatever she did. She knew the value of hard work and had the determination to finish the task.

I drove back to New York, where Coach Flaherty would be coming back to work after beating cancer's ass. It meant we would work together in coaching the offensive line.

Our next game was versus the Detroit Lions, now one of the worst teams in the league. They beat us. It was an upset. The next game, we bounced back and beat the Minnesota Vikings. We were now 5-2, but with a couple of key players hurt, our season was in jeopardy. We lost the next game to the Chicago Bears, then lost to the Arizona Cardinals and the Atlanta Falcons. With each loss, Coach Coughlin was handing his frustration and depressing attitude to the team. We were in turmoil—the NY Giants were on life support.

Coach Coughlin won because he was detailed and a task master. But he had the same problem a lot of head coaches have, which is that when things went bad, he fueled a negative culture. He was quick to blame others, which caused him to run into the arms of toxicity.

With two more losses to the Philadelphia Eagles and the Washington Redskins, we were now 5-7. It was mid-December, and Sabra's volleyball banquet was on Thursday night. I was unable to go because of preparation for our upcoming Baltimore Ravens game. Marti left work early to be there.

It was late Thursday night, and I still hadn't heard from them, so I called Marti, but there was no answer. I assumed they were already in bed. The next morning, I was up early and in the office when Coach Coughlin's secretary stopped by.

"Coach, your wife is in the hospital, and your daughter wants you to call," she said. A bit of panic was running through me as I began to regret taking this job. I called Sabra right away.

"What's going on, Sabra?" I asked as soon as she answered.

"Mom was at the banquet and suffering from pain in her abdomen. She left the banquet to go lie down in her car. After the banquet, I went out to the car and she was hurting bad, so I took her to the hospital where she waited for three hours to get admitted." I felt a little relieved that it wasn't a car accident, and from what Sabra was saying, it sounded like it was under control.

"What was it?" I asked.

"She had appendicitis, and they found out it had burst. It was an emergency surgery."

I took a deep breath and said, "I'm coming home as soon as I can get flight arrangements."

On my way to my position meeting with the players, I ran into Coach Coughlin, who already knew what was going on. "After practice and film evaluation, you can catch a flight to Buffalo," he said. I was expecting a do-what-you-need-to-do attitude, but instead it was typical Coach Coughlin—he was so laser-focused on his job that he couldn't see beyond it.

On the way out to practice, Coach Gilbride grabbed me. "You need to take care of your wife," he said. "Why are you here?" His empathy was soothing.

"Coach Coughlin wanted me to stay till after film evaluation," I replied.

Kevin shook his head in disbelief. "What? You should go now," he said. I had already asked Coach Coughlin's secretary to get me a flight and a ride to the airport immediately after practice. I figured I would deal with the consequences of missing film evaluation later. When I explained this to Kevin, he gave me the go-ahead nod.

It wasn't until I got on the plane that anxiety over Marti's health kicked in. I worried that a ruptured appendix could lead to something more serious. I was preparing myself to be strong, but by the time we landed in Buffalo, it was like I was riding the "What could go wrong?" train. Sabra was waiting for me at the airport, and as we headed to the hospital, she began answering my questions and filling me in. I was getting more and more confident that everything was okay.

As we got out of the car, I suddenly asked, "How did your volleyball banquet go?"

"I was named the Most Valuable Player," Sabra said.

I felt like a failed parent. Neither Marti nor I was there to witness her receiving the award. She made it to the top of the mountain with a broken hand, and her parents weren't there to celebrate her achievement, but I couldn't have been prouder.

She didn't mention it until I asked her because her mom was the most important thing to her at the time. Sabra always had an extraordinary emotional intelligence—never mind her 4.0 GPA.

Marti was in recovery, and when we were finally allowed to visit, I could tell she was already back to normal. "How are you doing?" I asked.

"Pat, I was sitting in the emergency room lobby in horrible pain watching *Saving Private Ryan*, and you know how much I love war movies," she said, being totally sarcastic.

"Maybe it was to make you feel better—knowing someone has it worse."

She winced and said, "Don't make me laugh."

We got Marti home and resting with Sabra playing nurse as I returned to New York for our away game versus the Baltimore Ravens. We would lose three more times before finally beating the Dallas Cowboys at home to finish 6-10 after a 5-2 start.

I respected Coach Coughlin's dedication to his job, his singular focus, his honesty, toughness, and the opportunity he gave me, but he lacked compassion and empathy. Those last two qualities are the glue that hold us all together, especially in tough times.

Some jobs make you speed to work—other jobs make you speed home. I packed my bags and started hunting for that speed-to-work treasure.

CHAPTER 23

I FOUND GOLD

Finding a good culture is not the question; it's the answer, the treasure. It's where your attitude maintains a good altitude. My phrase that I used to combat a negative environment was, "Don't get captured." It was getting used much too often.

I began looking around the NFL to see what possibilities existed. It only takes a few phone calls to the assistant coaches or players to find out where I don't want to be. But the reality was that I needed a job, and it wasn't always my choice.

My main concern was to get our family back together and get rid of long-distance commutes. It was mid-February; I had my eyes on the Cleveland Browns offensive line job. They'd just hired Romeo Crennel as their head coach, and Marti was from Amherst, Ohio, which was about 30 miles west of Cleveland. It might be a good fit. I sent my resume to the Cleveland Browns and began contacting coaches to find out about Romeo Crennel. Their answers fired me up as they all had complimentary things to say about him as both a person and a coach.

While waiting for an interview with Cleveland, I got a call from Pete Carroll, who was now the head coach at the University of Southern California. "Golden, what are you doing?"

I had not coached with Pete Carroll since our time at Arkansas 27 years earlier. We had stayed in touch over the years, and he was the one person where instant friendship was forged and had stuck over the years. Pete was the only coach who called me by my real first name. When I was a kid, I always wrote my name as G. Patrick Ruel, because I got teased. Then when I was 6'4" and 220 pounds in my senior year, I changed it back to Golden because I was able to defend it. I liked that Pete called me Golden because he acknowledged it with sincerity.

Pete was enormously kinetic and had an unwavering attitude of positivity. He was a groomsman in my wedding, and I had only known him for eight months, but in that short time, he'd made an enormous impact on me.

"I am trying to get the offensive line job with the Cleveland Browns."

Pete didn't miss a beat. "You need to come out here first."

This wasn't the first time he had reached out to me. He had called me when he first got the job at Southern California three years earlier. I was at Green Bay at the time. I told him I didn't want Sabra to go to school in Los Angeles. Plus, it was a college job, and I had my sights on staying in the NFL. I still had reservations about moving my family to LA, but a piece of me was thinking that Coach Carroll was exactly what I was looking for.

"Okay, sounds great, Pete. When do you want me there?"

When I arrived at the Los Angeles airport, he picked me up and, instead of getting on the freeway toward downtown LA, he turned west on the Imperial Highway heading toward the ocean. It was a gorgeous day. There was not a cloud in the sky, and when I saw the sun rays sparkling on the ocean's surface, I thought, *Wow, how beautiful is that?*

We went to lunch down by the water. I was thrilled to see him again. It was why I had asked him to be my groomsman after knowing him for only eight months.

We were old friends uniting and immediately fell into a comfortable conversation. Like me, Pete also had his share of moves, including two brief stints as an NFL head coach. I was amazed at his resilience. Despite being fired from the New York Jets and the New England Patriots, he had managed to land a coveted head coaching job at USC.

"What did you do after you got let go by the Patriots?" I asked as I dipped my French fry into the ketchup.

Pete flashed his boyish grin; he seemed eager to tell me. "I intentionally took the year off and wanted to develop a strategy of success. It was critical for me to have a philosophy in terms of how to develop players, the best methods of instruction, managing people, and working with the press. I read a lot, and I was influenced by several accomplished people." His curiosity to succeed was evident; he was researching who and what he wanted to be. I was so impressed with his self-awareness.

"Who are those who impacted you?" I asked.

Pete began to rattle off his list: "John Wooden, the UCLA basketball coach who won ten national championships, Tim Gallwey, who wrote the book *Inner Game of Tennis*, Lou Tice, the founder of the Pacific Institute, and a few others. They all were experts at how to manage the mental part of the game. How we think and act."

The more he talked, the more I could feel his vortex sucking me in. As a psychology major, I knew the mental part of the game was a primary ingredient to successful performance, and it was refreshing to have a head coach who valued it.

I looked out at the vast body of water glistening under the clear skies and said, "You're doing a great job of recruiting me, Pete." I smiled, and he nodded his affirmation. It was a bit more enticing than New York or Cleveland.

"Golden, USC is a great place to coach, and it has a rich tradition. You'll love it here."

We made our way back to the car and headed to the University. I had recruited southern California for Michigan State, but now the smog had disappeared, and LA seemed much cleaner.

When we arrived on campus, we parked the car and started walking toward Heritage Hall, where the football offices were located. A student yelled, "Pete! Pete!" Other students chimed in as well. They were obviously not only proud of their coach, but they seemed connected to him. After years of previous coaches struggling at USC, Coach Carroll and his staff had taken them to the top of the mountain—twice.

I got a quick tour of the practice fields and the weight room and then headed to Pete's office. He spent a few minutes filling me in on personnel, and then he asked what I was making with the NY Giants.

"You can't pay me what I made with the Giants," I said, knowing there had to be difference between college and professional football.

"Yes, I can," he replied. Just as I was processing that statement, his secretary appeared in the doorway.

"Bill Belichick is here to see you," she said. *You have got to be kidding*, I thought. I couldn't believe it. What was the three-time winning Super Bowl coach doing on the West Coast visiting Pete?

"Tell him to come in," Pete said. When he walked in, we stood up and shook hands. Then we all took a seat, and Pete motioned to me as he turned to Belichick.

"Pat's trying to get a job with the Browns, and I would like him to come here." He didn't say Golden this time.

Coach Belichick looked at me and shook his head. "It's hard to win in Cleveland and, if I were you, I would come here." Pete smiled, Belichick grinned, and I thought, *I'm sitting here with two head coaches who are at the top of their game!*

I nodded affirmatively, but I was processing. Sabra was finishing her senior year. Marti was tired of the long-distance commutes, and I wanted to find my treasure.

After Coach Belichick left, Pete and I resumed our conversation.

"Pete, I need to tell you that I damaged my shoulders lifting weights, and I need to get them fixed, so maybe I should take the year off."

"What are you talking about? We have excellent doctors at USC. You can get it repaired here with the Trojans," he shot back. Those words were like a virtual hug.

Pete continued, "Your daughter can go to USC and receive free tuition if she has an A average and good test scores."

I proudly blurted out, "She has a 4.0 GPA and scored very high on her SAT." Wow, free tuition at USC, one of the top academic schools in the country. That was a huge plus, but I still wasn't ready to commit.

"I need to talk with Marti, so give me a day," I said as we wrapped up our meeting.

"Pat, we'll have a blast. You come coach the offensive line, and I'll be in charge of the fun."

By the time I arrived at the airport, my phone was on low battery, and I needed to call Marti. But before I could make that call, my phone rang. It was Pete. "Hey, you know that last time the Browns were any good, Jim Brown was there?" He paused, as if to let me respond, and before I could, he asked, "Is Jim Brown still there?"

I laughed and said, "No, Pete, he's not."

I needed to find my treasure, my phone was almost out of juice, and Pete had shot me one more reason to think about. Suddenly, there was gush of words spilling out of my mouth; it was as if my brain had made the decision without me.

"Coach Carroll, I'm coming—I just need to tell Marti."

I knew who Pete was; he was highly competitive, full of energy, and respected everyone. Maybe this was my treasure.

"I'm fired up, Golden. Take a couple of days to get things together, then get back here and get your shoulders fixed. We're going win and have a fun doing it."

When I hung up the phone, I thought about how odd it was that the entire time he never brought up winning two national championships. You would think his sales pitch would have included those achievements.

I needed to call Marti, but my phone died. I would have to tell her and Sabra when I got home.

When I arrived back at our house in Buffalo, it was around 10 p.m. on Friday night. Marti and Sabra were in the family room on the couch watching a movie. I wanted to ease into this conversation because they were not part of the decision. I had decided to let them ask me questions about my trip to the West Coast. I was looking for some small talk before I broke the news.

"How was Pete?" Marti asked.

"He was great. We had an excellent visit, and I also met Bill Belichick, the New England Patriots head coach."

"Wow, that's cool. Are you interested?" Marti continued.

I had to tell her—it might as well be now. "I took the job." I saw her forehead wrinkle and her lips scrunch, and her eyes were penetrating my soul; she was upset. "Pat, why didn't you call me to discuss it?"

"I know I should have, but it all seemed right, and I just pulled the trigger. You'll love it."

I glanced over to Sabra, who was smiling with excitement, and then back at Marti, whose smoke was dissipating.

"I'm just concerned about my career and living in LA."

I gave her a reassuring smile and wrapped her in a hug. "Trust me," I whispered. "You'll love it."

Sabra was up for a new adventure. She was already looking at several colleges, so I told her to add USC to the list.

* * *

When I returned to USC, we went to work evaluating film and seeing where we could improve. It was a young but very energetic staff. We were in our off-season program, and I was in the weight room watching the players lift. The place was antiquated; it looked as if it were built in the 60s, and nothing had been done to it since.

Later that day, I asked Coach Carroll, "Don't you think the weight room could use some remodeling?"

He met my question with one of his own. "Do you know how many great athletes, All-Americans, and special people have trained in that weight room?"

"No, but I do know it's a large number." I shrugged.

"Golden, it's about the people and the tradition, not the equipment and the buildings."

Those were words I totally understood. Heritage Hall's lobby was a large collection of trophies representing 11 national championships, the 34 Rose Bowls, and 7 Heismans (the college's most valuable players), all in glass enclosures. They even had a case honoring their Olympians. USC, since 1904, had had 510 athletes compete in the Olympics. They had 153 Gold medals, which would rank them 11th if the University was a country. The tradition and history of USC was almost unimaginable.

I remembered sitting with my dad when I was 12 years old, watching USC play Wisconsin in the Rose Bowl on New Year's Day in 1963. That day, I was wondering if I would ever get to play in a Rose Bowl game.

Now, here I was. Not as an athlete, but as a coach. My opportunity to participate in the Rose Bowl game had improved immensely.

Like the weight room, the football offices and staff room were filled with furniture from yesteryear. The staffroom was small, and its 20-year-old conference table occupied 90% of the room. Some coaches sat in conference table chairs, others sat on metal folding chairs. The room was packed with coaches, graduate assistants, and a few administrative personnel. Whenever Coach Carrol called someone's name to get their opinion, he would toss them a baseball. Once they caught it, they would deliver their opinions or state their facts and then throw it back. It was an atmosphere of enjoyment, and it made me feel at ease sharing my thoughts.

Spring practice had ended, and it was mid-April when Coach made a surprise announcement. "Before we get busy with spring recruiting, we have an all-expenses paid trip to Hawaii as a reward for our last season."

The coaches erupted into cheers and clapping. After the meeting, I pulled Coach Carroll aside. "Coach, I can't go. I wasn't part of it."

He looked at me like I was crazy. "You're going," he stressed. "You're part of the team now, and I want you to be there."

I was already feeling I had made a good decision, and his attitude was like putting icing on the cake. But as much as I would have liked to make that trip, there was another reason I had to bow out. "Coach, my daughter has a college trip to the University of Wisconsin that week."

This time, he gave me the go-ahead nod, as he understood the importance of family.

* * *

Two weeks later, after working late one night, I was strolling across campus to my hotel across the street from the University. The USC football staff was on its way to Hawaii. I suddenly felt nauseous, so I stopped and started looking for a place to throw up. I found a flower bed. I hadn't felt right all day. As I emptied my stomach, all I could think about was, *Why did I pick a beautiful flower bed?* Maybe it was the nearest opportunity, and I wanted to avoid doing it all over the walkway.

Feeling better, I continued to my hotel room and started packing for our family college trip to Madison, Wisconsin. Sabra was interested in meteorology, and the University of Wisconsin offered it as a major.

After a flight from LA to Madison via Chicago, I was excited to see Marti and Sabra, who had flown in from Buffalo. Sabra looked adorable. I could see the excitement on her face for our new adventure. Marti acted like she was all-in to see her daughter off to college, but I detected some apprehension in those blue-gray eyes of hers.

I was like Marti; I didn't want to let go. I thought back to one time when she was five years old. I had picked her up and said, "You're my little gherkin." She never forgot it and would often leave me messages that were signed "Love, Gherk."

We went out to dinner, settling into our room at the Marriott. I woke up around midnight with a sharp pain in my abdomen. I paced the room, trying to settle the pain.

Marti woke up and asked, "Are you okay?"

I wasn't, but I didn't want to alarm her or my daughter.

"Go back to asleep. I'm fine." She rolled over and I continued my pacing. Only, now, beads of sweat were covering my forehead. The pain was getting more severe. My muffled moans turned to muffled profanity.

"Sounds to me like you're getting worse," Marti said as she sat up in bed.

This time I did not reassure her. "I need to go to the hospital."

We woke up Sabra and threw on our clothes. My mind was racing. I knew it wasn't a heart attack, but whatever it was wasn't good.

"We need to find out where the hospital is," I told Marti as we rode down the elevator. I went over to the front desk and asked a young woman for directions.

"Get on the freeway and there's one on the right two exits away."

"Thank you," I replied, like she was my best friend. I wanted to drive and be in control, hoping that my focus would minimize the pain. I was wrong—when we got to the second exit, I was drenched in my own sweat. I jumped out of the car and told Marti to park it. When I turned back to see Marti and Sabra, our car was the only car in the parking lot. The front door said that the urgent care was open 8 a.m. to 6 p.m. It was 12:30 a.m.

I turned to go back to the car, but then realized I had no idea where the real hospital was. I laid down on the grass and said, "Marti, call 911."

I heard her trying to explain where we were, and she stayed on the phone. Sabra was upset. I assured her I would be fine, but that was to calm her. I had no idea what was happening.

Just then, I heard the sirens, and a bit of relief blanketed me. The paramedics arrived and their first concern was my heart, but I kept telling them, "It's not my heart, just get me to the hospital."

Ten minutes later, we arrived at the University of Wisconsin hospital. Who would have ever thought that our daughter's tour of Wisconsin would start here?

They rolled me into the emergency room. A beautiful nurse with blond hair and blue eyes dressed in scrubs with a stethoscope around her neck started asking me questions about the pain. Her diagnosis was that I had gall stones.

"Can you please get me a doctor?" I demanded.

Marti was standing at the end of the gurney, shaking her head, when the nurse announced, "I am the doctor."

I laughed sheepishly. "I am so sorry. I was looking for a man with gray hair and glasses." I was truly embarrassed.

She smiled. "We have a gallbladder specialist, and he's a man." She winked.

They gave me something to ease the pain. I told Marti and Sabra to check back in the morning. I would spend the night being monitored. By the time I woke up at 7 a.m., my pain had subsided and I decided to hold off on my surgery until I got back to USC. I called Marti to tell her the plan.

"You go start the campus tour, and I'll catch up to you when I get checked out." I didn't want them to miss anything.

"Pat, we can wait," she argued.

"Marti, the pain has subsided. They said it was gall stones. Just go. I'll call you when I get checked out."

An hour later, another doctor entered my room and said, "Hi, I'm Dr. Mack."

"When can I get out of here?" I asked.

He looked at me and shook his head. "You have a large gall stone, and you're risking another attack if you don't get it fixed."

"I would prefer to go to USC for my surgery." I felt safer there. I could tell Dr. Mack was more concerned about me than I was.

"What do you do for the University?"

"I'm a football coach, and as a matter of fact, I coached for the Green Bay Packers, too." His eyes lit up like the glare of the sun on a tin roof.

"I love my Packers," he replied joyously, then added, "I don't think it's prudent to risk having another attack on the airplane. Besides, I developed a non-invasive surgery for it." His words finally penetrated.

"Okay, Dr. Mack. When can we do it?" I felt his love for the Packers meant he would take good care of an ex Packers coach.

"We can go in about two hours, around 9:30 a.m."

"Perfect, let's do it."

I saw all this as a minor bump in the road, and I would join Marti and Sabra in the afternoon.

They rolled me into the operating room, and the first thing he asked was, "Where is your wife and daughter?"

"They're on the campus tour."

"What?" He paused, looking at me like I was nuts, then pulled out his phone. "What is your wife's number?" He tapped in the number I gave him.

"We have Pat in the O.R., and you should come back here," he said as soon as Marti answered.

Then he handed me the phone. Marti was mad. "Why wouldn't you tell me this?"

I never wanted to be the one who slowed down progress, but not communicating was selfish. "It was a last-minute decision," I said, hoping she would understand.

The huge light in the O.R. was hovering over me as I handed the phone back to Dr. Mack. "Thank you, Doc. Could you please get me my sunglasses? This light is really bright."

He laughed. "Where you're going, you won't need sunglasses."

It was my turn to laugh.

"We're going to administer the anesthesia, and then let's see if you can count from a hundred backward. For your information, no one has made it to eighty-nine."

They put the mask carrying the gas over my face and nose. I started counting. "One-hundred, ninety-nine, ninety-eight, ninety-seven-" I could feel myself slipping away. "... ninety... six, ninety... five... ninety... four... eighty... niiiiiiine." I could hear laughter, then I was gone into the abyss.

* * *

When I woke up in my hospital room, the nurse gave me water and said, "Dr. Mack told me to tell you that you are the first one to make it to eighty-nine, but you left out some numbers."

I was still groggy; every word she spoke seemed to be on a two-second delay.

Then she added, "Dr. Mack got you a corner room with a view."

"I won't be here long enough to enjoy it," I slurred.

When she left, I got up and was walking up and down the hallway with my IV medical pole on rollers. A nurse tried to get me to go back to the room, and I told her I was fine. Then a couple minutes later, another nurse appeared. I assumed it was the head nurse, as she was older and had a no-nonsense look on her face.

"Get back in your bed. It's too soon to be up walking around." Her voice carried a commanding tone.

"I was just heading that way." I made light of it, knowing full well she was in charge.

I was ready to leave. But I had to wait for Dr. Mack and the discharge procedures. It was now 2:00 p.m., so I called Marti and asked her and Sabra to come back to the hospital to pick me up.

Dr. Mack arrived. "You're all fixed. Everything looked great, Coach. I know you want out of here, and I'm going to let you go, but you must promise me you'll take it easy. And no climbing stairs."

"You got it, Dr. Mack."

Marti was downstairs at the pharmacy picking up my pain medication, which I knew I would refuse to take.

We quickly joined the campus tour, where I found it was impossible not to climb steps. Wisconsin was impressive, and our daughter loved it.

Our flight to Buffalo via Chicago was at leaving at 7 p.m. When we arrived in Chicago, the gods of perseverance and determination were testing me; our connecting flight to Buffalo was on the other side of the airport. I was feeling the pain of carrying luggage.

Finally, I thought it was time to pop a pain pill. Then I realized I had left my pharmacy bag at the airport in Madison. Oh well.

After arriving in Buffalo, I packed up a few things and headed back to USC the next day. Three days later, I was back in the hospital to repair my shoulders. I had asked Dr. Tiboni, the orthopedic physician at USC, to do both of my shoulders at the same time.

He said, "Is your wife okay with that?"

I quickly responded, "What does she have to do with it?"

"Who's going to wipe your ass?" He smiled.

"Like I said, Doc, let's just fix the right shoulder. I know she loves me, but that might be pushing it too far." We both laughed.

I didn't tell Dr. Tiboni that I had my gallbladder removed. When he was fixing my shoulder, I woke up during the stitching. He was amazed and then upset that I didn't tell him. My anesthesia from my gallbladder surgery had caused my body to be less reactive to the second round of anesthesia in five days.

Rehab went fast. I was always a fast healer, it seemed. A large part of healing quickly seems to be having a good attitude.

It was early May. Spring recruiting and finding a home were next on my agenda. I recruited during the week and looked for a house on the weekends.

I bought a house down by the ocean in Hermosa Beach. It was 20 minutes from campus in non-traffic time. Marti was always concerned about the dog, Rup, our German shepherd, having a yard. This time, I came first, and I wanted a view of that magnificent ocean.

Marti, who was still in Buffalo, had resigned from her job and was waiting for Sabra to finish school before coming to LA. She was pissed that I bought a house without her. I didn't have time to consult her because the house I bought wasn't even listed yet, and it was a seller's market. I had to act quickly, and I placed my bet and gambled that it would pay off.

Marti was still fuming when she arrived in early June. She softened her attitude as we entered the house and climbed the marble circular steps to the family room and kitchen. She walked toward the sliding glass doors that led to a deck with a gorgeous view of the ocean.

"Oh my god, it's beautiful," she gasped. I hugged her. *Fuck the dog*, I thought, *I can find some grass somewhere.*

Sabra was getting ready to make her decision on college. We took her out to dinner and began discussing the pros and cons of Wisconsin and USC. Marti told me to leave the free tuition out of the discussion.

"Sabra, if you decide to go to Wisconsin, your mom and I will be there at your graduation. I'll have an air horn, and when you walk across that stage, I'll blow it and yell your name. Then we'll take you out to dinner and tell you that we love you, we're proud of you, and we'll always be there for you."

She smiled. "Thank you, Dad."

"Now, if you decide on USC, your mom and I will also be there for your graduation. I'll have an air horn, and when you walk across the stage, I'll blow it and yell your name. Then we'll go out to dinner and tell you that we love you, we're proud of you, and we'll always be there for you. And… that there's a new car in the parking lot with ten thousand dollars stashed in the back seat, and it's yours." I never mentioned free tuition.

I looked at Marti, whose jaw had dropped into her lap, but before she could say anything, Sabra said, "Dad, you're a great recruiter. Go Trojans."

When we left the restaurant, I felt like we had just boarded the Happy Train.

I had the family back together, an awesome place to coach, and a head coach who valued the culture.

I had found my treasure.

CHAPTER 24

CARROLL'S MAGIC

I had been dragging my family around the country like tin cans tied to the back bumper of a newlywed's car. I wanted it to stop. I could see and feel the stress it was causing Marti. Once again, she would have to resign from her job, monitor the packing of our house, then load up our dog and our car. This time, for a 2,800-mile trek across America.

I hoped that a beautiful house with spectacular views of the Pacific Ocean and Sabra's acceptance to USC would buffer any anxiety Marti was feeling. With my gallbladder gone and my shoulder fixed, I was ready for my job at the best college program in the country.

I was drawn to Pete by his extraordinary energy when we were pups. But now, 26 years later, he had found a way to convert his energy into a power grid called USC. His journey before USC was a bit tumultuous. Coach Carroll was terminated at two NFL jobs that wanted instant results. He landed the USC job only after Dennis Erickson of Oregon State, Mike Bellotti of the University of Oregon, and Mike Riley of the San Diego Chargers turned it down. Many criticized the choice by Mike Garrett, the USC athletic director, but Pete, in his second year at USC, proved he had the winning formula.

I admired his resilience and persistence. I was jealous of his passion to march against the odds. He was not deterred. He went after what he wanted with a purpose. In most cases, I had let jobs come to me. I sold myself short. I should have kept trying. But I also would have needed to recognize that my determination to put the team first and create a good culture came at a cost.

I often acted like a German shepherd policing bad attitudes. On a few occasions, I felt it was necessary to bark. The head coaches knew there were issues, but it could damage them politically, so I became the fixer. It didn't matter to me whose toes I stepped on or whose feelings were hurt if we solved the problem. I was never afraid of confronting my superiors. But I learned that, although those confrontations resulted in good outcomes for the team, it really wasn't my place to intervene.

In the days to come, I would learn the magic of Coach Carroll.

We were in an organizational meeting reviewing schedules for spring training and recruiting.

"Spring practice and in-season practices are open to your families," Coach Carroll said after a few minutes. He paused for a few seconds, then said, "It's important to be there for your kids' athletic and academic events, so let me know, and we'll try and work it out." I was amazed at how important it was to him that the coaches' families were part of the team.

In training camp four months later, he once again illustrated his need to create a great atmosphere. Halfway through training camp, we boarded a bus for Manhattan Beach for their annual ATP Volleyball Tournament. The players were free to get lunch on their own and watch the volleyball games. After two hours, we boarded the buses back to USC.

I had never done anything like this during training camp.

"Coach Carroll," I said, my curiosity driving me, "What is the purpose of this volleyball field trip?"

He flashed me a knowing smile like a friend about to impart a secret. "They've been working and competing hard for two weeks, so we take them away from their everyday activity and let them enjoy being together in a different environment. It's a good mental and physical break." He seemed to be constantly working on the mental and physical health of his team and his coaches. I was about to see how far he would go.

We were ten days away from our opener versus Hawaii in Honolulu. Coach Carroll stepped into my office.

"Golden, we're going to have the graduate assistant coaches be the opener for our team meeting at the end of the week. They're called the Wild Bunch."

I looked at him and wondered where he was going with this. "Got it, Coach."

"Since you're in charge of the field goal team, come up with a name for them that makes them special."

"How about Trojan Wall?" I offered.

"That's great, and you should stand by the basement door to signal the Wild Bunch when I motion you to do so. They'll be hiding in the stairwell." I felt like Coach was Stephen Spielberg and we were making a movie. Ironically, Hollywood was just a few miles from campus.

The preparation for our game was in its final stages, and it was time for the Wild Bunch production. Our team meeting was on the ground floor of Heritage Hall. The meeting room was tiered like an amphitheater. The seats were cushioned and colored in Trojan cardinal. Like the rest of the building, it had character, and it was old. The room was too small to hold all of us, but Coach Carroll loved the intimacy of a room too small.

I took my place by the basement door and waited for Coach Carroll to enter the room. I had no idea what the Wild Bunch was going to do. I just knew Coach Carroll believed you should always start team meetings with energy. Lots of energy.

Once the team was seated and the door to the basement was closed, I waited for Coach Carroll to enter the room. As he did, he turned and gave me the go-ahead nod. I pounded on the door forcibly, which was my cue for the Wild Bunch. The door flew open.

The Wild Bunch came sprinting out yelling, "ST Wild Bunch, ST Wild Bunch, ST Wild Bunch!" The players joined in; it was deafening. The ST stood for Special Teams.

I looked around the room. The players were jumping up and down, commanding their chant. Their eyes conveyed an intensity usually reserved for the highest level of competition or war. The electricity in the room surged off the charts as the yelling melded into one steady but loud chant.

Then one of Wild Bunch yelled, "What do you do when you get in a fight?"

The players loudly proclaimed, "You take your shirt off!" Then everyone, including coaches, discarded their shirts. I thought, *If we're going to do this every week, I should try and lose a couple of pounds.*

There were many chants that the players had made up that all revolved around the alpha dog-ish environment, like "Jacked up, shit right," and "Don't start no shit, won't be no shit."

As the energy began to dissipate, Coach Carroll took command of the room and reviewed Special Teams assignments. When I got up to review the field goal and extra point team, the whole team chanted, "Trojan Wall... Trojan Wall ...Trojan Wall," while rocking back and forth in their chairs with their right arms extended and their hands in a fist. They were simulating that the wall couldn't be broken.

"Sam Baker is hurt," I yelled out.

"I got it," his back-up, Kyle Williams, said. It was our way of making sure everyone knew their responsibilities. When Special Teams was done, we reviewed the highlights of the previous day's practice. More player participation ensued.

That same energy was visible in practice. It was all about competition. Coach Carroll would keep score of all the team drills. We always practiced situational football—first down plays, third down plays, blitz calls, red zone calls, short yardage, and goal line calls. If it was a ten-play period and the score between the offense and defense was 5-5, we would go into sudden death to see who won. He loved creating a tie, so we would have to play one more play. Like in a real game, everything was on the line. Coaches and players were encouraged to hoot and holler.

As the highlights were shown, it became a beautiful display of onomatopoeias. There were *ooohs* and *ahhhs*, *booms* and *zooms*, or someone would make the ESPN sound, or verbal taunts like, "Goodbye, Felecia," and "You're toast," or "Strike up the band." It was all about competing. They were being highlighted or made fun of, and it was all done in a spirit of unity. Coach Carroll said this often to the team: "We don't compete against each other. We compete with each other to make each other better."

After a quick walkthrough, we went to the airport, boarded the team charter, and headed to Hawaii. I reflected on my time at the University of Kansas. I had participated in two winning Aloha Bowls, beating BYU and UCLA. I loved the memories I had of Hawaii and was looking forward to creating a new one. USC was coming off two National Championships, so there was external and internal pressure to win a third one. When you're ranked number one for two years and have a 22-game winning streak, you can expect everybody's best shot.

We beat Hawaii 63-17. We had 518 yards to their 437 yards. It was suddenly clear to me that we would have to grow into a good defense. Hawaii dominated time of possession with 33 minutes to our 27 minutes. USC returned 14 starters to the 2005 team. Ten on offense and four on defense. It looked like the offense would have to carry the team.

* * *

When I returned home, Marti and Sabra were there to greet me. Sabra was already attending USC, and Marti was busy organizing the house and explaining to our German shepherd dog, Rup, that beach homes don't have grass. Being back together felt good.

We were getting ready to play Arkansas in the LA Coliseum on Saturday. Coach Carroll gave us Friday morning off before a 1 p.m. staff meeting. But, of course, I got there early. I walked into my office, which was an 8' by 8' brick enclosure with no windows. It was more suited for solitary confinement. Three walls were red brick, and the other was plaster board and a door. It was ideal for working and had a maximum capacity of two people. Then I saw it—a note on my chair.

> *Dad, I dropped by to say hi. I like my classes, and knowing I can come by and see you makes it special. We should make Fridays our rendezvous. Call me. LaLaLaLa, Sabra.*

She used the line from the Delfonics song, "La-La Means I Love you." I instantly started to tear up, because she was no longer a little girl. She was a young adult about to experience college life. My daughter stole my heart when she was born, and she still had it. I wanted her to know that there would always be a daddy hug nearby. Phones didn't cut it.

* * *

We had our crazy Friday team meeting, which seemed to be getting crazier.

Game day was awesome at the Coliseum. We had a full stadium and beautiful weather. After the pregame, we returned to the locker room, running up a hundred-yard ramp. We ran because Coach Carroll saw it as a sign of passion and strength. After a few words from Coach, we headed back down the ramp. We were all locked arm-in-arm as we walked. The only sound came from the players' cleats hitting the cement. The clicking and clacking noise was a universal symbol of football players marching to the field of battle.

Then, about halfway, the team captains started a slow whisper. "Waarrrrtime, waarrrtime, waarrrtime..."

It slowly got louder. The sound of the mantra reverberated off the walls of the ramp. It was an eerie moment where we were no longer just us—we were a part of something much bigger. It felt special to be locked arm-in-arm with these men who had trained all week long.

We scored five touchdowns off our first 12 plays. We won 70-17. We had 745 yards of offense. We ran the ball 33 times for 291 yards, 8.8 yards per rush, and passed it 34 times for 454 yards, 13.4 yards per attempt. It was USC's 24th straight victory. I had never witnessed such dominance by an offensive team.

The following week, we traveled to Eugene to play University of Oregon, who was ranked number 24. We were behind 13-10 at halftime. We didn't play like the number one team in the nation. Coach Carroll woke our team up in the locker room at halftime, and we beat them 45-13, our 25th straight win.

The following week, we were on the road again, this time to the 14th ranked Arizona State Sun Devils. It was October 1st and game time was 12:30 p.m. It was unusually hot with temperatures in the high 90s. Like with Oregon, we were getting their best shot and were behind 21-3 at halftime. When we went into the locker room, we looked like a MASH unit.

"This is not good," Coach Carroll said as he walked up to me. "We have nine players getting IVs, and your offensive line is lying on the floor like wounded rhinos."

"They'll be fine, Coach. We just need to run the ball more." I was ignoring the problem of heat because I felt in my heart that they would rise to the level of their training. Our practices were challenging. Besides, running the ball is an expression of dominance.

Coach Carroll addressed the team. "We need to play better and stay hydrated. Can you win the game in the first quarter?"

The team said, "No."

"Can win the game in the second quarter?"

The team shouted, "No!"

"Can you win the game in the third quarter?"

The team yelled, "NO!"

Coach paused. "Can you win the game in the fourth quarter?"

The team screamed, "YES!"

One moment we looked out of gas; the next moment was like a Formula I pit stop. In a matter of minutes, we had changed the tires, refueled, and told the driver to put the pedal to the floorboard.

Looking at Deuce Lutui lying on the floor made me wonder if he had enough to finish. He was my biggest player. During the spring, Deuce was 6'4" and 375 pounds and played right tackle, but he was too heavy and lacked stamina.

I had called him into my office.

"Deuce, I'm moving you to guard, and you need to lose fifty pounds before training camp if you want to have a great season and eventually play in the NFL." I knew that was setting the bar high, but it would make a huge difference in his explosiveness and stamina.

"Okay, Coach, I will," he replied. He was a soft-spoken Tongan with the most sincere and genuine disposition. He had an infectious laugh and was a magnet to his teammates.

"You have four months to do it, and I know you can."

I monitored him with phone calls during the summer. I had told players before to lose weight, but never this much.

When he reported for camp at 335 pounds, I was the proudest coach ever.

When we got back on the field to start the second half, I grabbed Deuce and asked, "Are you okay?"

"I'm fine. Thank God you made me lose that weight, Coach."

We scored 14 points in the third quarter, and Arizona State was shut out. Midway into the fourth quarter, we scored 21 more points and were ahead 38-21. I took Fred Matua, our right guard, out of the game to get his backup some experience. He was visibly upset because he and Deuce were in a competitive battle for the most knockdowns. He pleaded with me to go back in the game.

"In a minute," I said.

Fred and I were standing together when the team broke the huddle. We called an outside zone play to the left. Deuce exploded off the ball and shoved the defensive end to the ground and then climbed up and pancaked the linebacker. He turned toward the bench while on a knee and flashed us two fingers, adding to his knockdown count.

I turned to say, "Fred, did you see that?" But before the words got out of my mouth, Fred had run back into the game. It appeared that between Coach's halftime talk and good work by our trainers, we could play all day in searing heat. Both our running backs, Reggie Bush and Lindell White, had over 150 yards rushing. We had 373 yards rushing and 258 yards passing for 631 total yards and a 26-game winning streak.

Coach Carroll was a master of making his team stay in the moment and love the journey.

Our next game was the Arizona Wildcats. We were again slow to start but won 42-21 for a 27-game winning streak.

Next up was Notre Dame, the Fighting Irish in South Bend. We pulled up to the stadium for the usual Friday walkthrough, which is a non-event. As our buses neared the entrance to the stadium, we were met by 3,000 rabid Notre Dame fans. They had derogatory signs about OJ Simpson and the usual imaginative signs you get from the students. They started chanting, and a few banged the buses with their hands; that's when the players on bus one started rocking the bus. Bus two followed suit. I worried that the bus would tip over. The students' chants had stopped, their enthusiasm diminished. The rocking of the bus became a symbol of defiance and intimidation. It was eerily quiet as we deboarded. It reminded me of that moment in the movie *Butch Cassidy and the Sundance Kid*; I could hear the Notre Dame students whispering, *Who are those guys?*

Pre-game warm-up was like the red carpet for the Oscars. It was a virtual who's-who on the sidelines. It was a collection of former great players from USC and ND, famous sports announcers, and political hacks.

We all noticed the grass field hadn't been cut. It was three inches long—twice the length of the normal game day grass. The rumor was that they did it to slow down the Trojans' team speed.

"Wouldn't that make a slow team slower?" One of the players asked. We all shook our heads because it made no sense at all.

By game time, the atmosphere was so emotionally charged that goosebumps had turned into goosehills. The game went back and forth, and for the third straight week, we were behind at halftime, 21-14. Matt Leinart, our quarterback, threw two interceptions as the Irish blitzed him and the offensive line failed to adequately protect him. At the end of the third quarter, we were tied 21-21.

I was reviewing protections with the offensive line on a knee with my players on the bench in front of me. They had shown some new blitzes for our game.

"Coach, behind me," Sam Baker said. I looked up, and there were five men leaning over the players, watching me make corrections.

I calmly said from my kneeling position, "You guys need to move back, thank you." They stepped back about three feet.

I went back to instruction when Ryan Kalil, our center, signaled to me that those same guys were leaning in on the players again, trying to hear.

I jumped to my feet and yelled, "Get the fuck back... NOW." My eyes pierced theirs like angry lasers. It was my workspace. They moved back ten feet this time.

"That's the Coach Ruel I know," Ryan said, with his usual mischievous grin.

The fourth quarter was back and forth. It was USC 28-24 with 5:09 left.

Then Brady Quinn, the ND quarterback, engineered an eight play, 87-yard drive for a touchdown to put ND ahead 31-28 with 2:04 left in the game. After the kick-off, we started at our own 25-yard line with a minute and 54 seconds left to play. The first play was an incomplete pass. Now it was second down and 10, and Matt Leinart was sacked for a 10-yard loss.

ND ran a line stunt, and we didn't pick it up. *Why didn't I remind the offensive line to be aware of line stunts by Notre Dame? That was poor coaching on my part.*

Was this winning streak coming to an end?

It was third down and 20, and having the ball on your own 26-yard line is not a fun down. Leinart threw it to Reggie Bush for an 11-yard gain. Coach Carroll called a time-out. This time, I reminded them of line stunts. Matt was given the option to change the play if they showed man coverage.

Then it was fourth down and nine yards to go. My eyes were glued to the offensive line. Matt Leinart spotted man coverage and switched the play to a one-on-one fade route to Dwayne Jarrett. Notre Dame brought pressure, and we picked up on it. Dwayne Jarrett was running with the ball for a 61-yard gain to ND's 13-yard line.

A field goal would tie the game. On first and 10, we threw an incomplete pass. It was now second and 10. We gave the ball to Reggie Bush, and he ran for six yards. On third and four, we chose to give the ball to Bush again. He rushed for five more yards, giving us a first down at the ND two-yard line with 13 seconds left. On first and goal, we called a pass.

Matt Leinart scrambled to his left and hurled his body with a dive toward the end zone, but he was hit at the goal line and fumbled the ball out of bounds. I was practically hyperventilating on the sideline. The clock continued to run, hitting 0:00. The game was over as ND players, coaches, and fans rushed the field. Meanwhile, every USC coach was headed down to tell the officials that the clock should have been stopped. Coach Carroll sent us all back, as it was his job to talk to officials, not ours.

The officials convened and decided they should put seven seconds back on the clock. The Notre Dame fans were clueless, as they hadn't seen the fumble. There was a mixture of boos and cheers as they cleared the field of ND students, players, and coaches. Coach Carroll signaled Leinart to clock it—to spike the ball and stop the clock. Leinart also had the option to quarterback sneak it. Only the players on the field knew what was going on. The stadium went deathly quiet, as everyone knew this would possibly be the defining play.

With seven seconds left, Leinart took the snap and executed maybe the worst quarterback sneak of all time. Instead of bending his knees and dropping his shoulder pads for leverage, he stood straight up like he was going for a walk in the park. That's when Reggie Bush decided Matt needed a little help. He rushed up and pushed Leinart forward into the endzone for a touchdown. It became known as the Bush-Push by the media.

We kicked off with three seconds left and tackled ND deep in their own territory as the clock ran out. The game was now officially over. This time, it was USC players, coaches, and fans celebrating. There was jumping, bouncing, hugging, and a few players rolling in the grass; it was pandemonium on the field as our band played the fight song. The Notre Dame field of extra tall grass became a trampoline for everyone who believed in the USC Trojans.

It was our 28th straight win.

* * *

When we boarded the plane to return home, I immediately recognized one of the men I yelled at for getting too close during my reminder and correction period.

"Hey, sorry I yelled at you, but you were in my workspace." I was still high on my dopamine, oxytocin, serotonin, and endorphins.

"I am so sorry, Coach. I came all the way from Australia to see the most exciting game ever."

So you could be on the sideline aggravating me, I thought. "What were you doing in Australia?" I asked.

"I was working on a film called *Ghost Rider*," he said.

I shot him a curious look.

"You have heard of Nicholas Cage, haven't you?"

"Of course, but do you have any movies that I would recognize?"

"Sure." He nodded. "I produced *The Score, Tin Cup,* and *Sleepless in Seattle*."

Suddenly he had my full attention. "Oh my god! Don't ever tell my wife that I yelled at the man who produced *Sleepless in Seattle*. That could be grounds for divorce." We both laughed.

"Don't worry, Coach, I got your back."

In the following weeks, we would beat the University of Washington 51-24 for our 29th straight win. Then Washington State University 55-13, bringing the streak to 30 wins in a row.

Marti called me at the office while we were preparing for Stanford University.

"Pat, there is a huge gift basket with a *Sleepless in Seattle* DVD, coffee cups, and other paraphernalia, and it was addressed to me and signed by Gary Foster. Do you know him?" Her voiced was filled with joy.

I could feel myself smiling. The producer had somehow managed to obtain my address and my wife's name. He was making amends; he was my type of guy.

"Yes, I'll explain it later."

* * *

We beat Stanford University 51-21, University of California 35-10, and Fresno State 50-42. They were our 31st, 32nd and 33rd straight wins.

Next up was our cross-town rival, the number 11 ranked UCLA. This time, we led at halftime 31-6 and won 66-10. We had 448 yards rushing and 249 yards passing. The total was 649 yards. Our streak was now at 34 straight wins.

With the win, we clinched the Pac-10 title and maintained our number one ranking and an invitation to the Rose Bowl to play Texas, ranked number two, in the National Championship game.

My dream to play in a Rose Bowl when I was 13 years old sitting with my dad in Coral Gables, Florida on January 1, 1963, never came true. But 42 years later, I was going to coach in it for the National Championship. Just the thought of it was awesome. Texas and USC were the only unbeaten teams in the nation.

USC ranked 35th in total defense, while Texas ranked ninth in total defense. The Texas offense ranked number one in points per game with 50.2 points, and USC ranked number two at 49.1 points. Our total yardage per game was number one at 579.8 yards per game, and Texas was number two at 512.1 yards per game.

After studying the Texas defensive schemes in my office, I turned off the tape. I leaned back in my chair, closed my eyes, and thought about how lucky I was to be part of a great culture, USC, and the Rose Bowl. Then I snapped back, returning to my preparation.

We prepared for the game like kids before Christmas Day. Coach Carroll wanted our practices the week of the Rose Bowl to be a review of our install for Texas.

Game day arrived. We boarded the bus to the Rose Bowl and rocked it as it pulled up to the Rose Bowl stadium. It had become our signature for our arrival. Walking toward our locker room, we passed by the Texas credentials hut, where someone stepped out and waved—Matthew McConaughey!

"Hey, T-Mac," I said to Todd McNair, our running back coach who was walking beside me, "You see McConaughey? I didn't know he was a Texas alum."

"Yes I did, Pat, but we've got Neil Armstrong, John Wayne, George Lucas, and the USC Song Girls." That sounded like a good recruiting line to me.

"You're right. We win," I said. We had the first man on the moon; an iconic Hollywood cowboy; the creator of *Star Wars*, *Indiana Jones*, and *American Graffiti*; and our made-for-Hollywood Song Girls.

I could feel the hair on my arms rise to attention. Reddy Kilowatt had taken his place deep in our souls. The atmosphere was so charged up that it felt like we were positrons hunting for an electron to collide with. Every game carries an anticipation of what the future holds. This game was different. It was the pinnacle; it was the ultimate prize. "The Natty," as the players referred to it.

There was an ocean of cardinal red on one side and a sea of orange on the other. We were more than ready to go head-to-head for what would hopefully be our 35th straight win.

CHAPTER 25

THE CHARGE TO THE NATTY

I gathered the offensive line in the locker room. A magical season was about to culminate in a single 60-minute contest where winner took all. I was convinced there was no one good enough to stop us. There was confidence and determination running through my veins, and as I looked at my players' faces, their eyes conveyed to me a message: "Fight or get out of the way." They didn't need any motivation, and neither did I.

"Play physical, play smart, and no penalties," I said. We all reached forward, putting our hands together in the middle. "Dominate on three—one, two, three, DOMINATE!" Even the tone in their voices told me they were ready.

When Coach Carroll entered the locker room, the team quickly gathered around him. The room went eerily quiet. I could see the glowing confidence in his eyes.

As he scanned the room, he repeated our proven philosophy: "Take care of the football, and just be you. We don't need to make shit up—you're enough."

With that, we charged out of the locker room door to prepare our entrance to the field. We locked arms, and the sound of cleats hitting the pavement was soon drowned out by our traditional wartime chant.

There was a loud roar as we entered the playing field. There wasn't an empty seat anywhere.

93,988 in attendance and 35 million watching. They had Vince Young as their quarterback; he was 6'5", 233 pounds and ran a 4.58 40-yard dash time. He looked more like a big-ass linebacker. We had Matt Leinart at 6'5", 220 pounds, who ran a 4.95. He looked more like a model for GQ magazine. Both were the catalyst for their teams.

Texas won the toss and elected to play defense. They were going to test their ninth rank defense against the Trojan offense. They stopped us on the opening series and we were forced to punt, but their punt returner fumbled the ball and Scott Ware, one of our defensive backs who covered kicks, recovered for the Trojans. Our sideline was jumping like oil on a hot skillet.

We went three plays for 42 yards to the Texas four-yard line. It was first and goal and we handed it to Lindell White on a power play, who walked into the end zone practically untouched. Trojans 7-0.

The Longhorns started at their own 20-yard line after the kickoff. Their dive stalled at their 49-yard line. It was fourth, a long yard from their own 49-yard line. It was a normal punting situation, but Mac Brown, the head coach for Texas, elected to go for it. You could feel the tension in the air between our two storied programs. It was King Kong versus Godzilla. Texas ran an option play, and Vince Young was tackled for a yard loss. The ocean of cardinal red was euphoric.

We drove the ball down the Texas 23-yard line and faced a third down and seven. We were the number one offense in third down conversions at over 50%. Leinart threw a swing screen to Reggie Bush, who ended up a half yard short. Rather than kick a field goal, Coach Carroll decided to go for it. It was now our turn to execute a fourth and one at the Texas 17-yard line. We called a quarterback sneak. I held my breath, knowing he might need another push from Bush, but Reggie wasn't there; this time, he was lined up outside as a receiver. The ball was snapped, and again he was too tall and not using leg drive. Leinart was two inches short, as his feet slipped out from underneath him. The sea of orange was rocking.

We exchanged possessions. The score at the end of the first quarter was 7-0. At the start of the second quarter, we ran a screen to Reggie Bush, who exploded into the Texas secondary. After running 35 yards to the Texas 20-yard line, he tried to lateral the ball to Brad Walker, who was trailing to his right.

What the fuck? I thought. *We don't do that.* Taking care of the football was our mantra, our pledge, and our vow. Texas recovered. Reggie was visibly shaken, as he knew it wasn't like us. He did what coach preached against: "Just be you—you are enough. Don't make shit up." Reggie made shit up, and it was now the Texas Longhorns' ball.

The Vince Young Show was now underway. He was nine for ten throwing the ball. We slowed him down and forced a field goal. Score was 7-3.

After receiving the kickoff, we took over possession on our own 27-yard line and moved right down the field. Then Leinart, on second and nine, threw deep to Steve Smith, who had beaten the coverage. The ball hung in the air for what seemed like an eternity. Everything seemed to slow down. I could feel the rhythm of my heart beating. I could see the rotation of the ball as it traveled through the warm Southern California air.

Just then, Texas defensive back, Michael Huff, their All-American safety, leapt in front of it like a Tiger pouncing on its prey—intercepted at the goal line! The sudden turn of momentum momentarily produced a gasp from our sideline. It was our second turnover of the game, and both had occurred with the Trojans in scoring position.

My inner voice was screaming our philosophy: "It's all about the ball." Coach Carroll said it constantly in the locker room, in the meeting rooms, on the practice field, before breakfast, during lunch, at dinner, and before bed. The offense must protect it and take care of it, and the defense must attack it and steal it.

There was a breakdown of the replay equipment, and oddly two plays were unable to be reviewed. The first one was Vince Young pitching the ball to a teammate on an option play with his knee clearly on the ground, which resulted in a Texas touchdown, and the second play was the Texas linebacker Drew Kelson intercepting a Leinart pass and then landing on his back; the ball popped out, and we recovered, so it was called an incomplete pass. It suddenly felt like Texas was getting all the breaks. Coach had trained us not to let a bad call or a bad play affect us; we knew who we were, and we were on a mission. Even though it was a hard pill to swallow, we knew we had to just keep competing.

Texas scored twice, marching through our defense like a hot knife through butter. We managed a field goal and went in at halftime down 16-10. We had certainly been in this position before. Coach Carroll always did a great job of summarizing why we were ahead or why we were behind and what needed to happen to finish with a victory, and it was no different this time. You win the game in the fourth quarter.

We stopped Texas' opening possession of the second half. We took the ball 62 yards in seven plays to take the lead, 17-16. Texas went 80 yards in even plays to get back ahead, 23-17.

We received the kick-off from Texas and went 74 yards in nine plays to retake the lead, 24-23. The third quarter was over. The National Championship and a 35-game winning streak was on the line. We were all in. We drove the ball 52 yards in nine plays and increased our lead, 31-23. Texas managed a field goal, making it 31-26. We went 80 yards in four plays to make it 38-26.

Trailing by two scores with 6:42 left to play, the Vince Young Show came in full view as Texas went 69 yards to make the score 38-33 with all of it being Young running or throwing.

We managed to get to the Texas 45-yard line; it was fourth and two with 2:13 left in the game. Texas called time-out and Coach Carroll decided to go for it because we had been unable to stop Vince Young. We called the power play, which the Longhorns had been unable to stop. Our right tackle, Winston Justice, was responsible for sealing backside pursuit. He threw up his inside arm, but didn't stop the Texas Linebacker who blitzed, and it caused our running back, Lindell White, to bounce away from a big hole. We were stopped a half yard short. I felt like I was in quicksand, watching my body slowly sink into a dark hole. It was a guy that I had coached and depended on who failed. I felt like I'd just let down the entire Trojan nation.

Now with a short field, the Longhorns drove down to the Trojan 14-yard line. Facing fourth down and five, Vince Young, in shotgun formation, couldn't find anyone to throw to, so instead he scrambled to his right.

My mind was screaming, *Where is our defensive end? He's supposed to contain the quarterback. Oh, my God, there's no one to stop him.*

Then a roar from the orange sea—I looked at the clock, and there were 19 seconds left. I tried to console myself with a reminder that we still had time. The score was now 39-38, and Texas went for two to make it 41-38. Now, with no timeouts left, we got to the Texas 43-yard line, and time expired.

We made shit up, we lost the ball twice, and we ended our 34-game win streak, losing what would have been a third straight National Championship.

But it was a great game. It was played with a competitive spirit that was off the charts. It was not a time to cry, but to realize what it takes to be a great team, to cherish the journey, and to realize how vulnerable we were and how strong we could be.

Vince Young finished with 200 yards rushing on 19 carries and 267 yards passing for a total of 467 yards. The rest of his team got 89 yards. The statistics at the end of the game were pretty much even. We had more total yards, but they had one less turnover.

After congratulating Texas coaches and players, we made our way to the locker room. I felt empty; it was as if I had not eaten in a week. It was like a piece of me had vanished into the air, like a helium balloon lost at a fair. I felt like it was my fault. What if I had told my right tackle during the time-out that he should aggressively protect the backside? He had executed this assignment perfectly in previous games, but the critic in me was saying that it didn't matter; I should have reminded him. Would we have made a first down and stopped Vince Young from getting another opportunity?

When I entered the locker room, the team was swimming in a funk. I was right there with them, but I knew I had to say something. I walked over to each of the offensive linemen. They were all sitting in front of their lockers with their heads down, slowly peeling off their uniforms. I thanked each of them for their effort and commitment. Coach Carroll signaled me to call them up. 34 games of celebration, and now he had to give them direction on how to handle this moment of despair.

We had only three rules in Coach Carroll's program, and they could be applied to family, the organization, and the team.

Rule one: Always protect the team. This was about your actions and helping others.

Rule two: No whining, no complaining, and no excuses. This was about how we talked and communicated.

Rule three: Be early. This was about our preparation and our passion to learn.

The game was over. We lost, and rule two was now in full effect. Coach Carroll started off by reminding us of the rule, and then he praised the effort of the whole team. He thanked the seniors for an extraordinary string of victories. He thanked the service (scout) team that prepared our team each week. He thanked the staff and reminded everyone that we were Trojans, and we took care of each other.

We were proud and accountable men, and we accepted our loss like men.

As I showered and dressed to go to the post-game party, I heard coaches and players say they weren't going. I understood, but why would we pass on our sorrow to those we loved? It was a time to put on the husband and dad hat and move on.

When I came out of the locker room, I saw Marti and Sabra. We advanced toward each other. My arms opened wide, and they snuggled in close for a group hug. Hardly a word was spoken—we just melded into each other.

After a good 60-second hug, Marti asked, "Are you okay?"

"I'm fine. I felt like we just ran out of time." My emptiness was not going away. I had to fake it.

"Why didn't we punt the ball instead of going for it?" Marti wondered out loud. I hated losing, and I really hated the whys from family, friends, and alumni. They had every right to ask, but I only wanted to relive it with those who'd fought the fight.

"Marti, we lost, and it's over. There will be a lot of second guessing, but let's leave that to the critics." I was already shifting into my "Don't get captured" mode and was ready to move on.

She nodded empathetically. "I know. I just hate losing to Texas because we have friends on their staff."

"Well, today they're not my friends," I shot back. Once again, I needed to shift gear. "Let's go to the post-game party and try to enjoy it."

Marti and Sabra followed me into the big tent where the party of gloom was underway. We walked around a bit aimlessly. The spread of food and drinks was intended for the champions, only that wasn't us, and nothing looked good. I kept thinking about those rules; they were the foundation for building good character and maintaining discipline needed to win championships. But they were also a reminder of how to handle losing.

* * *

Coach Carroll gave us a few days off before we would go back to recruiting. I was in an all-out effort to get my happiness back. The hole in my soul was still huge. My brother Ron, who worked as a nurse in South Florida, had flown in for the game. He had always supported me through my career and was my biggest fan. I wanted to take him and his friend Marty to the 3rd Street Promenade in Santa Monica to show my appreciation for his caring and to start my climb out of the abyss.

The Promenade was an upscale outdoor shopping area filled with excellent restaurants and high-end shops. We walked around a bit and decided on Italian food. We requested a table for outdoor dining where we could enjoy a beautiful day and soak up the sounds of live music and magic acts by street performers. Our table was next to the decorative wrought-iron fencing that separated the restaurant from the buzz of activity around us. It was a perfect spot for people watching.

We ordered wine and were studying the menu when a young man in his mid-twenties caught my eye. He was walking straight to our table and stopped on the other side of the fence.

"Hey, can I see a menu?" he asked. He was a handsome young man with black hair and forest green eyes. I couldn't place it for sure, but his accent sounded British.

"Sure, here you go," I replied, handing him the menu. As he scanned the sheet, he commented, "Wow, the wine is expensive in California."

I laughed.

"Yes. You're not only paying for the wine, you're paying for the weather, too."

He smiled and handed me back the menu. I wanted to continue the conversation, as I sensed that he had no idea we had just lost a National Championship game. I felt safe.

"Where are you from?" I asked.

"South Africa, just outside of Cape Town," he replied.

That piqued my interest. "What are you doing here?"

"I'm a musician whose absolutely gorgeous girlfriend left me in the middle of the night because I wasn't making very much money, so I came to the U.S., and specifically California, to chase my passion for music."

I was amazed at his frankness, now totally engaged. "What's your name?"

"Liam."

"Well, Liam, why don't you come in and sit with us? I'll get you some wine and a meal on me." I could see he was excited, and I could feel the hole inside me starting to close.

As Liam went around the fencing to the entrance of the restaurant, Marti's face displayed unease.

"Pat, what are you doing?"

"We have an extra seat, and he needs a meal." I paused. "Are you okay with that?"

"Whatever," Marti shot back.

Unlike Marti, Ron was clearly amused. "This might be fun."

My brother's friend looked at me like I was nuts.

When Liam sat down, we toasted a glass of wine to his future. He seemed to fit in like a long-lost brother.

As we enjoyed conversation, I suddenly said, "Let's see if we can find someone for you."

Liam laughed as I signaled two older ladies from the Promenade to our table.

"Love or money?" I asked.

They both quickly said, "Money."

"Thank you for your input," I said as they walked away, discussing the question.

I proceeded to flag down more and more women and posed the same question. They all kept saying, "Show me the money."

Then, finally, this woman said, "Love." But she was twice as old as Liam.

Everyone, including Marti, was getting was kick out of my polling.

Finally, I spotted a very athletic-looking girl, about Liam's age. She was tall and had a beautiful smile. I waved her over to the table.

"I need you to answer a question," I said.

She smiled and responded, "Go ahead."

"Love or money?"

She didn't even blink as she replied, "Love, absolutely."

"Meet Liam," I said, as we all laughed. He got up and shook her hand, leaning over the iron fence.

"Go," I said, as I handed him twenty dollars.

When we left the restaurant, we all wondered if they would really find love. That small event killed my emptiness; I was whole again. I realized that making others happy was the key to getting my mojo back.

Now I was ready to recruit.

CHAPTER 26

LEARNING ABOUT GREED AND EFFORT

We kicked off recruiting with a gaping void. The Heisman Trophy winner, Reggie Bush, and an extraordinary power back, Lindale White, were leaving as juniors. To offset this, we signed four running backs to replace White and Bush, or, as the press called them, Thunder and Lightning.

Those would be tough shoes to fill. In addition, Matt Leinart, our quarterback and another Heisman Trophy winner, was a senior. He too would be entering the NFL draft.

Losing Bush, White, and Leinart was bad enough, but I now had juniors Winston Justice, my starting right tackle, and Sam Baker, my starting left tackle, also talking about opting out to the NFL. It was the downfall of a highly successful program. I had to stop the bleeding. I failed to convince Justice to stay, but through an extraordinary effort by me and his family, I was able to convince Sam Baker to hold on, get his degree, and be a first-round pick next year. When players opt out of their senior year, it means their degree is put on the back-burner. The NFL, money, and their agents take priority. It's very sad, as many of them don't ever finish their education. They start the quest for their degree and quit on the home stretch.

I loved coaching and developing players. We kicked off spring practice excited to get a new team ready to play.

There was no stress of preparing for a game. All I had to do was concentrate on teaching them skills and the value of competition. Coach Carroll always said, "You are competing with each other, not against each other. Competing to make each other better and make the team better." It was never an us-versus-them attitude, which can often result in an unhealthy environment.

I was busy at practice demanding my philosophy of foot-work, fundamentals, and finish to put them in the proper place and leverage positions, and to show who they were. I constantly focused on that order. There was no compromise.

Once we reached the teamwork part of practice, I pulled Sam Baker aside and told him he was stepping underneath himself and needed to open his hips more. I loved coaching Sam because he demanded perfection from himself.

As he went back to the huddle, Coach Carroll walked toward me, and in a light and soft voice said, "Make sure you coach effort first."

His words immediately took me back to the summer of 1964. I was 13 years old, sitting in the living room and watching the Olympics being held in Tokyo with my dad. I remember my father specifically pointing out the Olympic marathon, which I thought was rather boring. We watched the first, second, and third place runners cross the finish line. I was ready to bolt, but Dad insisted we wait for the last marathon runner.

"Dad, why are we watching the last guy finish? He's the ultimate loser," I said brashly.

"Just hold on—you need you to see this."

The telecast had switched to review other events. As I waited, I looked at my dad like he might be playing a trick on me. my head was tilted, and I was confused as to where this was leading. The telecast finally switched back after what seemed like an hour. Then it happened; the television cameras pointed at the tunnel to catch the last marathon runner as he entered the stadium.

"Here he comes. The last guy," Dad said proudly. I was about to ask what was wrong with him when the stadium full of people rose out of their seats and erupted in applause.

I was completely confused. There was no real cheering, just people standing and clapping. I looked up at my dad.

"Without effort, nothing can be accomplished," he said. "You see, Pat, that man is special because he made it to the Olympics, and he finished the race. The fans are showing their respect for his effort to finish. He didn't quit because he didn't win, he continued, and he finished what he'd started. It's about the effort."

I knew Coach Carroll was right. Effort is an essential ingredient that gives gave us value. Great coaches teach effort every day. Yes, it can be taught, and it's more important than math or English because it's effort that will determine a person's success in everything.

It was part of Coach Carroll's formula for success; whether we were in a staff room, team meeting, or practice, the message was always the same.

"When my friends watch us play, I want them to say that my team plays with great effort, great enthusiasm (passion), and great toughness (grit), and that they play smart (proper decisions/no penalties)." He never mentioned winning—it was a product of those traits.

For Coach Carroll, effort and enthusiasm were brothers. During games, he would often turn to our backups and red-shirted players who weren't playing and say, "You better enjoy these moments of being in the Coliseum and winning—they might not be here forever."

Those players then knew they had the freedom to be our own fans and would often be jumping up and down or locking arms and swaying back and forth on the sideline to exhibit their enthusiasm. Coach Carroll wanted them to be in the present and participate.

This year, with all the new players, we were going to need full-on participation. Josh Booty, who was a junior quarterback, had been patiently waiting for three years and was chomping at the bit to take over. He didn't disappoint; he was calm, cool, and confident. He led us to an 11-2 season. It was a successful season, but for me, it spelled the end of an extraordinary run. We lost to Oregon State on the road 33-31. Oregon State had forced three fumbles and an interception. What did that loss signify?

It ended a 38-game winning streak over regular season opponents, 27 straight wins over Pac-10 opponents, and 18 straight road wins. It was devastating to see all those streaks come to an end.

We were playing a multitude of running backs. It was like being a kid in a candy store. We had options on who to choose, but we never made the choice. Rather than choose, we played them all. Coach Todd McNair was trying to keep them all happy. The truth was that they all became increasingly frustrated. Chauncy Washington (a junior), Stafon Johnson, Emanuel Moody, CJ Gable, and Allen Bradford (freshman), all wanted to be the next Reggie Bush. Great coaches don't make individuals happy; they make the team happy. Pick one and let him prove himself worthy. By not choosing, we sent the message, "None of you are good enough." By choosing, we told the others to prove us wrong. If he chose not to compete, then the player was never worthy of a starting position.

We never did it with the quarterback position, because we wanted them to know who the captain of the ship was.

Later that year, with two games to go and another National Championship game on the horizon, our offensive coordinator, Lane Kiffin, made a remark that incensed me.

"If I was head coach, we wouldn't have lost a game."

I looked around at the other assistant coaches in the locker room for their reactions. Some rolled their eyes, and a few shook their heads. Within a minute, Coach Carroll came into the locker room.

"Hey, Lane," I said, "Tell Coach Carroll what you just told us."

He declined, saying it was nothing as he quickly left the dressing room.

Coach knew I was up to something.

"What did Lane say?" he asked.

"He said that if he was head coach, he wouldn't have lost a game." I replied.

Coach Carroll laughed. "That's Kiff." I appreciated that Coach was above Kiff's surliness, but to me, it was an acceptance of him glorifying himself and stroking his ego.

I was in my office a few hours later when Kiffin stepped in to confront me. "You threw me under the bus, Pat."

I could tell he was pissed. I didn't care. "More like an eighteen-wheeler, Kiff, and you deserve it, as it was a ridiculous statement," I said.

Kiff grumbled, but he knew I was right. He left my office without another word.

We spent the final week of the regular season preparing to play our cross-town rival, UCLA. It was the only game that stood in the way of competing for another National Championship opportunity. Our fourth in four years.

That game week was unlike any other in preparation. We were in disarray. Kiff, who was an excellent game planner, seemed to be mentally absent. On top of fighting a bad cold, he was consumed with getting the Oakland Raider head coaching job. Normally, he was present in the staffroom strategizing. Instead, he was in his office making phone calls

It felt disorganized, and that was further emphasized by his decision to move Thomas Williams, a linebacker, to fullback after we had lost our first and second team fullbacks to injury. *Why would we put a player with no experience playing fullback in a position to fail?* It was a horrendous decision and one of the cardinal sins of coaching: asking a player to perform in a new position with no experience.

By the time game day arrived, it was also obvious that I'd done a poor job of preparing the offensive line. We were struggling to run the ball and completely abandoned the run in the second half. We didn't look anything like a ten-win team. We lost to UCLA 13-9. Pathetic. This snapped an NCAA record streak of 63 consecutive games with scores over 20.

We went on to play in the Rose Bowl, defeating Michigan 33-18 and ending up ranked fourth in the final poll. Despite that, I was struggling to leave some of those potholes behind.

Although we won our fifth straight Pac-10 title, I felt completely frustrated losing to UCLA and missing another shot at the Natty. The Trojans were starting to show some cracks in their armor.

After the season, we headed out to recruit and found parents and high school coaches who were asking about an investigation that the NCAA was doing on USC athletics. We blew it off. We knew it was nothing serious and told the recruits, parents, and high school coaches that there was nothing to be concerned about.

But I still couldn't wrap my head around what we were being investigated for. The NCAA was very secretive.

CHAPTER 27

NCAA AMBUSH

Coach Kiffin got the job with the Oakland Raiders three weeks after the Rose Bowl. It was my view that we would miss Coach Kiffin about as much as a rock in a shoe. I still hadn't gotten over how he put himself before the team.

But there were bigger problems ahead with the NCAA. Although they remained secretive as to what they were looking at, Coach Carroll was convinced it was a wild goose chase. Why would we even think of breaking rules? We were a top academic institution with great history and traditions, basking in the warmth of the California sun. With the Pacific Ocean and beaches 20 miles to the west and the southern tip of the Sierra Nevada Mountain range 100 miles to the east, it was a paradise with a huge recruiting base.

Regardless, the NCAA was like a storm with big, billowing black clouds visible from a distance. Why they were investigating was a huge mystery to the coaches and fans. But it was now becoming a major question asked by parents and high school coaches.

Our competitors in the Pac-10 and elsewhere were carefully stoking the fire—and rightfully so. If we were going to be penalized by the NCAA, USC wouldn't be the best place to attend.

It really pissed me off because when I was at Texas A&M under Coach Jackie Sherrill's tenure, we broke rules constantly. Coach Sherrill created a win-at-all-costs culture; truth and ethics were severely wounded soldiers in the ICU and of no use.

In contrast, Coach Carroll did everything perfectly. He was never promising anything other than a chance to compete at the highest level. He loved meeting the families and engaging in conversation about USC and a young man's future. Not once did I ever see anything that would be considered an NCAA violation. But the questions about the NCAA investigation were annoying and getting harder to answer as we had no idea what was going on.

Despite all the bullshit, I loved recruiting at USC because we were always a major consideration by the prospects. Recruiting at schools that were not on the national stage was like pulling teeth. Just getting the student athletes to commit to a visit was sometimes a huge task. At USC, I always felt we would be in the top two of a prospect's choices. Again, we beat back the rumors and recruited another good class of student athletes in 2007.

* * *

In the meantime, Sabra seemed to be getting recruited herself. I noticed a little sparkle in her eye when she dropped by my office for her usual Friday lunch time visit and I had to ask.

"Are you dating someone?"

"Yes, Dad. He's a business major."

I didn't care about his major, I wanted to meet him. "What's his name?" I pressed. I was now in daddy detective mode.

"His name is Dave."

That seemed to be a boring name. I hoped he had some personality; I was already looking for a reason not to like him. "How long has this been going on?" I was curious. Sabra, now 19, had grown into a beautiful young woman, but she was still my little girl.

"About four weeks or so," Sabra replied with a bit of impudence. I teased her when she was young trying to get her to engage me in a bit of banter. As a result, she could hold her own.

"When do your mom and I get a face-to-face?" I was intent on meeting this Dave fella.

"I'll bring him by the house, but I'm not sure when."

"Good, can't wait," I shot back. For the next month, I was calling him Davy Doo-Doo. Every time I talked to her on the phone or saw her at school I asked, "So, when do we get to meet Davy Doo-Doo?" I could tell she was getting annoyed.

"Dad, don't call him that."

Oohhhhh, she was protecting him now... *Hmmmmm, she must like him more than a little*, I thought. "Well, that's who he is until I meet him."

Six weeks had passed, and it was now late spring. I had been bugging her constantly. Marti and I had gone out of town, and when we returned, Sabra and Davy Doo-Doo were at the house. He was about six feet tall with dark brown hair and an athletic build. We stepped toward each other and extended our hands.

"Hi, Mr. Ruel. I'm Davy Doo-Doo," he said, giving me a firm handshake.

On one hand, I was shocked that my name for him had been revealed, and on the other hand, I was impressed with his sense of humor. "Very nice to meet you, David." I paused for a moment before continuing. "You can break my daughter's heart, and I'm okay with that, but if you ever verbally or physically abuse her, I want you to know I'm going to jail. Do you understand that?"

David didn't miss a beat. "Yes, I do."

Marti and Sabra both looked horrified that I would say such a thing on our first introduction.

"Do you really think that was appropriate?" Marti let loose as soon as they were gone.

"All great teachers hand out the syllabus before class," I said, smiling. I knew I came on strong, but I wanted them both to know exactly how I felt. I looked at Marti and she nodded her approval.

Nevertheless, I liked his sincerity, and I was pleased that Sabra was happy.

* * *

We kicked off the 2007 season with our trademark of energy and enthusiasm that was bolstered by our new offensive coordinator, Steve Sarkisian, who had replaced Kiffin. We raced through the first three games in usual fashion.

We were 3-0, playing the Washington Huskies on the road, when we hit our first detour. Midway through the second quarter, I heard Coach Carroll shout:

"Pat! Chilo and Kristopher are hurt."

I was looking at two Trojans lying on the ground—Chilo Rachal, our guard, and Kristopher O'Dowd, our center. Two offensive linemen hurt on the same play—*Jesus Christ*. I glanced at the bench and spotted Zach Heberer and Matt Spanos running toward me. It gave me a shot of confidence that they were ready. Our head athletic trainer, Russ Romano, was on the field checking out the injured players.

"Will they be alright?" I asked.

"Don't know yet, but it looks like they'll definitely be out for a couple of weeks." I gave Zach and Matt the go-ahead nod as Chilo and Kristopher limped off the field. We defeated Washington and headed home 4-0.

The following week, we were playing the Stanford Cardinals, and according to the oddsmakers, they were a 41-point underdog.

We entered the game with 35 straight home game victories. We were up 9-0 in the second quarter when our calm and cool quarterback, John David Booty, fractured the tip of the middle finger of his passing hand. His hand had hit a Cardinal helmet while throwing. At halftime, he assured us he was okay, but his passes would sometimes sail on him. His first errant throw was intercepted and returned for a touchdown. He was clearly struggling, as he threw four interceptions in the second half. We needed to run the ball, but we were inconsistent and ineffective when we did. We had 459 yards to their 235 yards and lost the game 24-23.

The loss to Stanford was possibly one of the greatest upsets ever in the history of college football.

My soul was buried somewhere deep in the Mariana Trench. How could this have happened? It wasn't the players' fault; the blame rested solely on us, the coaches. We chose to let Booty stay in the game when he was clearly struggling. It was another record-ending game.

When we lost, we often reflected on things we could do to get better. I started thinking about the toll it took on my family. Sometimes I didn't see things before it was too late.

I was enjoying having my family with me. I was very proud of Sabra—she was practically a straight-A student and had made some good friends. Marti, although frustrated about not being able to find the job she wanted, was loving being close to the beach and drinking coffee on the rooftop deck as she perused job opportunities.

But the life of a football coach's family, whether it's college or the NFL, is totally centered around their job. During the season, I left early in the morning, between 5:30 a.m. and 6:30 a.m., and arrived back home between 10 p.m. and midnight, just in time to sleep. So, for 3-4 days a week, the majority of our communication was done over the phone, or during a lunch or dinner break. The other three days are normal eight-to-ten-hour days. It is a 24-7 job. To be a coach, you've got to love football, love the competition, and love being an impact on those you coach, but it comes at a cost to your family. Winning is like a Band-Aid; it covers all your wounds. Losing rips that Band-Aid off and exposes everything that's wrong with your life.

Coach Carroll tried to offset the imbalance of a coach's life by hosting weekly family dinners at the office. It was one of his ingredients to creating a great culture. I made sure we took special summer vacations. It was my way of saying, "Thank you for being there for me." We went to the Orlando theme parks, Atlantis in the Bahamas, Key West, and Cuba. After the season, Coach Carroll and some awesome USC alumni would provide us expense-free trips to Cabo or Hawaii. It was an opportunity to re-energize with our families.

But these escapes didn't solve the six months of neglect. Everything became a bit more normal in the off-season, but we still were on the road recruiting, looking for the next great player, and it was all beginning to crash down on Marti.

Marti had worked my entire coaching career, and she was somewhat insulated. It was perfect in some ways, because she had value and growth being on her own team. But now, with a stalled career, our daughter at college, and a sometimes-husband, she was like a singular flower in the desert.

After a day or two at the bottom of the ocean, I relied on one of my favorite sayings: Don't get captured. I surfaced with a renewed attitude. I was more aware to be more supportive of Marti and to help us get back on track.

* * *

We recovered from the loss to Stanford and beat Arizona at home 20-13. Then Notre Dame on the road, 38-0.

Then came a loss to Oregon. Like other rare losses, we were again plagued by turnovers. Oregon was a good team, and the team with the least mistakes won... Oregon 24, USC 17. Later, however, we dominated the rest of the teams and finished the season by beating UCLA 24-7. Sweet fucking revenge.

We ended the season 11-2, winning our sixth straight Pac-10 title and ending up in the Rose Bowl. We beat 13th-ranked Illinois 49-17, finishing third in the final national rankings.

We again signed another great class of student athletes. We were all excited about the 2008 season as the staff remained intact.

That April, when the NFL draft was underway, I was worried about Sam Baker, our All-American left tackle, who I had convinced to stay for his senior year by dangling the promise of being drafted in the first-round pick. But now I was concerned because he had missed several games due to a severe hamstring injury. The draft was rolling along, and I was nervous. Then my phone rang.

It was Sam. "I'm a first-round pick, and I graduated!" he yelled with excitement, "Thanks, Coach!"

At that moment, there could not have been a happier coach in the universe. Sam was drafted by the Atlanta Falcons. I felt as though I was part of his great accomplishment.

As we prepared for the 2008 season, the NCAA investigation—which had been going on for three years—continued to loom in the background. Everything had gone so quiet that I wondered if it was the calm before the storm. Were they that intent on taking USC down, or were they that inept? I was beginning to think it was both.

But the longer it went, the less concerned we became, instead shifting our thoughts to the season ahead. We had an excellent team coming back: a company of juniors who chose to stay. Maybe Sam Baker's decision influenced the others.

With the graduation of quarterback John David Booty, our biggest concern was finding someone to replace him. That someone turned out to be Mark Sanchez, who had been waiting for three years to take center stage. That stage was previously occupied by three nationally recognized players: Palmer, Leinart, and Booty.

As it turned out, those three years of preparation made Mark more than ready, as he performed extraordinarily well. The 2008 season was a blast; we went 12-1. We dominated our opponents, with the highlight of the season being a crushing defeat of fith-ranked Ohio State at home, 35-3. The lowlight was the one loss on the road to Oregon State; we were down 21-0 at the half. They had played the perfect game, rushing the ball for 176 yards and controlling the time of possession. They had the ball almost a full ten minutes more than us and had no turnovers. We had two turnovers and lost 27-21.

Coach Carroll was quite remarkable after a loss. He simply identified the problems and went about fixing them. He didn't blame players or coaches. I was always amazed at his ability to get to the source or cause of the problem and then tell us how we were going to solve it.

This team was not as talented as the 2005 team, especially on offense, but it had a sense of purpose. We won our seventh consecutive Pac-10 championship and another Rose Bowl versus sixth-ranked Penn State. We led Penn State 31-7 at halftime; the final score was 38-24.

That year, we played six teams with nine plus wins: Oregon, Oregon State, Cal, Ohio State, and Penn State. It was a National-Championship-type team. We finished second in the Coaches poll and third in the Associated Press poll. But our success came at a huge price. There was a mass exodus at the end of the season with 11 players entering the NFL 2009 draft class. All 11 were drafted.

Sanchez, our quarterback, was fifth pick in the first round. He left as a junior; he was one and done. It was a horrible decision for USC. We now had to play someone with little or no experience at the quarterback position. We lost our offensive coordinator, Steve Sarkisian, who became the new head coach at the University of Washington and took Nick Holt, our defensive coordinator, as his own.

Reloading this time would not be easy. The NCAA investigation was heating up. There were rumors flying about Reggie Bush's stepdad, LaMar Griffin. He apparently accepted a house from some agent in San Diego 130 miles from campus. Pete had questioned the staff, but no one knew anything.

Three years of an investigation, and all they had produced was rumors. It took a year and a half to build Disney World; the Empire State building was built in a year; the Benghazi Investigation took two years and four months; and NCAA found nothing. The investigation was sounding more and more like a union job. It was becoming obvious to me that they had put Inspector Gadget, Detective Clouseau, and Maxwell Smart in charge.

CHAPTER 28

THE GOOD, THE BAD AND THE UGLY

I walked into Coach Carroll's office like a I had just discovered gold. "Coach, you weren't accounting for Michael Vick's (Atlanta's QB) scrambles, and it was over a thousand yards. So they finished twenty-seventh in the NFL in rushing offense, not first."

Coach Carroll loved Alex Gibbs, Atlanta's offensive line coach and former Denver Broncos offensive line coach. He had tried for two years to get me to run outside zone exclusively, just like the Atlanta Falcons offense. He thought it was the secret to Atlanta's success. I had watched a couple Atlanta games; the outside zone looked consistently average. The magic was Michael Vick, who would scramble on pass plays. Since most quarterbacks don't have those kinds of yards, I gave him the NFL average of 200 yards. That adjustment—taking away hidden quarterback scrambles that vaunted Atlanta's rushing attack—dropped them from first to 27th out of 32 teams in the NFL.

He looked as disgusted as I had ever seen him. I was going against him, which I almost never did.

"You don't get it. They went to two Super Bowls while at Denver." He shot me a look of disdain.

Nevertheless, I continued. "It looks like the NFL has caught up with the outside zone," I barked. My experienced and evidence told me that the inside zone had always averaged better consistency and multiple run schemes were much harder to prepare for.

Coach disagreed, saying there was genius behind its purity. "You will never be as pure as Alex," Coach said. He then motioned me to go.

He had issued me a challenge. I took it. I went back to my office and wrote on my board in big letters, WWAD (what would Alex do).

I love Pete because he was honest and created a wonderful culture, but that was my way to dig at him. He never acknowledged it, so after a month, I wrote WWPD (what would Pat do). I was hurt that he brushed me off, but I knew he was swamped with the exodus of two coordinators and a quarterback coach.

Coach Carroll announced a new defensive coordinator and a new offensive coordinator. Both were on staff. They were well respected and solid choices. With one spot to fill, he chose Jeremy Bates from the Denver Broncos to be assistant head coach and quarterback coach. It became immediately apparent that the culture was on an unstable cliff.

Bates, who had a surly attitude, let us know early and often he was not going to entertain our points of view. I was confused. He had taken over the offensive coordinator position that Coach Carroll gave to John Morton. John, who was on staff previously, was well organized and an excellent coach. Who told who what? That was the question of the day. Did Coach Carroll turn everything over to Bates? Coach Morton was upset. He felt as if Carroll's offer to be the offensive coordinator lacked substance. Because of our success and belief in coach, none of us complained.

Whoever recommended Bates to coach didn't tell him the complete story. Bates knew what he wanted, and we would be the adjusters. We now needed to learn the Broncos' way of doing things. Within one week, I knew we were looking at a little dictator.

I recognized that he was going into a program that won two national titles and seven straight Pac-10 titles. It had to be difficult for Bates. He had the stress of maintaining a high standard. I loved that he had principles, but when he was challenged, he would denounce players and coaches alike. It was evident that the chemistry we once had was gone.

Coach Carroll was busy with the new defense coordinator Rocky Seto. None of the offensive staff would communicate to coach that that Bates was hard to work with and that he was often a Debbie Downer. However, let's be clear; he joined a program that had 80 wins and nine losses, and we thought we had the answers to stay that way. It was a tough situation for Bates, and he lacked the people skills to navigate it successfully.

He was not a Pete-Carroll-type coach. He took the fun out of the culture. Everyone seemed to be getting frustrated. My rule, "Don't get captured," was being tested regularly.

Spring practice had started, and on this day, it was pouring. Despite Albert Hammond's song, "It Never Rains in Southern California," there were exceptions. We didn't have an indoor facility. We stretched as the rain began to dissipate. A huge puddle had formed on the side of the field. It was about two inches deep and stretched for 30 yards.

I yelled, "Watch this!" It was time for me to create a little juice. I lined up ten yards in front of the puddle and ran as fast as I could, diving and laying out like the start of the freestyle event at the Summer Olympics. I slid for 20 yards, and the players all laughed as water shot up around me like a speed boat.

At the end of practice, Coach Carroll, having seen me slide, wanted to take the next step. Competition was his favorite word, and his fun meter was always at ten. He called the team up. "I think we should have a slide-off between Coach Ruel and Coach Franklin." The team cheered.

Coach Franklin was our defensive line coach. He would go first. He was 6'1" and 255 pounds. The players cheered as he sprinted, then he dove and slid about 22 yards. Water was spraying everywhere. My turn to take my 6'3", 250-pound self for the win. I was running at a speed only I could appreciate. As the players cheered, I dove and slid, but I ended up a yard short. I immediately called for a rematch. Coach Carroll loved it.

This time, instead of bending to make a smooth transition from running to sliding, I dove without dropping down, and when I hit, it felt like I'd just belly flopped off a three-meter diving board. The sudden impact took my breath away. Coach Franklin beat me again by a yard.

That night, I noticed pain around my rib cage on the left side. It would come and go for the next several weeks. I mostly felt it doing sit-ups or boogie boarding at the beach. After a month and a half, I knew it was time to see the doctor.

As a coach in college for the NFL, I had very well qualified doctors at my service any time I needed them.

I drove to USC med on a Friday. In less than 20 minutes, I was lying on my back with my shirt off. The nurse/technician had spread a cold jelly on my chest and proceeded to do an ultrasound of my rib cage.

As the technician moved the device around my torso, she made barely audible discovery sounds; "Mmmmmm," and "Ohhhhhh," and "Okaaaaaay."

"What are you seeing?" I asked. My mind was racing.

She said, "The doctor will discuss this with you."

I put my shirt back on and we headed to the doctor's office.

"Go home, Coach. I'll call you with the results," the doctor said.

I proceeded out to the parking lot when a nurse yelled, "Coach Ruel, come back!"

What the hell? Did I leave something? I thought.

When I got close to her, she said, "The doctor wants you to have an MRI immediately." The arrow of anxiety planted itself deep inside me.

"Why's that?" I almost didn't want to ask, and she wasn't able to say. I was suddenly very quiet as we entered the doctor's office.

"Coach, you have what appears to be a large mass on your liver, so the MRI will give us a better look. Don't worry—it's possible that it's benign."

The doctor left and the nurse took me to the MRI room. The MRI technician handing me a hospital gown and socks said, "Get undressed and put these on."

In less than two minutes, I was lying face up on the table. Before sliding me into the tube, the technician asked, "Are you claustrophobic?"

"No," I responded. I was wondering how long I would have to be in that tube. "How long will this take?" I asked, as if I was in a hurry. There was no hurry; I felt the pain of that arrow.

"Around 30-40 minutes," he said.

"That's easy—I'll probably fall asleep." I was trying to add some humor to this moment, but I was a bit scared.

The technician laughed and said, "Just be still, no movement."

There was a bit of noise, and I concentrated on not moving. Where would this fateful day lead me? *Is my coaching life over? Am I now entering the world of surgery and chemo? I don't want people to have to take care of me.* It was my job to help them. Again, I was trying to employ "Don't get captured." As I told my daughter many times, "Life is just a bunch of hurdles. Just be a great hurdler."

When the technician announced, "You're done," I was momentarily relieved.

The nurse appeared with matter-of-fact instructions. "Go home, and the doctor will call you around five p.m. after they read your MRI." I looked at my watch. It was 3 p.m. *No way am I going back to the office,* I thought. I heeded her advice and headed home.

I was driving down the 110 freeway heading west. I was about 20 minutes from our home in Hermosa Beach. I usually played music, but this time I wanted to be with my body. I was talking to my body. *You're going to be ok. You're a survivor. You're tough. Help me help you.* I believe the mind is extremely powerful, and I was issuing instructions to my body.

I arrived home and was surprised to find Sabra there. She had her own apartment but had decided to come home for the weekend. I was excited to see her, but I didn't want to expose her to any bad news just yet.

I took a seat in the living room and turned on the TV. I was aimlessly perusing the guide looking for anything to amuse me while I waited. I turned on ESPN and was trying to lose myself in a women's college volleyball match. Sabra watched with me, commenting on the game. I wasn't listening; my mind had parked itself in the "what if" room.

It was 4:35. Every second became a minute; every minute became an hour. I was constantly glancing at my phone for the time. My ringtone was the theme song from the movie *The Good, The Bad and The Ugly.* I don't have to tell you who I was rooting for.

As five o'clock neared, my mind suddenly had kicked into conquering mode. *It doesn't matter. I will fight this, and I will win.* I got up to get a drink, then it dawned on me: I didn't want to have the conversation with the doctor in front of my daughter. After all, he sent me home because he didn't want to tell me face-to-face. My thoughts were shifting back and forth like a switchback trail up the mountain. One minute I was standing on top of the mountain as the conquering hero, and the next moment I was hanging on a cliff by my fingers, hoping somebody would rescue me.

"Sabra, I can't find what I want to drink in the refrigerator. I'm going to run to the store," I said.

"Dad, there's plenty enough to drink here."

I was at a loss to make up what I wanted to drink. I moved toward the door as though I hadn't heard her.

I got in the car and drove it to a nearby park. It was 4:50. Marti had found her dream job at San Diego State; she was the associate vice president for student services and was heading home as well. She got the job before the 2008 season. It required her to leave on Monday morning early at 5 a.m. and she would return on Thursday night or Friday afternoon, depending on her schedule. I was ambivalent; I liked that she had her own team, but I wanted her to have a job that would allow her to sleep in our bed.

I parked and waited for the doctor's call. Five o'clock. I took a deep breath. 5:02; no call yet. If I was a doctor, I wouldn't want to make these calls either. *It's probably nothing, but what do I do if it is?* I needed to have plan on what to do and how to do it. Finally, at 5:08, my phone rang.

"Hi, Doc, what's up?" I was trying to sound upbeat.

"You want the good news first or the bad news?"

"Good news first, Doc." I wanted the good news first; it would buffer the bad news. Everything seemed to be in slow motion.

"Your liver is one and half times the size of a normal liver. So, no mass. Just an extremely big liver." Every word was imaged phonetically in my brain as he spoke. I was elated as I waited for the bad news.

"The bad news is that you have torn cartilage in your rib cage, which might take up to three months to fully heal," Doc laughed. I think he felt my anxiety bubble had popped.

Oh my god, that's it! My yo-yo ride was over! "Thanks Doc! You're the best." I started the car and headed home.

Why is it that our minds seem to run out of control without facts? I was already spreading my ashes in the ocean. Now, with an uninterrupted attitude of gratitude, I was back to my old self.

* * *

The dark clouds of the NCAA that had been billowing off in the distance were suddenly here. Before the start of the 2009 season, the NCAA was interviewing the coaching staff. Four years, and finally I had two investigators in my office. They asked, "Who have you seen go into Todd McNair's office (Reggie Bush's coach)?"

I had a clear view of his doorway. "The only people I have ever seen in that office were his players, his kids, and occasionally a recruiting host to get info on a visiting prospect."

"What about alums or agents?"

"No," I responded.

"Are you telling us the truth?"

"Yes. I'm insulted that you would imply I wasn't. Which brings me to a point—I have a few questions I want to ask you."

"No, we will not answer any of your questions because you don't have due process under the NCAA." The investigator's face turned red with anger, and mine did too.

"Well then, I guess we're through. Why should I even talk with you? You accused me of lying, and I have to sit here and take it? I don't think so."

About two days later, they came into my office and said, "We need your recruiting logs."

I explained that I'd turned them in a week earlier.

"We can't find them. Do them over."

I was infuriated, as I knew that there was no way that they were that careless. I knew they were trying pressure me. I glared at them. "How is it that I do what I'm supposed to do, and you lose my recruiting logs, and now I'm responsible for your incompetence?"

They leaned back in their chairs, looking a bit disgusted. I knew we ran a clean program, and I wasn't about to be their piñata.

The investigation centered around an ex-con, Lloyd Lake, who was a sports agent wannabe giving Reggie's stepdad, LaMar Griffin, a house in San Diego in hopes that Reggie would sign his future away to a man with a checkered past and no qualifications. Basketball's top player OJ Mayo was under investigation as well; he too had two vultures with questionable pasts, Rodney Guillory and Louis Johnson, possibly providing him with gifts. In return, he would sign with them. These were violations by vultures preying on athletes and virtually impossible for coaches and administrators to monitor.

Things were heating up, and the picture was getting clearer to me. The NCAA was starting to look like they were manipulating an investigation to purposefully bring USC down. And they had several characterless suspects whose words they accepted. It felt like the NCAA had some sort of vendetta. I had been in a cheating program, and I knew what it looked like, smelled like, and felt like. USC was not even close to that atmosphere.

It felt like a tsunami was on its way. First, it was the athletic director who was unsupportive of his football and basketball coach. Next was Bates, who didn't buy into the coach's culture and was changing the offense to his way only, which I accepted even though I felt like we were being sabotaged. Moreover, our star quarterback, Mark Sanchez, was one and done, leaving after his junior year, which meant we were going to play with an inexperienced quarterback. Teams can get away with some inexperience, but not at the quarterback position. The method at USC for quarterbacks was to train for two to three years, break records, graduate, and play in the NFL.

I had hoped it would sort itself out. But as the season got underway, the rushing waters of that tsunami had clearly taken over.

We were having a difficult time as coaches changing from what we once knew to the Denver Broncos' offense. Then, on top of all that, our athletic director was questioning the veracity of his coaches. All of this was sowing the seeds of discontent. The magic of our culture and style was on life support.

We ended up 9-4, beating Boston College in the Emerald Bowl 24-13. We finished fifth in the conference and Oregon won the Pac-10 title. That was a good season for most, but for USC, it was the beginning of the end.

Rumors were flying about Coach Carroll leaving for the NFL, like every year, only this time he was quiet. He loved USC. He brought them back to their rightful place. But now there was a bogus, phony, and spurious NCAA investigation, and Athletic Director Mike Garrett, who forgot the meaning of the Trojan motto, "Fight On." He abandoned them.

The cracks in the Trojan armor were now crevices and canyons.

CHAPTER 29

NOT INVITED

I was buzzing with anticipation as I worked on my recruiting list, waiting for my phone to ring. It was mid-January, and after weeks of intensifying rumors, we had just learned that Coach Carroll had accepted a job with the Seattle Seahawks. I knew Coach Carroll wouldn't take any job in the NFL without full control. He had been there and done that, and was not about to make that mistake again. Again, like Bill Parcells said, "If they want you to cook the dinner, at least they ought to let you shop for some of the groceries." This was important to Coach, and I was excited to be a part of that environment in an NFL setting.

I glanced at my phone, willing it to ring. I'd heard he had already called some of the coaches. I was anxiously waiting for my turn. After an excruciating hour, my phone finally lit up.

"Hey, Coach," I said excitedly.

Coach Carroll quickly responded, "Pat, I've decided to move in a different direction." Wow, it was like being hit on the head by a hammer. I was stunned and could feel anger creeping its way in. Another "Don't get captured" moment.

"I understand," I quickly told Coach, forcing the words out of my mouth. I was hurt. All the coaches I had worked for had always wanted me to stay or go with them. First time for everything. Coach Carroll wanted Alex Gibbs, whom he admired greatly.

"I'll be fine. I have six months left on my contract," I said. *Was it me or was it Bates?* I thought. He and I had our conflicts.

Then there was a pause; two friends taking different paths, neither sure what to say.

Finally, I said, "Thanks for the opportunity. It was great."

Another pause. "You should come up and visit sometime."

"Will do," I said. I was still in shock as I ended the call. The guy I admired for his ability to fix and maintain a good culture was now telling me I wasn't good enough, or that he had found something better. Marti was upset, and I was too, but I was relieved that I didn't have to be in the same room as Bates. We were just different.

With all that had transpired, I knew I needed to find something that would give me a purpose. It was time to finish the offensive line manual. I knew it would keep me from feeling lost. As the spring approached, I even thought of going into private business, but I realized the love of coaching might not let that happen.

I enjoyed the freedom of planning my own schedule and spent hours in my basement working on my manual. By the time May rolled around, I had a massive amount of material, but I needed pictures to illustrate proper techniques. My only problem was that I didn't have any players to demonstrate.

Even so, I was feeling accomplished. It was matched by a bigger accomplishment—Sabra had just graduated from USC with a degree in film and critical studies. I would miss those days Sabra would drop by my office for a chat or leave a traditional note signed, "LaLaLaLa, Sabra." But I was so proud of her, as she had a 3.7 GPA. Oh yes, she got her car—a Volkswagen Jetta—and the 10K, as I promised.

Sabra was excited about finding her dream job. She went to all the big studios: Universal, Warner Brothers, Sony, 20th Century Fox, and Paramount. When she returned, she was clearly deflated. She said, "No one is hiring. I'm going to work for The Gap." She knew it was a fallback. She had worked there in the summers past.

I was not about to let her take the easy way out. It would only hurt her in the end. "No, you're not. You're going to go back and tell them you'll work for free. We'll take care of your gas and food. Nobody goes to USC to work at The Gap."

She laughed and said, "Maybe you can find a free job too, and Mom can pay for both of us." I always encouraged her wit—it showed she was engaged in the conversation—but with that comment, she may have been too engaged.

She went back to all the ones that turned her down. That showed some perseverance, and Sony hired her for free. I knew that if she were performing well inside the organization, she had a better chance of being hired with pay later.

Sabra found her job, but I knew I would have to wait until December when coaches were being fired and hired at the end of the football season. I was a bit distraught because USC was a special time for us as a family. We were winning and my family was together. Now, we were interrupted again with concerns about the future and possible new job opportunities.

Amidst it all, the NCAA released its sanctions against USC: two years post-season ban; 30 scholarship losses over a three-year period; vacating old games including the BCS

Championship; and USC had to disassociate itself from Reggie Bush and return his Heisman Trophy.

I was so mad my inner soul blurted, *Those corrupt motherfuckers!* Not one coach, player, or booster did anything illegal. It was unprecedented. The NCAA had acted egregiously and with malice toward USC. They tried to place blame on Todd McNair, our running back coach, with no evidence. The only justice came ten years later when the NCAA was forced to settle a suit brought on by Todd McNair for an undisclosed amount (reportedly eight figures).

But I wasn't happy with USC either, whose fight song had these primary words: "Fight on." Well, they didn't. They were cowering. But it was no longer my problem, and I, like Reggie Bush, became disassociated with the Trojans.

My contract ended in June. I was getting anxious because I was 60 years old, and it was a young man's game. The fact that I had worked for some of the very best coaches and produced many NFL players and All-Americans may not have been enough.

I started calling my coaching friends to stay in the loop. I wanted them to know I was available. Then, in mid-July, I got a call from Jeff Jagodzinski. He coached tight ends at Green Bay where he and I worked together. He was now the new head coach of the Omaha Nighthawks in Nebraska, a professional team in the UFL (United Football League).

"Hey Pat," he boomed into the phone, "I want you to come out here and coach the offensive line." At first, I wasn't interested, but he was a close friend, and he needed me, and I was missing being on a team.

Jeff filled me in; the league was a start-up. That was scary, but then he informed that we had Jeff Garcia, the former quarterback of the San Francisco 49ers, and Ahman Green, former running back of the Green Bay Packers. *Well*, I thought, *if it's good enough for those former NFL players, it's good enough for me.* My salary wasn't enough to get admittance to Disneyland, but I was doing what I loved.

When I told Marti about this unique opportunity to coach former pro players, she looked at me like I was an alien who had just landed in the living room. "Pat, it sounds like a player and coach graveyard."

"No," I responded. "It's where we can all do what we love doing for free." I laughed and said, "Besides, it's only a nine-week season." I was doing my best to make it sound like an awesome opportunity.

She snickered. "When does the 'I Am Desperate League' start?"

"September," I said, knowing there was some truth in what she said.

"Wonderful. Are you competing with the NFL and college?" she asked sarcastically.

"Well, not exactly. We're not in their markets," I said with a bit of trepidation. "I'll be home before Thanksgiving."

Marti's eyes rolled. We both knew that I was already in Fantasyland, but I felt wanted and needed.

Leaving my family again? What the hell is wrong with me?

I thought about *Paint Your Wagon*, a musical that my first love, Margie Parker, dragged me to in high school. I fell in love with the music and went out immediately and bought the eight track. I played it a lot. A particular song grabbed my soul; the song was called, "Wand'rin' Star." It seemed to fit me because I was addicted to the next challenge or adventure.

The lyrics were sung by Lee Marvin, who can't sing, but his raspy voice fit the song perfectly. The final lines spoke to me like a voice from above.

And where am I wand'rin'? Omaha, Nebraska...

By mid-August, I was on the plane. I paid for my flight, and I had no car. It felt like my first job. Nevertheless, I was excited and was not going to let those things deter me. I landed in a place where summers are hot and humidity runs wild, and where winters are cold and snow runs deep. On the way to our hotel, it was evident the Earth was flat in Nebraska. I gave up the ocean, the mountains, and the constant 75-degree weather to coach for free in Omaha. Wand'rin' star? More like a Wand'rin' Nut.

Our coaches, players, and trainers all lived at the Ramada Inn. They called it a resort because it had a water slide in the pool area. It was super convenient; we used the hotel's meeting rooms for our staff and players. We had vans that took everybody to the practice field.

I realized more than ever it wasn't the salary, facilities, and the perks that made coaching so enjoyable; it was the relationships and the friendships it afforded. Most of the players had already played in the NFL. Some had a desire to get back to the NFL, but their real motivation was the love of the game that they all played as kids. It was the esprit de corps, the togetherness and camaraderie, that gave us a natural social wealth in the core of the human soul.

Training camp was in full throttle. We were three weeks away from our opening game against the Hartford Colonials.

Although the humidity made me sweat like a turkey at Thanksgiving, I couldn't believe how much fun it was to coach again. Within a week, I could see the improvement the offensive line was making.

With twelve days before our first game, I had a great meeting with my offensive line. We covered all the install and then told a few jokes. I went back to my room and looked over practice plans. It was a full day, and I was ready for bed when my phone rang. It was Coach Carroll.

We made small talk for a couple of minutes, which was unlike him. Then he blurted it out. "I need you to come to Seattle."

Once again, I was stunned by his words. It had been almost eight months since he dropped the bomb on me.

"Why?" I asked. I was confused. *Did the Seahawk mascot die?*

"Alex Gibbs quit."

I couldn't help but wonder, did he quit or was he fired? I knew Alex to be a great coach, but I also knew that, like me, he had certain things he believed in.

"Coach, why did he quit?" I pushed.

"I don't want to talk about that." I could feel his anger and disappointment. Anger was an emotion Coach Carroll rarely carried.

"So, you want me back?" I only asked to him to hear him say it.

"Yes, and I need you right away. We have one week before our opening game." I could hear the sense of urgency in his voice, but I felt like a desert flower getting the first rain.

"Is Bates okay with this?" I asked.

"He doesn't have a say," he shot back. I knew instantly to drop that subject.

"I should get bonus compensation," I said kiddingly.

Apparently, Coach was in no mood to joke around. "Of course. How much?" he responded.

After giving him a figure and discussing travel arrangements, I hung up the phone and began processing the enormity of what had just happened.

After months of worrying about how I could have done things better and wondering if my coaching career was taking a U-turn, I was given a golden ticket. I was back in the NFL! I was headed to a beautiful city, and the icing on the cake was that I'd be back in the culture I loved.

I couldn't wait to share the news with Marti. I grabbed my phone and called her. "Guess who had a moment of clarity?" I announced as soon as she answered.

"You?" she shot back. Not what I was fishing for, but I understood.

"No, Coach Carroll. He wants me back."

There was a moment of silence. "Your profession is for crazy people," she said, and then added, "and that makes me crazy." After 14 moves, she was just as convinced that I was born under a wand'rin' star.

"Are we going to sell the house?" she asked. "Do you want me to..."

I immediately cut her off, "Absolutely not. That's where we're going to retire." We had gorgeous views of the Pacific Ocean, Catalina, Malibu, and our family safety spot. I wasn't about to give that up.

"I was also trying to ask you about my job," Marti interjected. I could hear the frustration in her voice. As much as I wanted to be together, I knew that Marti didn't want to quit her job; that was her team, and she loved working with the college students. I never wanted to hold her back from growth or achievement.

"Marti, I know you want to keep your job. It's your decision."

Suddenly, her voice changed from frustration to excitement. She wanted me to say it was up to her. "We can fly up for home games and go to games here in LA."

Sabra, like Marti, was a veteran of the coaching lifestyle, and, like me, she craved the next adventure. She was already checking flights. I always wanted the best for everybody, but I knew that didn't always translate to what was best for the team, especially our family team. I told myself that it was only a three-hour flight from Los Angeles to Seattle and convinced myself we would manage—we had done this before.

Here we go again. Sabra and Marti would stay in Hermosa, and I would take my wandering self to Seattle.

CHAPTER 30

SEATTLE SEAHAWKS

I stared out my plane window thinking about my morning meeting with the Nighthawks offensive line. After being on the job for less than two weeks, I was bailing on Jeff and my players. I had already spoken to Coach Jagodzinski earlier; he was gracious and supportive, like a true friend. Now I had to tell my players, and I felt horrible about it.

I headed down the hallway of the hotel, trying to formulate how to break the news. When I entered the meeting room, my players were already there.

"What's up, Coach?" George Foster said as he and the others took their seats. He had been drafted as the 20th pick overall by the Denver Broncos.

I assumed my spot in the front of the room, took a deep breath, and forced the words out. "Coach Carroll called me last night and offered me a job with the Seattle Seahawks."

They all looked at me, stunned. The room was quiet.

"Are you taking the job?" PJ Alexander, another former NFL player, asked. Before I could respond, he gave me the go-ahead nod. "You'd be crazy not to."

I had so many mixed emotions that all I could do was nod my head.

In a matter of a few seconds, the room erupted, and they were on their feet congratulating me. "Don't forget me, Coach," several players echoed. They all wanted to play again in the NFL.

I loved their enthusiasm for me; it showed how selfless offensive linemen were. They rarely got credit and were often criticized. They were the epitome of the word "team." I truly had an attitude of gratitude because they were not only supporting me, but they were also excited for me.

* * *

The flight attendant was busy telling us to put our tray tables up and return our seats to the upright position. We would be landing soon, and I was thrilled to start my new adventure. As I perused the terrain out my window, Mt. Rainier suddenly appeared. It loomed majestically over the city of Seattle. It was a gorgeous day, and the sunlight glistened off the small amount of snow on the peak. I was replacing the Midwest flat plains and farmland with the imposing Cascade and Olympic mountain ranges.

The plane landed, and I hurried off like a kid on the last day of school knowing summer vacation was about to begin. While I was hustling to baggage claim, Coach texted me that he was outside. I couldn't wait to see him.

As soon as I stepped out the door, I spotted him standing by his car, excitingly waving me over. It was good to be back—we were connected on so many levels, like a peanut butter and jelly sandwich. The minute we pulled out of the airport area, he began filling me in on the offensive line. I was emotionally charged up to be back with Coach.

As we drove down the 405 freeway, I couldn't help but be in awe of the large Douglas fir trees that lined the highway. This feeling was only magnified when we pulled into the Seahawks parking lot. Directly in front of me was a huge body of water that was as smooth as glass. Lake Washington was decorated with giant pines and multi-million-dollar homes. On the north side of the lake, I could see the I-90 bridge to Seattle and the stunning skyline of the city of Bellevue. It was so beautiful it belonged on a postcard, or at least a vacation album. I immediately understood this was one of the sweeteners that lured Coach Carroll to the Seahawks; like me, he loved the water.

After getting settled in my office, I headed down the hall to see Coach Bates. I popped my head into his office, unsure of what to expect. He seemed happy to see me, but I felt he had been mentored by Coach. Either way, I felt needed and wanted by Coach Carroll, and that was all I cared about.

Early the next morning, I took a seat in the team meeting room to watch the players file in. As soon as they were situated, Coach Carroll began to address them.

"We have a new coach who was with me at USC and will be working with the offensive line... Coach Ruel," he announced. As he pointed to me, I stood up, and the players responded with some light clapping.

I quickly observed how upbeat and engaging the players were—the first sign that they had bought in. The culture he developed and produced at USC with college kids seemed to be working beautifully with the pro players.

It was like I had never left. We jumped right into game week. We had deficiencies at almost every position. As the season progressed, it became apparent that we were not a particularly talented team, but we had an awesome attitude.

We played hard. We found ways to score on special teams and defenses. We even designed trick plays to help us get an edge, but it wasn't enough. The holidays had arrived, and we were 6-8 with two games left to our season.

It was a Thursday night around 10 p.m. on December 23. I had worked a 16-hour day and was exhausted as I pulled into the Marriott Residence Inn where the Seahawks had been putting me up. It was three miles from the facility.

"Home sweet hotel."

My family had arrived that day and were waiting for me in my room. When I entered the hotel, it was like a ghost town. There was nobody in the lobby and just one girl behind the reservation desk.

I waved and she smiled. "You, a rabbi, and an atheist are the only people staying here." She laughed, and so did I. "It sounds like the opening line of a joke."

Everybody was off for the holidays, but my family would be basically spending it by themselves in the Marriott, with intermittent visits from me.

A vacuum of silence filled the elevator as I rode it to the fifth floor. The same desertedness filled the hallway as I walked to my room. There was something very sad about it, but as I opened the door, I could hear "The Little Drummer Boy." Only Christmas music could warm my heart like this.

My family got up from the couch to greet me. In the corner was a perfectly shaped tree about three feet high with lights, ornaments, and presents under the tree—but my family was the only gift I wanted.

As Marti and I embraced, Sabra and Dave, who had become a fixture in our lives, joined in for a group hug. It made my eyes water. The old saying, "Absence makes the heart grow fonder," was in play.

We indulged in Christmas cookies and fudge that they had brought from California. We enjoyed the treats, listened to a few more Christmas carols, and went to bed. When we got up, it was Christmas Eve. I had five hours to enjoy with my family. By 1 p.m., I was back in the office getting things finalized for our trip to Tampa to play the Buccaneers.

The team traveled on Christmas day. The charter plane was decorated by the flight attendants. Some players even had on Santa hats. Coach Carroll was about living in the moment; he wanted the players and coaches to enjoy it as much as possible. He believed that if they felt good, they would perform better.

It was unusually cold for Florida; 49 degrees at game time. We scored first, on a boot play. Our quarterback, Matt Hasselback, chose to run it in, but he looked like Chester from the TV show *Gunsmoke* as he limped his way for a touchdown.

"What's wrong with Matt?" Coach Carroll asked. We all wanted to know.

One of the trainers filled us in. "He pulled his gluteus maximus."

The coaches on the sideline were looking at each other in disbelief.

Kippy Brown, our receivers' coach, glanced at me and smirked. "Who pulls their ass jogging untouched into the end zone?"

It was a good question, but we could tell Matt was in pain. The coaches were all asking, "Is he okay? Can he play?" He was unable to continue, and our execution suffered.

I was already seeing the headline in the Seattle Times: *Seahawks Defeated by Gluteus Maximus*

We lost 38-15.

Our five-hour, 2,539-mile plane trip back to Seattle was like a ride in a flying funeral home. Players slept, and coaches reviewed the game. Amazingly, we still had a chance to win the division in our last game of the season playing the LA Rams at home. They were 7-8 and we were 6-9.

Even though we had no chance at a winning season, we were still upbeat. This was the mark of a good culture—regardless of setbacks, we kept going. In good cultures, hope is eternal.

Going into our final game of the regular season, Coach Carroll maintained his positive ways. He was always telling us where we needed to get better and did so in a cerebral way. It was such a 180-degree turn from my time with the NY Giants. I was part of a 6-10 losing season, and it was the longest season of my life. After each game, Coach Coughlin would demonstrably bring the disappointment of losing to center stage, often chastising coaches and players. But I was told there was more than one way to skin a cat.

My family toured Seattle in my absence. They visited the Space Needle, Pike's Market, and Post Alley with its Gum Wall, featuring 250,000 pieces of chewed-up gum. Totally gross, but you must see it to believe it.

With a win over the Rams, we could clinch the division. Matt Hasselback was back from his butt injury and led us to victory 16-6. We won our division. Holy cannoli—we were in the playoffs! The Seahawks were the first team in NFL history to win their division with a losing record 7-9. Our opponents were the New Orleans Saints and Drew Brees, the reigning Super Bowl Champions.

The week of preparation flew by at the speed of sound. Entering the stadium at game time, I could feel the electricity of the crowd. The hair on my arm was standing at attention. Seattle was starving for a winning team. Our fans, the 12s, took their role in helping us win very seriously; they often made it impossible for the opposing teams to hear.

My family and the fans were on their feet most of the game, making it challenging for the Saints' quarterback to communicate.

It became known as the Beast Quake game. Marshawn Lynch ran for a 67-yard touchdown in the fourth quarter. At least seven Saints players had a chance to stop him but, on this play, he was truly a beast. The run produced crowd noise so loud that it created a mini earthquake.

Another first: We became the only sub-.500 team to win a playoff game, and we did it against last year's Super Bowl Champion 41-38. Working an 80-hour week and losing is an abyss, but winning is heaven. We were standing at the gates.

My family left on Monday at 5 a.m. to get back to their jobs. They were hoarse and emotionally elevated.

The following week, we traveled to Chicago to play the Bears and lost 35-24 on a cloudy, blustery, 24-degree day. Our season was over. But there were many reasons to be excited.

I was done wandering for now—I had found a new home.

CHAPTER 31

THE DRAFT

We were less than 24 hours away from the start of the 2012 NFL draft, and I needed to discuss JR Sweezy, a defensive lineman from North Carolina State. We had been thinking we could develop him into an offensive guard. He had average skills for defensive line but excellent skills for offensive line.

I approached the draft room and smiled at the sign on the door that read "Authorized Personnel Only." The room was off-limits to outsiders year-round. It was like our own CIA room.

This was where we kept detailed information on each NFL team. Every pro team's roster was on the side and rear walls. The rosters would show us areas of weakness, clues to what they needed. The front of the room had a board list of possible college draftees by rank and position on magnetic strips. Each placard listed the prospect's name, school, physical dimensions, and a symbol which stood for his character. It was all about information. It could dictate a trade up for a prospect and losing your pick, or trade back and gaining a pick. The room also contained a large television screen with the draft in real time.

Information was being tabulated constantly. It was where we quietly negotiated who we thought could help our team and why. The draft room had a similar mantra as Las Vegas: "What goes on in this room stays in this room."

I was excited because I could feel a sense of purpose. We were improving our team. I couldn't help but think back to the year before when we practically cleaned house. By the time the 2011 season started, we had seven new starters on offense, eight new starters on defense, and a few coaching changes. One of those coaching changes was Bates. He was not a good fit for coach. Older players were cut or not re-signed. Now we just needed a few more solid picks to take us to the promised land.

I went to bed wondering who would be joining us. When I woke up at 6 a.m., I sat up in my bed with images of John and Coach making the phone call to a college player and popping the question, "Are you ready to be a Seahawk?" It was a life-changing moment for those young men to be drafted into the NFL.

Would we get the right young men that could help our team? So much work went into picking the players we liked and being in position to select them. We were looking for men with good character that were self-starters and had a craving to be special.

The coaches did their evaluations by position. I had written summaries on all the college offensive linemen who were given to us by the college scouting team. Now it was up to John and Coach Carroll to perform their magic.

Draft day was here, the countdown had started, and we could feel the oxygen ions colliding in the air around us. There was food everywhere—sandwiches, chips, veggies, fruit, and cookies—symbolic of the all-day process.

The room was filled with chatter, but once the draft was underway, the room fell silent like a movie theater when the feature begins while college scouts reviewed their evaluations and coaches' assessments. Coach Carroll and John would quietly converse about prospects. In the meantime, the other coaches and I went somewhere where we could be loud, make comments, and express our thoughts on each player drafted. Coach Carroll would call for us if and when we were drafting a player for our position. The draft emphasis this year was on defense, but we also needed a quarterback that we could develop.

The offensive coaches were assembled in the staff meeting room, sitting at a long table with whiteboards, depth charts on the side walls, and viewing screens on the front and back walls with our grading system for every player on our team.

When the draft began, we anxiously waited for our pick. We took Bruce Irvin, a defensive end from West Virginia with the 15th pick in the first round. We needed a pass rusher, and we got one.

Day two would be rounds two and three. We took Bobby Wagner, a linebacker from Utah State in the second round, an exceptional player with all the intangibles.

Then as the third round was underway, Coach Carroll stepped into the staff room and announced, "We're picking Russell Wilson, a quarterback from Wisconsin." No one said a word. Then coach continued, "I don't want you guys criticizing this pick. John loves his abilities and his intangibles, and I am in agreement."

Several weeks before the draft, Coach Carroll made it clear not to argue with the scouts, saying, "If there's a difference of opinion, John and I will make the final decision." It was easy to deduce there would be no arguing with him either—that time had come and gone.

We all nodded like a bunch of bobble-head dolls. When he left, we all turned toward the TV. "Seattle is on the clock," they announced. Then, within three minutes, the announcer said, "With the seventy-fifth pick in the third round, Seattle Seahawks select Russell Wilson, quarterback from Wisconsin."

Carl Smith, our quarterback coach, was grinning ear to ear. He had done his homework on Russell by watching all his games.

"Russell has Sacagawea," Carl said.

"What the hell is Sacagawea?" I asked. I wasn't the only one perplexed.

"I don't know exactly what it means—I just know he's an exceptional football player who is kind of short," Coach Smith chuckled.

"I've never heard of that—I'm looking that up."

Grabbing my phone and diving deep into Google, I found it. It was the name of the Shoshone Native woman who guided the Lewis and Clark expedition. She was known for endurance, selflessness, and dedication. Sacagawea had a famous quote, "Everything I do is for my people."

"Wow, I would like to be thought of like that," I said to myself.

Coach Smith said, "That's Russell, but he's kind of short at five foot eleven. But what's too short?" I guessed we would find out.

I was concerned. "Do they make platform football shoes? How is he going to see over those six-foot-four plus offensive linemen?" I suddenly realized I was reaching for some humor but was guilty of doing what coach asked us not to do.

The draft was over, and in less than a week, all the rookies had reported for off-season training.

Every time Wilson threw the ball, our eyes lit up. We glanced at each other with non-verbal communication: *Did you see that? How far did he just throw that ball? Oh boy, I think we got a good one.*

We could even hear other players making comments about his talent.

Russell would throw deep balls with remarkable accuracy, but what blew us all away was his attention to detail. He would miss a throw at practice, then stay out after practice and repeat the throw over and over until he was satisfied. *Sacagawea*?

Carl Smith, whose emotions were normally reserved, was bubbling with joy. "This one's going to be fun to coach."

As the offensive staff stood there and watched, Coach Carroll delivered his I-told-you-so moment. "This is why he'll be a great player." We were all in awe. His focus to be exceptional was there.

Our team was now a mixture of rookies and veterans obtained in free agency. There was lots of excitement about new faces, especially the rookies.

Between our new draft picks and the 2011 draft selections—including KJ Wright, linebacker; Richard Sherman, corner; Byron Maxwell, corner; and Malcolm Smith, linebacker; as well as undrafted free agent Doug Baldwin, wide receiver—we were on our way.

The last two years felt like the famous line in the *Wizard of OZ* from Dorothy, "My! People come and go so quickly here."

It felt like a subway station. Some were just arriving in Seahawkville, while others were leaving for a new destination.

We prepared for OTAs and a required minicamp.

Coach Carroll had his own style; we had a sign over the door of the team meeting room and the door that opened to the practice field that said, "I'M IN." We would all tap the sign and say the words. It was an affirmation that our minds were clear, and we were committed to the mission of excellence. It was important that the coaches, players, and administrators bought in. Coach always tried to make each day a fun experience that always began with giving our best effort.

We could feel the focus and intensity of this new group of players, and as they became closer, they practiced with a purpose and passion. It was as if every day was game day.

Finally, it was late June, which meant four weeks of a much-needed summer break. Like every year, I always planned a surprise vacation because I knew the toll that my job was taking on my family. After many years, they knew the drill: Save the first three weeks of July.

Three weeks prior, I had called my brother, Ron, who lived in Miami, and invited him and his family to go with us.

"You just get there by plane, boat, or swim. I'll take care of rooms and meals. And, by the way, you're hereby sworn to secrecy because Marti and Sabra don't know yet."

On the Fourth of July, while we were watching fireworks from our rooftop deck in Hermosa, I asked, "Does anybody know how to make a Bahama Mama?"

They shook their heads.

"Well, I guess we're going to have to go to the Bahamas and find out." This caused a mini explosion of joy mixed in with the fireworks. I glanced at David; he looked concerned. "That includes you too, David." His sad face had left and was replaced with a wide smile as he thanked me and hugged Sabra.

A week later, we landed in the Bahamas and headed for Atlantis, an exclusive beachside resort that left nothing to be yearned for. It featured an aquarium, beaches, a casino, and my favorites: the water park and jet skis. It was our family's holiday season; we were all together enjoying life to its fullest.

Every morning in this paradise, I was jumping off the bed to be the first at the water park. I have always loved the water. Marti would often say about me, "He's sixty-four, looks like forty-four, and acts like twelve-year-old." I literally would race kids to the water slide, start splash fights in the lazy river, play football in the pool, and buzz around in the ocean on a jet ski. No vacation day was left behind—I tried to capture all of them.

When recess was almost over, I had a couple of days left to spend in Hermosa Beach before heading back to Seattle for training camp. I was relaxing on our deck watching the sun's rays flickering off the ocean's surface when my phone rang. It was David asking if he could see me before I left.

"Sure, what time were you thinking?" I asked.

"In an hour," he responded. That answer caused me concern. What was the urgency? My thoughts immediately jumped to the warning that I issued to him when I first met him three years earlier. "You can break my daughters' heart, but if you verbally or physically abuse her, I'm going to jail."

What is this about? I wondered. *Surely, he's not breaking up with her.* Did he want my advice on something?

When he entered the house, he looked a little nervous. I was a bit on edge myself.

"What's up, David?" I asked, trying to make him feel at ease.

Then, without a hint of what was to come, he blurted out, "I wanted to ask you—" *Oh no, here it comes.* "—if I could take your daughter's hand in marriage?"

Happy, sad, excited, somber, you name it—I had all the emotions. Happy and excited for Sabra, sad and somber for me. I thought, *Wow, his style is kind of formal, kind of cool.* I knew this day was coming.

I had listened to Clint Bruce, a former Navy Seal and excellent life coach. He said, "Anyone who marries one of my three daughters must have the four P's: Purpose, Passion, Provider, and Protector." I was confident that Dave was all that.

I extended my hand to shake his, but we naturally turned it into a momentary embrace. "Yes, and welcome to the family."

I looked at Marti. She seemed very happy and a lot more aware of what was going on. I suspected Marti, Sabra, and David had planned this ambush.

After David left, I asked her, "Did you know about this?"

"What do you mean?" she shot back with a grin. Marti wouldn't say, but her smile told a different story.

It didn't matter. I found myself thinking, *Are we losing a daughter or gaining a son?* All the players I coached were like my sons, but there was only one Sabra. For now, it wasn't real, but it would soon be a reality. I hoped I could hold it together.

CHAPTER 32

SUPER BOWL

It was our third season in Seattle, and I was reminded that the monogram NFL really stood for "not for long." Coaching at the college or professional level meant "Win, now." The owners and the media were not patient characters. We were in the age of instant pudding, instant soup, instant rice, instant noodles and, yes, instant wins. Based on my knowledge of these instants, I am inclined to believe instant sucks. Cutting corners to mimic real progress is a recipe for the ordinary.

Having missed the playoffs in our second year, it was time to show significant progress.

It was Monday morning, September 10, 2012, and the offensive staff was meeting to discuss our opening season loss to Arizona.

"We can't protect Russell if he keeps bailing out of his protection," I announced. I wasn't trying to deflect blame from the offensive line, but after 40 years of coaching, I knew that about three and half seconds was all the time we would get in the pocket, and if any one of those linemen had a breakdown, it was even less.

"We're working on it," Tater (Coach Carl Smith's nickname) shot back. Tater was the guru of quarterback play.

Kippy Brown, our receiver coach, joined in, "Maybe he can't see—after all, he's barely five foot eleven."

"Let me show you." Kippy grabbed two six-inch bottles of water and a three-inch saltshaker that was sitting on our meeting room table. He then picked up the saltshaker and placed it behind the bottles of water.

"Here's Russell," he said, as he picked up the saltshaker. We all cracked up at Kippy's demonstration. It had merit.

Tater asked, "Hey Siri, how tall is Drew Brees?" One thing about Siri was that she was good at giving you an answer, but if you wanted to know why or how, you needed to do the research.

"Drew Brees is six feet tall," Siri said. We all knew he was an exceptional pocket passer because he moved around in the pocket finding his throwing lanes like a jeweler crafting perfection.

Russell Wilson was a natural scrambler. He had a panic button. Good coaches always designed their offense and defense to take advantage of a player's talent.

Tater had made his point. "He'll be fine. We'll keep working on it."

After we instructed him to stay in the pocket for three weeks, Russell kept his timely scrambles going and continued making big plays. After beating the Dallas Cowboys and the Green Bay Packers, Coach Carroll said, "Let Russell keep doing what he's doing." It was evident that every time he scrambled, he made big plays with his feet or with his arm, or he was sacked.

By mid-season, we were 4-4.

The final eight games of the season, we went 7-1 to finish 11-5 and secured a wild card spot in the playoffs. We were becoming a great team. We played Washington on the road and won; it was the first road playoff win since 1983. We lost the following week to Atlanta on the road 30-28 to end our playoff run.

Suddenly, everything was falling into place like the last three pieces of a thousand-piece jigsaw puzzle. By the time the 2013 season had rolled around, Russell mania had grabbed the entire Northwest. It all felt magical. We went 13-3 and had home-field advantage throughout the playoffs.

We beat New Orleans and San Francisco at home to punch our ticket to New York, home of the 2013 Super Bowl.

I reflected on a reoccurring dream I had where I raised my arms and levitated, circling around the room like a hawk eyeing its prey. It was almost a spiritual event. I hated waking up from dreams like that. Oddly, I rarely dreamt about football. But I thought about the symbolism. Our team was that hawk positioning itself over the greatest prize in sports.

Forty-eight years earlier, when I played for Coral Gables High School, we were declared National Champions. Now I was a coach with the Seattle Seahawks, and we were preparing for a chance to be the World Champions.

We arrived at our New York hotel five days before the game. The players had received their room keys and dashed for the elevator. Fifty players and two elevators meant we had to wait our turn to get to our rooms. While we waited our turn, I reminded the players why we were there.

"We're a team of destiny. Nothing can stop us." It's one thing to say it, but it's another to believe it. We sensed we were meant to be in this moment.

With so much media attention and external buzz, the week was moving fast. We managed to stay in a mindful cocoon of purpose. Nothing else mattered; we were talking like the only thing that could stop us would be us. No team, no media report, no consensus could stop our mission.

Our fans were proudly walking around in Seahawk gear, some of them from head to toe. We had taken them with us on this journey, and they certainly deserved it because it was their passion and participation that helped thrust us to reach that magical ridgeline called the Super Bowl.

"The day before the day before," was a phrase Coach Carroll and the staff would use to emphasize the sense of urgency to finish our preparation. We reviewed the game plan and our schedules. Like many of the successful teams I was previously on, the anxiety, unease, and nervousness were not visible. We had discarded those emotions in a dumpster at the Seahawk facility.

The only emotions we wore on our sleeves were our love and trust for each other that we'd developed on our journey. We knew we were good.

Game day was finally here. The hay was in the barn, the ship had docked, and we were in a holding pattern high above MetLife stadium waiting for our moment to show the world who we were.

I hopped out of my bed like a kangaroo. I needed to move. I went outside and walked the city streets. No signs of snow, even though they'd predicted it the day before. So many Denver and Seattle fans. I could tell by their clothes where their hearts resided. In the meantime, I was like a set of jumper cables looking for anyone who needed a jump. My energy level was off the charts.

When I returned to the hotel, we had the traditional pre-game meal at five hours before the game. I was not interested in eating. I wanted to get on the bus to the stadium.

The police checked our credentials and security dogs checked our briefcases and backpacks. We boarded the buses and headed to MetLife Stadium. The bus was deathly quiet. Coaches were reviewing notes and players had headphones on, listening to their favorite music.

Snow had been predicted for the game, but they adjusted the forecast; it now called for snow to hit late that night, with game time temperatures at a balmy 50 degrees.

We arrived at the stadium four hours before game time. It was already a mass of people. I wondered about all the tail-gaters. It was game day for them, too, but their highs would never be as high as ours, and their lows would never be as low as ours. This was what happened when we worked 70-80 hours a week and there was an enormous amount of people counting on us to win. We were either the hero or the goat.

As I was taking it all in, my soul ached for my father—how I wished he could have been here. He would have his Seahawk hat on, with his embracing smile ready to participate. When I was young, he was my counsel and my mentor, and now I would be his ambassador.

Fans were proudly displaying their team's flag as our bus entered the stadium parking lot. I looked at faces, trying to recognize any of my Seattle friends. The vendors were buzzing around selling game paraphernalia. Security personnel were directing us to the locker rooms.

I thought about the game we had played here six weeks earlier against the New York Giants; we had beaten them 23-0. After the game, one of the employees of MetLife stadium had said, "Thank you for coming." Then, smiling, "I'll see you in February." He'd been talking about the Super Bowl, and I'd been listening.

As we got off the bus, the cool air was refreshing.

I was instantly grabbed by the thought, *It's really happening!*

Huge banners hung above the lockers that read, "NFC Champions" and "Super Bowl XLVIII." They were like billboards screaming our achievement. Everybody had an individualized Super Bowl name plate over their locker. I stared at my own name plate. It had "Pat Ruel" written on it, sitting on top of a picture of the New York City skyline at night. To the left of my name, the Lombardi Trophy with "Super Bowl XLVIII" was written underneath it. So many who dream of this would never get here, and yet here I was—the sense of accomplishment was overwhelming.

My game day ritual was running the stadium steps. I did this to dissipate the powerful storm in my heart to calm down.

The fans were filing in. As I continued my stroll around the field, I could hear the Seahawk fans chanting, "Seahawks, Seahawks, Seahawks!"

To myself, I asked, "Where are you, Dad?" I wished with all my heart that he could have been there. Even my mom, who'd once walked by our TV set while we were watching a football game at home asking, "Would you neanderthals like some raptor wings and wooly mammoth chips?" We'd all laughed because mom viewed the game as legalized violence. Nevertheless, I knew she would have been so delighted to be here, and Dad would have been so proud that the "courage to participate and passion required" was successfully passed to his first born. I knew that, somewhere in the heavens, they were both in attendance.

The stadium was growing with people and, like time-lapse photography, the flower of humanity was blooming rapidly.

Game time had arrived. Both teams ran onto the field; it was already dark. The stadium lights were on, and it felt as if everything was slowing down. Seconds felt like minutes. From the moment we kicked off, it was all Seahawks. Everything we did was successful.

On Denver's first play of the game, Peyton Manning was in shotgun formation and an errant snap rolled into the end zone for a safety. Then it became the Russell Wilson and Legion of Boom Show—this was the name our dominant defense had given themselves.

We were the underdogs to Denver and Peyton Manning's record setting offense.

Toward the end of the fourth quarter, we were leading 43-8 and Coach Carroll called up to the press box, where the other coaches and I were conveying information or calling plays.

"You guys in the press box can come down now," he said.

I raced down like I was holding a winning lottery ticket that was about to be cashed. All the coaches' families were being ushered to the field.

As I connected with Marti, Sabra, and Dave, the blue and green sea of confetti rained from above. The stadium address system belted out a song that Frank Sinatra made famous, "New York, New York." As we all sang, tears of happiness streamed down our faces. I tried to wipe my leaking eyes, but it was as if someone had left the faucet on; I couldn't stop it. The stadium was lit with emotion as players and coaches hugged each other and their families. I even hugged a few people I didn't know—in that moment, we were drawn to each other like powerful magnets of joy.

* * *

Three months later, the Seahawks were in the White House for the traditional visit for the Champions. The history and the portraits were awe-inspiring. I thought their furniture could use some updating, but it also represented so much of our country's past. I walked over to look at President John F. Kennedy's portrait. They called his time in office Camelot, after the famous musical. My dad bought that record, and I'd heard it a thousand times.

All of us were floating in the wonderful dream of history and sports until one player came back from the restroom and announced in a quiet voice, "I just dropped a number two in the White House bathroom." I shook my head, realizing that they may look like adults, but looks can be deceiving.

President Obama was extremely cordial. We gave him a Seahawk Football Jersey with the number 44 on it. We all took quick pictures with him. Meeting him was a gift. He exuded caring and confidence. He was articulate and made everyone feel like there was no one in the room but them and him. It was an extraordinary experience.

I had reached the top of the mountain in high school, college, and professional football partially because I chose to be around good characters and positive-thinking people.

On June 19, our Super Bowl Ring ceremony was held at the EMP Museum in downtown Seattle. Paul Allen, our owner, spared no expense.

After a beautiful dinner and receiving the rings, the famous Usher performed for two hours in front of the team and a few coaches. Some of the coaches and administrators left, as they had no idea who Usher was, leaving him to be singing to about 60 people. It was unbelievable—our own private concert.

The rings had an estimated value of $40,000. Wow, talk about gaudy; 172 diamonds, 40 sapphires, and a green tsavorite (the eye of the Seahawk) on a large, solid gold ring. I wore it long enough to snap a picture, then it took its place in my drawer as winner of the most ostentatious piece of jewelry I have ever owned. The ring represented the past; I preferred the present.

Speaking of the here and now, we were one month away from W-Day: Sabra's wedding.

CHAPTER 33

THE WEDDING

This summer would be all about the wedding. I had already announced that I, as father of the bride, would provide $50,000 dollars for expenses. There went my Super Bowl check. It was barely enough, as the costs climbed like Spiderman on a skyscraper. The wedding was slated to be held at the Auberge du Soleil Hotel in Napa, a beautiful resort that sat halfway up a small mountain overlooking the valley of wine.

We needed an officiant, and I knew just the right person: Jerry Pettibone. He was a principled man with high standards. He was 5'11" with dark hair and the squarest jaw on the planet. Put him in a dark suit and his look had "preacher" written all over it. Besides, we had history, having coached together at Texas A&M and Northern Illinois University. I presided over his own daughter's wedding three years earlier.

Sabra gave me the task of picking the song for the father-daughter dance. I had asked friends and acquaintances, and I even surveyed the internet. I found the song "I Loved Her First" by Heartland. It started a stream of tears on my face. I kept playing it over and over, hoping I would be so tired of it I would not get emotional. I didn't want that stream to turn into a river on the dance floor.

I told Sabra my selection. She loved the song. We both said, like reading each other's minds, "We'll be crying on that one." Just to be safe, I had a backup plan.

"Sabra, seriously, we should both wear sunglasses for the father-daughter spin around the dance floor."

Sabra laughed. "I know, Dad. There's no way we'll make it through that song without crying."

I spent the month leading up to the wedding working out and getting in shape. I wanted to look good in my tux.

Things were moving fast; I was as excited as the moment before the start of a Seattle Seahawks game. I was also in excruciating distress knowing I was losing my little girl. Marti seemed to be much more grounded than I was. She handled all the things daughters needed before their wedding.

The wedding date was July 18th, four days before I had to report back to Seattle for training camp. I was happy and excited for our daughter, sad and gloomy that we were losing her, and pleased that she was happy. In other words, I was an emotional mess. I could not help but think, *This David dude better treat her right and not take her too far away.*

W-Day was here. It was a gorgeous day. Clear skies, 84 degrees, a light breeze, and the sun rays dancing on the fields of grapes. To the residents of Napa Valley, it may have been a typical summer day. To Marti and me, it was the day we would gain a son-in-law and hopefully look forward to a grandchild. Truly the circle of life.

The morning of the wedding, David arranged for his groomsmen and the father of the bride to go to the Olde-Town Barbershop in Napa. There we would get heat packs put on our faces, then lathered with shaving cream and shaved with a straight razor, just like the old days. I had seen enough movies of men sitting in a barber chair with heated towels on their faces when the bad guy walks in. It seemed like an extremely vulnerable position. Nevertheless, it was a unique experience. Now with my face as smooth as a baby's butt and my tux fitting beautifully, I was ready.

It was time to get this spectacle started. The wedding guests and the families of the bride and groom had taken their seats. Jerry Pettibone, our officiant, and David had found their rightful place. The wedding march started, and I was in my special place, arm-in-arm, walking our daughter down the aisle. I was excited yet composed. I was doing better because I realized what our daughter saw in David was real. He was authentic and loving.

I took my seat and held Marti's hand. I was fine until they started their vows. My insides felt like a vast, lifeless canyon. My heart was pounding, and the tears started their journey down my face. Marti handed me a tissue.

After Jerry announced them as man and wife, I felt there was so much more that should be said. I don't know why, but I stood up and pronounced, "I have something to say." I was breaking the norm for a wedding, but it wasn't enough. My heart wanted to give David and the guests a peak from Sabra's father's eyes, now drenched in tears for this wonderful girl David was marrying.

"David, let me tell you a few things you and others might not know," I began. "When she was two, she stood in the middle of the living room in only a diaper and bounced up and down to Billy Ocean's song 'Caribbean Queen.' She has style."

I was already leaking tears and my voice was cracking. I needed help. I called Ryan, Dave's best man, up and said, "Slap me."

Ryan looked puzzled.

I said, "Trust me, it's ok."

Ryan slapped me gently but efficiently across my face, and I told him to stand by. The wedding guests laughed.

"When she was three, she carried a pink blanket with her, and our German shepherd dog named Santa would often snatch her blankie, as she called it. Sabra would waddle after Santa trying to get it back. She became frustrated because she couldn't catch the dog. Marti said, 'Pat, would you please get her blankie from Santa?' I shot back, 'Let her figure it out.' She said, 'Pat, she's two! That's ridiculous!' I responded, 'Just give her chance.'

"Sabra toddled into the kitchen and grabbed Santa's bone, holding it above her shoulders and walking toward the basement steps blocked by a child gate. All eyes were on Sabra— mine, Marti's, and Santa's. Santa watched her intently, and when Sabra got to the barricade, she tossed his bone over the gate and down the stairs. Santa sprung to all fours, charged the child gate, leapt over it, and crashed down the stairs. Sabra, using a speed-waddle this time, retrieved her pink blankie and crawled into my lap. Marti and I were in a state of disbelief. Sabra had her blankie, and Santa was stuck on the stairs of the basement with his bone in his mouth.

"She's a problem solver."

I looked around, and I felt that the guests were thinking, *He's not going to go through her whole life, is he?*

I continued, explaining the tornado story, when Sabra had better sense than I did and told us to turn back from the danger. I was fighting back the tears. I called for Ryan again, "I need another slap." This time, he smacked me so good that my left cheek was stinging. I guess he was tired of seeing a winning Super Bowl coach emotionally breaking down. The guests this time grunted in concern, but laughed when I said, "Ryan, that was good. You're done."

I continued. "David, you're getting a wonderful girl. Take care of her." What I did was totally spontaneous. I can be impetuous when I know in my heart that I'm doing the right thing.

It was now time for the wedding party to take pictures. While we were there, I told Ryan, "You played your part too well." We both laughed.

It was time to shift into reception mode. I was completely in charge of my emotions now. Back to my old self. I walked around to each table thanking them for being part of a wonderful day. I was so lucky to have married the right woman and to have a beautiful daughter to be so proud of. When I sat down at the head table, I sighed in relief that I had gotten through the hard part.

Then as we finished the meal, the DJ said, "It's time for the father-daughter dance."

"Oh, fuck," I whispered to myself. I hadn't cried this much since I lost my father. I held my hand out to Sabra, and we walked onto the dance floor. All the guests were clapping.

"It's time," I said. I gave her the go-head nod for us to put on our sunglasses. Our tears peaked out beneath them as we danced to "I Loved Her First" by Heartland.

As we twirled around the dance floor. The words reached deep into my heart. "I loved her first."

When the music stopped, Sabra looked at me with tears cascading down her cheeks and said, "I love you, Dad."

I smiled and hugged her. I held her tight, then whispered in her ear, "I love you too."

With my emotions splattered all over the dance floor, I immediately went to the bathroom and threw some cold water on my face. When I looked in the mirror, I saw a man who coached a rough sport with tough men who, in this moment, felt weak as a newborn child.

"Take deep breaths," I said to myself. *Why do I get so emotional?* What was wrong with me? It seemed like the older I got, the more love would grab my soul and my face should have come with a flood warning. It made me feel quite vulnerable, but in some ways, it was also a source of strength because it made me feel alive. I liked who I was.

As I went back out to the reception, the music was playing and everybody was dancing. Ties were no longer tied, suit jackets were off, shirt tails were out, hair was let down, and shoes were discarded—the July heat even forced a couple of cummerbunds to reside on the backs of chairs. We were in party mode. We danced and danced, followed by an occasional group hug which had as few as three and as many six. I was a sweaty and hot mess, but loving every minute of it.

When it all started to die down, we had buses to take guests back to the Yountville Hotel, where the post party was. As the father of the bride, I felt it was my duty to stay to the end and make sure that everyone survived. It was 2 a.m., and when I got back to our room, Marti was already in bed. I laid down next to her, grabbed her hand, and fell asleep immediately.

The next morning, the wedding party was scheduled for a wine tasting tour. I grabbed my headache, my abused tear ducts, and my wallet and headed to our first stop, the Camus Winery. By the time we got to Stags' Leap and Oakville Winery, it seemed as though all the wineries had a gossip line; they all knew I was a Seattle Seahawks coach. My ego enjoyed the attention, but my head wanted a bed. This day-after-the-wedding wine tour had to be a young person's idea. It was surely David's.

It was a beautiful wedding with so many good friends, but it was over, and I shifted into coaching mode. It was time to get back to work. I said goodbye to my family and got on a plane to Seattle.

When that plane took off, I stared into the future for a moment and thought about my dad. He never got to be a grandfather. It was then that I asked God, "Allow me to become a grandfather before you take me." My grandfather was fun and entertaining, and I wanted to complete the life cycle. It was my next goal as a father, even outshining my goals as a coach.

EPILOGUE

The hardest thing about going to the top of the mountain in sports is to repeat the feat. I could already see the problems with reaching the top. Players and agents wanted more money, there was free agency, coaches wanted more money or to be head coaches, and the fans wanted perfection. Often, we lost the concept of being a team, and greed became the general theme.

Coach Carroll had preached about maintaining our work ethic and team attitude. Even though we were faltering early in the 2014 season, Coach Carroll reminded us daily that we must recapture the work ethic and team attitude that got us to the first one. After six games, we were 3-3, then Coach Carroll's magic took over. We rallied and finished 9-1, making us 12-4, and we finished in a three-way tie with the Green Bay Packers and the Dallas Cowboys. Because we had beaten Green Bay earlier in the season, we earned the number one seat and home-field advantage throughout the playoffs. We beat the Carolina Panthers in the divisional round to advance to the NFC championship against the Packers.

Game day in Seattle was cold, windy, and full of intermittent rain. In front of 68,524 fans, we floundered like a fish out of water. We threw three interceptions in the first half. We went into our locker room at half time down 16-0. After an impassioned speech by Coach Carroll at halftime, I ran back to my designated spot in the press box where I kept track of defensive fronts and pressures.

I was back in my seat in the coach's booth overlooking a lot of worried, upset, and angry Seahawks fans. We scored late in the third quarter on a fake field goal, making it 16-7. Green Bay added a field goal in the fourth quarter, making it 19-7 with 5:04 left in the game. Green Bay's odds of winning were 99.3%.

I had been here before; it was déjà vu in 1992. I was the offensive coordinator at Kansas. We were 4-1 and went on the road to play Iowa State; some 10,000 Kansas Jayhawk fans joined us.

We jumped out to a 21-0 score in the first quarter. They scored 28 points in the second quarter. Behind at half time 28-21, we got the ball to start the second half. We fumbled on the first play; they took it in for the score and missed the extra point—34-21. They scored again and again, making it 47-21. 9,500 fans left for their four-hour ride back to Lawrence, Kansas. Iowa State's odds of winning were 99.9%.

I went over and scolded the offense. "I'm not interested in why this has happened. Let's just go out and execute and not embarrass ourselves."

As I started to turn away from the bench, Chris Powell, our fullback who played at Rockhurst High School in Kansas City, Missouri (the winningest program in the Midwest) said, "You think we're going to lose, don't you?"

He was right, I did, but I quickly caught myself and fired back, "No... we're not going to lose. We just have to score every fucking time we touch the ball."

Wow, did I get called out. An embarrassing moment for a coach who preached, "No signs of weakness," and "Don't get captured."

Down by 26 points and nearing the end of the third quarter, our team clawed back. We were now on the Iowa State four-yard line leading 50-47 with less than a minute to play. A 29-point comeback. Who could have ever imagined this? Chris Powell did.

Coach Mason, our head coach, wanted me to knock it in for another score, but I refused. First because it was a crazy game with fumbles, blocked kicks, and interceptions, second because the head coach for Iowa State was Jim Walden, who gave me my first chance as an offensive coordinator at Washington State. We took a knee and I realized that sometimes we need to be reminded that it's never over until the clock hits 0:00. Taking a knee is absolutely the right thing to do. Never give the opponent another chance.

Now, sitting in the press box in Seattle, I was wondering if this could be another improbable comeback. I sensed that we could pull this off, but I couldn't help but wonder, *Where is the team that got us here?* We already had coaches and players violating rule number two: no whining, no complaining, and no excuses. Time was running out.

On the field, some players and about 20,000 Seahawks fans had decided it was over. They broke my rule, *"Don't get captured,"* no matter how bad it gets. As the throngs of fans were leaving, Coach Carroll was running up and down the sidelines reminding players, "We have lots of time to win this. Stay positive." He chanted. "It's not over! Keep playing your asses off."

Suddenly, Russell Wilson, who had now thrown four interceptions, started connecting. He hit Doug Baldwin, and later Marshawn Lynch, for big plays. We scored to make it 19-14 with 2:09 left in the game. Coach Carroll called for an onside kick, and we recovered it. Quick like a bullet train, we scored again with 1:25 left to go, making it 20-19. We went for a two-point play and made it 22-19. Our odds of winning were now 91.1%

Green Bay and Aaron Rodgers tied the game up 22-22 with a field goal with 0:14 seconds left in regulation. We were headed to overtime.

Green Bay and Seattle captains went to midfield for the coin toss. It was the Packers' call; they called tails and it was heads.

The mass of Seahawks fans were outside pleading to get back into the stadium. Three plays into overtime, Russell Wilson threw a deep ball to Jermaine Kearse for the touchdown, and then it was pandemonium in the press box and on the sideline. Everybody was patting Darrell Bevel, our offensive coordinator, on the back. I looked over at the Green Bay bench—they were completely stunned. I've had that feeling before too. It's like the oxygen gets sucked out of your body, and you stand there as if in a bad dream, waiting to wake up and realize it's not true. Our fans, players, and coaches were in a euphoric frenzy. We sealed the deal for our second trip to the Super Bowl, this time in Glendale, Arizona. Yes, we did it again. Woohoo!

Like throwing a stone in the water and watching the ripple effect, positive people can produce a wave of belief which is extraordinarily powerful. Thank you, Chris Powell and Coach Carroll, for creating the highway of hope.

We were now preparing to play the New England Patriots and Tom Brady. A daunting task, but we'd had more success than most teams against them. The atmosphere in Glendale, Arizona didn't have the same magic as New York. Maybe because it was our second one. Nevertheless, it was the Super Bowl. It was a great game; we were tied 14-14 at halftime. Then the Seahawks surged ahead 24-14 at the end of three quarters. The fourth quarter was all Patriots. We got stopped on offense and the Patriots went 80 yards twice on the number one defense in the NFL. The score was now 28-24. The clock was at 2:02, and time was running away from us.

We got a couple of big plays by Marshawn Lynch and Jermaine Kearse to get us to first and goal at the New England five-yard line. We gave the ball to Marshawn, who looked like he was going to score but got tripped up and was down at the one-yard line. There were 36 seconds left. We knew defensive coaches sent everybody with the hopes of tackling in the backfield. We chose to throw it and called a perfect play for man to man, but we messed up the execution, and New England's Malcolm Butler intercepted Russ Wilson and saved the day for the Patriots.

We were all devasted by the outcome. We were so close to achieving back-to-back Super Bowl wins. Such an empty feeling. It was if the blood that was pumping through our bodies at high speed was suddenly shut down. It was like the brightest light was just unplugged, and we were embraced by darkness and despair.

While New England was celebrating, we hustled into our locker room at the end of the game. A few players slammed helmets on the ground, and the verbal barrage of emotional anger spewed like molten rock down the side of a volcano. It was the most horrible display of behavior I had ever seen in my coaching career. The inexcusable reactions by Marshawn Lynch, Richard Sherman, and a few others on the defense turned our locker room into a den of outrage and anger.

At that moment, we were no longer a team. We were playing the blame game. The hardest thing to watch as a coach is bad character tearing at the very fabric of team principles. Some coaches and players tried to calm things down, but it was a sign that we were only as strong as our weakest link. That powerful chain that got us there had snapped. One player was yelling about how much money this had cost him, another blaming the play-call, and yet another blaming the defense. It was emotionally charged bullshit.

Coach Carroll signaled me and a few other coaches to call the team up. I looked around at the faces and it was if we all had witnessed our own funeral. Coach Carroll, who looked pale but determined, stood up in front of the team and said, "I know this is hard to take, but we win as a team, and we lose as a team. I want to thank all the players and coaches for their efforts."

I can't even remember what Coach Carroll said after that. It was if a bomb had exploded, and we were all like soldiers wounded and disoriented. Our computers had crashed, and were waiting to be rebooted. It had left us staring at each other trying to understand what just happened. The one thing that was clear was the agents of selfishness and greed had permeated our team.

After two Super Bowls, the years that followed were successful, but we failed to reach the summit. It was not for lack of trying. We had good teams, we had a great culture, and our opponents were getting better. Coach Carroll was the guru of a great culture—a culture mechanic.

Some corporations, leaders, and bosses are consumed by money, self-gratification, and a lack of accountability and fail at their core, therefore ruining a good work environment. Their unbalanced drive to success causes them to be manipulators, users, and whiners. They lack a moral code. It is quite common to be consumed with success and accomplishments because it is gratifying. But to deny your inner soul of humility and appreciation lessens your value. It is never all you. It is a unique combination of all those who impacted you through their knowledge, caring, and empathy. Success can lead to our greatest failure, which is pride; failure is our best example of humility and learning.

After replacing both knees, I decided that it was time to move on. I decided to stop in and see Coach Carroll.

"Coach Carroll, do you have a minute?"

"Of course I do. Let's sit on the couch." Coach always did that to create an informal and comfortable atmosphere. "What's up, Golden?" he said inquisitively. He liked using my real first name; it always made me smile.

"QTR, coach," I responded.

"What is that?" he asked.

"Quality time remaining," I replied. "I am done. Thirty years of Division One football and fifteen years of NFL is enough."

I loved coaching, but I wanted to be more than coach; I wanted to write a book and do some public speaking. Take Marti to new places of non-work adventures and play with grandkids.

Coach called me that night and said, "Are you sure?"

"Yes," I replied.

FINAL THOUGHTS

We all should possess an ATTITUDE OF GRATITUDE. It is just a positive way to say I appreciate all the good I was taught and all the bad I was taught. Some teach us how not to do things and how not to act, while others teach us how to do things right and to be respectful.

A good culture's main ingredients are caring, humility, productivity, and achievement. Bad cultures lack humility and caring, and are mired in self-gratification. That is why I used the phrase, "Don't get captured." It allowed me to survive in a bad/toxic culture. It was a way of saying, "I will not carry my anger, and I will not participate in the ugliness of disrespect." Those who know me well know that I violated my own principles on occasion, but I always ran back to my inner soul.

Values and principles can be very fragile in moments suffering, adversity, and pain. We turn against the very thing that gave us unity, strength, and commitment. This can happen at your job or even in your personal life. Maintaining a great attitude in a toxic culture is paramount to fixing it and your survivability. Learn from the narcissist's lack of humility—don't emulate it. Learn from their disrespect—don't repeat it. Our running back coach at Seattle, Sherman Smith, was a very principled coach.

He would say, "The power of respect is to never disrespect."

I used to ask the players I coached, "Who is evaluating you?"

Their answers would include dads, teachers, coaches, wives, girlfriends, friends, kids, bosses, co-workers, teammates, even policemen, judges, dogs, cats—you get the idea.

We are all provided with canvas at birth; those who love and care for you will provide paint brushes. So go paint a great picture. Reveal your soul, stand up for what is right, and be the best you.

Those who impact your life in a successful way should be recognized and thanked.